The Digital Photography Handbook

An Easy-to-U

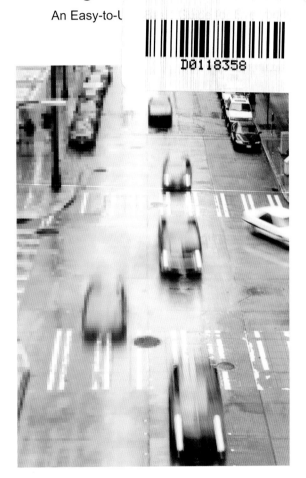

A QUINTET BOOK

First published in the United States in 2004 by
Amphoto Books
an imprint of Watson-Guptill Publications
a division of VNU Business Media Inc.
770 Broadway, New York, N Y 10003
www.amphotobooks.com
www.watsonguptill.com

ISBN 0-8174-3793-2

Library of Congress Control Number: 2003114167

1 2 3 4 5 6 7 / 09 08 07 06 05 04

This book was designed and produced by
Quintet Publishing Limited
6 Blundell Street
London N7 9BH

ENDP

Quintet Publishing Limited
6 Blundell Street
London N7 9BH

Project Editor: Anna Southgate
Project Manager: Corinne Masciocchi
Designer: Ian Hunt
Art Director: Sharanjit Dhol
Creative Director: Richard Dewing
Publisher: Oliver Salzmann

Manufactured in Singapore by Pica Digital Pte Ltd
Printed in China by Midas Printing International Ltd

The Digital Photography Handbook

An Easy-to-Use Basic Guide for Everybody

Tim Daly

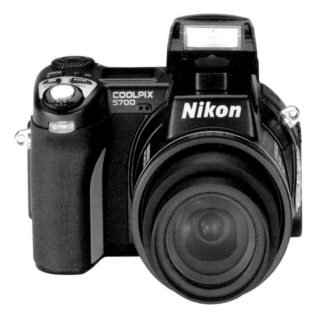

AMPHOTO BOOKS

An imprint of Watson-Guptill Publications / New York

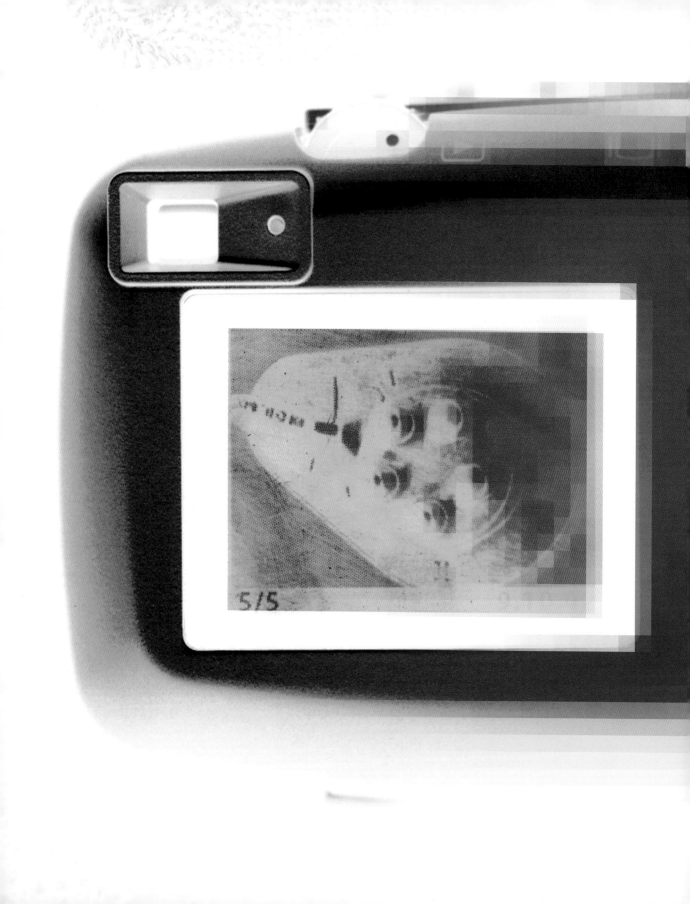

Contents

Introduction

As conventional photography enters its third century, the digital revolution is very much underway. With giant technological advances in cameras, software and desktop printers, today's digital photographers have an unparalleled range of sophisticated tools at their disposal. Quality has improved while corresponding prices have fallen, leaving good digital cameras within the range of most budgets.

In contrast to its chemical forerunners, the only creative boundaries to digital photography are those of the user's imagination. As technology starts to level out and standards become established, so the creative digital photographer can concentrate fully on the real work of making great pictures.

The digital image has to be the most multi-purpose artwork ever invented. Printed out, attached to an e-mail and sent instantly to the other side of the world, or uploaded to the Internet, images are fast becoming an essential part of the way we communicate with each other.

Now that information management is a task most employees have to deal with, digital photography is no longer the domain of creative individuals alone. Increasingly competent images are produced by non-specialists for work presentations, reports and other communication materials. Soon, digital images will be as widely shared as text messages and e-mails.

The Digital Photography Handbook is designed for users of all levels of confidence and ability. It focuses on the fundamental issues of making great photographs using the latest in digital photography equipment. The practical tasks included in the book are backed up with a jargon-free reference section. No previous knowledge of cameras or computer operations is assumed.

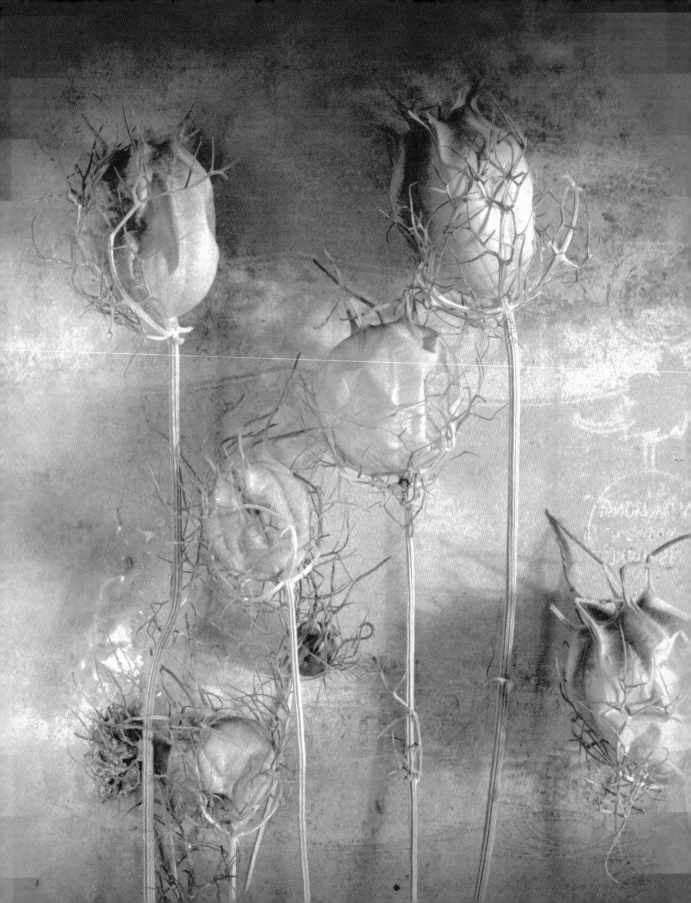

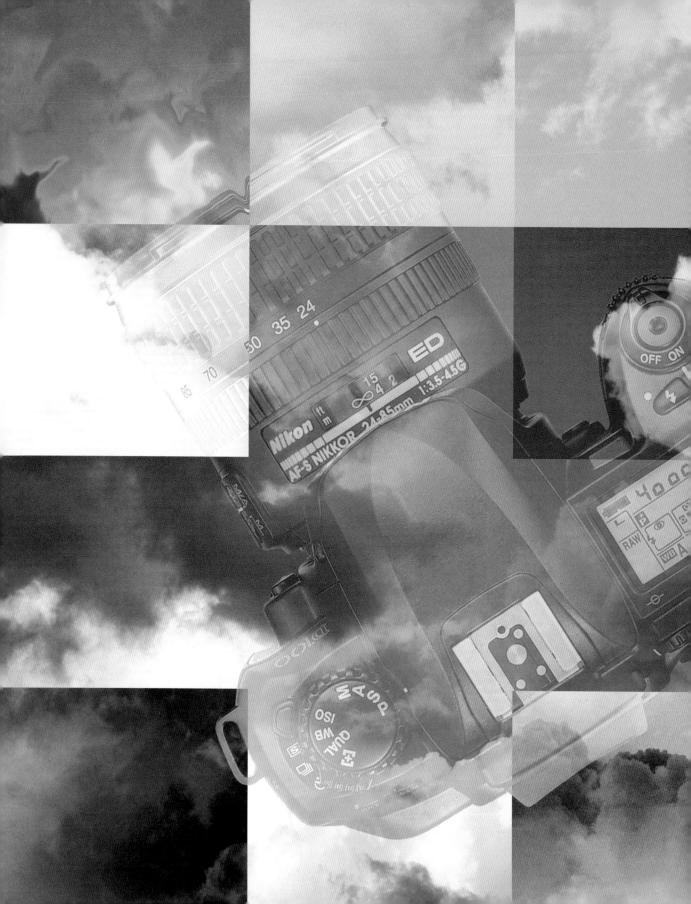

1 Digital Cameras

Anatomy of a digital camera

The confident photographer will have a good knowledge of the basic functions of a digital camera.

Lens 1

The image sensor, known as a Charge Coupled Device (CCD), is much smaller than 35mm film, so lens focal lengths are effectively shortened. An 8–24mm zoom lens on a digital camera corresponds to a 35–115mm zoom lens for a 35mm-film camera. Only a single lens reflex camera (SLR) and top-of-the-range compacts permit interchangeable lenses.

Digital zooms 2

Many digital compacts have a digital zoom function, which is not to be confused with an optical zoom lens. An image created with a digital zoom setting is enlarged by software trickery.

Flash 3

Built-in flash affords the ability to shoot in most low-light scenarios. This kind of flash unit is generally low in output compared to an external unit and can only work within a range of 16 feet (5m).

Shutter release 4

Many digital cameras have an electronically operated shutter instead of the moving mechanical curtain common to film cameras. This kind of shutter works without making the recognizable clunk, so it can be difficult to know if an exposure has been made.

Sensor 5

A digital camera uses a light-sensitive CCD instead of film. These sensors convert light waves into pixels and can produce digital images in a number of different pixel dimensions. Most cameras nowadays are referred to as "megapixel" cameras, as they produce image files with over one million (M) pixels.

Storage media 6

Once an image has been taken, it needs to be saved and stored for later printout. Digital cameras use rewritable memory cards for this purpose and they can be purchased with different storage capacities.

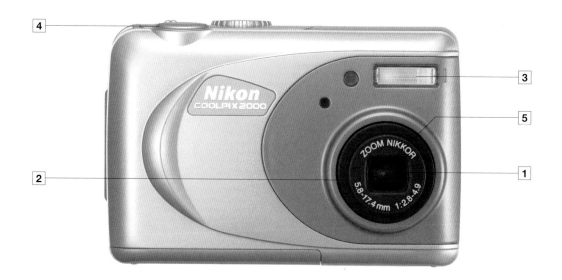

Computer connector 7

Once ready for enhancement, the image data must first be transferred from camera to computer. There are various types of cable connector available, including Universal Serial Bus (USB), FireWire and Small Computer Systems Interface (SCSI).

Liquid-crystal display monitor 8

The better cameras have a very useful liquid-crystal display (LCD) screen on the rear, which allows the user to preview pictures that have been captured, and to use the camera for real-time framing — like a camcorder. The LCD also gives access to menus and settings and has image playback options, including full frame, thumbnail and slide show.

Video out 9

With a video out function, a digital camera can be connected to a television set for previewing pictures. In the United States and Canada users can use a National Televison Standards Committee (NTSC) system for this, while those in the United Kingdom should look for cameras that have UK-compatible Phase Alternating Line (PAL) output.

Alternating current (AC) power supply 10

Digital cameras are power hungry, draining standard batteries quickly if both flash and LCD preview functions are in constant use. In order to minimize costs, users should aim for a model that accepts rechargeable batteries. Many cameras have an optional AC adaptor for running directly off an outlet, which is essential when transferring images to a PC.

Sound and video

Some cameras will allow the user to capture and create a short desktop-quality movie, which can then be played back via computer. Sound clips can be captured for adding verbal "memos" to pictures.

Optical viewfinder

Most digital cameras use a simple viewfinder window to frame and compose an image.

See also Memory cards *pages 34–35* / Connecting to a computer *pages 36–37* / Working with flash *pages 52–53* / Camera handling *pages 62–63* / Capture *pages 74–75* /

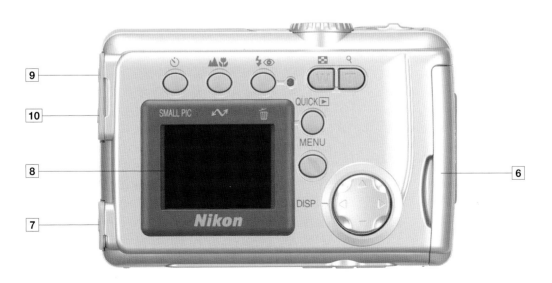

Camera functions: image-quality settings

It is vital to understand all the factors that influence digital-image quality.

ISO speed [1]

International Standards Organization (ISO) speed is a term used in traditional photography to indicate the light sensitivity of film materials. With conventional film, special light-sensitive emulsions are manufactured to work successfully under bright, normal or low-light conditions with respective speeds, for example, of ISO 50, ISO 100 and ISO 800. As each of these values doubles, the sensitive material needs only half the amount of light to work effectively. If the ISO value is halved, say from 400 to 200, then twice the amount of light is necessary. The best-quality images are produced using the lower ISO settings. Basic digital cameras are designed with just one ISO speed setting, usually ISO 200, but better digital cameras have a range of different ISO speeds that can be set to match a range of specific conditions, even those particular to an individual shot.

ISO by-products [2]

Inextricably connected to ISO is an aspect of digital-image quality called "noise." When high ISO settings are selected and images are shot under low lighting conditions, insufficient light causes the creation of error pixels, called noise. The sensor creates bright red or green pixels in order to fill in the missing data. A large number of these produces a visible loss of image detail and sharpness. Noise is most visible in the shadow areas of a digital image and the effects can be minimized, but not removed entirely, by filtering them out in a good imaging application such as Adobe Photoshop. Many professional photographers avoid noise by opting to shoot conventional film in low light, which is then scanned using a special film scanner.

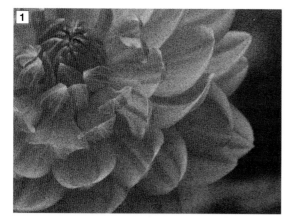

Noise is very evident when shooting at a high ISO.

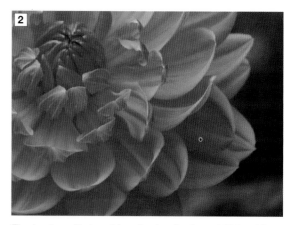

The best quality is achieved using the lowest ISO setting.

File formats 3

Many of the better cameras can package digital-image data directly using the universal Tagged Image File Format (TIFF). This is used throughout the print and publishing world and can be read by most image, graphics and desktop-publishing applications.
There are several different variations of a TIFF file, including a less universal compressed one. However, digital camera TIFF files are usually uncompressed and take up lots of storage space. In conjunction with this problem is the noticeable delay, or lag, between shots, as the camera tries to process and store the data and get ready to take the next picture. There is little visible difference between a TIFF image and a high-quality JPEG (see below).

See also What is a digital image? *pages 72–73* / File formats *pages 86–87* / Compression *pages 88–89* / Packaging image files *pages 90–91* /

Compression 4

The large data files that are created by digital images can be reduced in size using a compression routine such as JPEG. The JPEG routine was developed by the Joint Photographic Experts Group and involves a clever mathematical sequence which minimizes the need for a discrete instruction for each individual pixel. As a result, compressed images take up far less space on a removable memory card, thereby increasing the number of shots that can be stored there. Digital cameras usually have high-, normal- and low-quality JPEG settings, where the highest gives the best-quality images coupled with small data-saving; normal gives reasonable quality with more data-saving and a low setting gives the poorest quality but the greatest data-saving. The drawback with highly compressed images is a very visible blocky pattern, which cannot be removed using software processing. High-quality JPEGs have become the established standard file format for good-quality printouts.

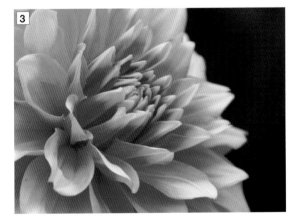

Saving as a TIFF file maintains maximum image quality.

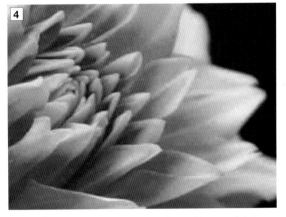

The trade-off with a JPEG file is a loss of image detail.

Camera functions: color settings

Without the need for screw-on color filters, digital cameras have a range of tools for managing light and color.

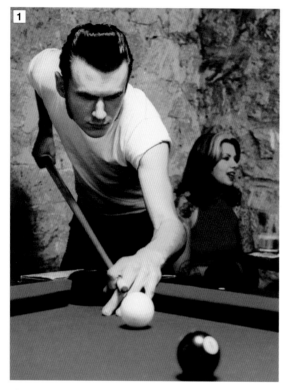

Uncorrected artificial light can cause strange color shifts.

METERING	MATRIX
SHUTTER	1/60
APERTURE	f4
EXP +/-	0.0
FOCAL LENGTH	40MM
EXP MODE	AUTO

Most settings can be set via the LCD panel.

White balance 1

Traditional photographic film is manufactured to work only within a specific range of natural daylight and will produce strange and unexpected colors if shooting under artificial illumination. Digital cameras have a white balance function, which provides invisible color correction to the effects of fluorescent tube or domestic tungsten lighting. The automatic white balance setting is perfectly acceptable for most photographic situations — including normal daylight shooting — but professional photographers should seek a camera that has precision color temperature controls using the Kelvin scale (K) for assignments where accurate color is critical.

Color space 2

The term color space is best thought of in terms of a color palette. Each color space or palette is defined by its own unique number of different colors and many good-quality digital devices such as printers, scanners, monitors and digital cameras can be set to create digital images using a common color space. The advantage of working within a consistent color space is to avoid unwanted color change when images are transferred between different devices, where some colors could convert with a far from exact match. The Red Green Blue (RGB) color space is a general palette used in most digital cameras, but better cameras can be set to shoot in the Adobe RGB (1998) color space, which draws upon a larger range. Professional image-editing software like Adobe Photoshop allows the management of images produced under a range of different color spaces, thereby minimizing the visible damage. If digital images consistently lack color or brightness, it is worth checking the color preferences of the imaging application to see how the files are being interpreted.

Image size and resolution

Many digital cameras allow images to be created in more than one size. This is especially useful if the camera is to be used for both print and Internet end products. There is no advantage in shooting an enormous image, say, 1800x1200 pixels, if the end use is for a web page or an e-mail attachment, in which cases a smaller size option, usually 640x480 pixels, is best. In general, the smaller the image size selected, the more images that can be stored on a camera's removable memory card. The drawback in shooting smaller images, however, is that they will not be suitable for photo-quality printout. Subjects to be photographed for both Internet and print use should be shot on the largest image size available with a second, smaller, version made by resizing the image in Photoshop or another imaging application.

Sharpening 3

The sharpening option on a digital camera is usually available in high, normal and off settings. The filter works by increasing the contrast at the edges of strong shapes within an image. It should only be used if files are to be printed directly or used on-screen without further processing or manipulation. Should sharpened images be manipulated further, error pixels, known as artifacts, will become apparent. For high-quality print work and commercial reproduction, leave the sharpening filter off, as this can be applied in Photoshop as the very final processing step.

See also Seeing in color *pages 58–59* / Resolution *pages 78–79* / Pixels and print size *pages 82–83* / Sharpening *pages 190–191* /

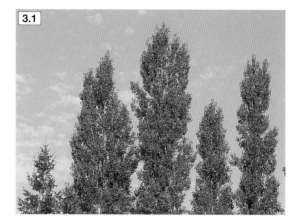

Oversharpened images can look very artificial.

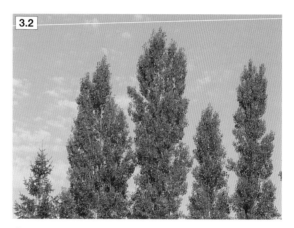

Correctly sharpened images display all available detail.

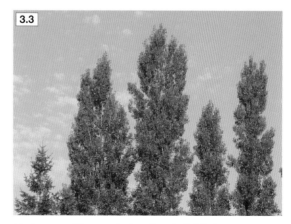

Unsharpened images look soft and slightly low-contrast.

Camera functions: creative settings

In addition to the various technical controls available, digital cameras can be used with creative settings, too.

Monochrome 1

Many digital cameras allow the user to shoot in a monochrome or sepia mode for making black-and-white photographs. Although monochrome photography is an attractive and stylish way to make digital images, the process is much better undertaken by converting RGB color images to monochrome using imaging software. This way, a wide range of contrast effects can be achieved with the added bonus of an identical color original to use, too.

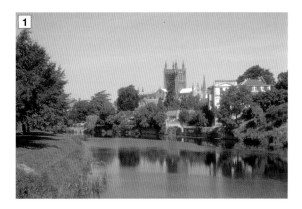

Contrast 2

Contrast is best defined as the amount of strong black and pure white in a photographic image. In certain lighting conditions, for example on a foggy or overcast day, natural light is said to be low-contrast — having many shades of gray, but no strong blacks and whites. Such circumstances will produce photographs lacking strong tones and colors.

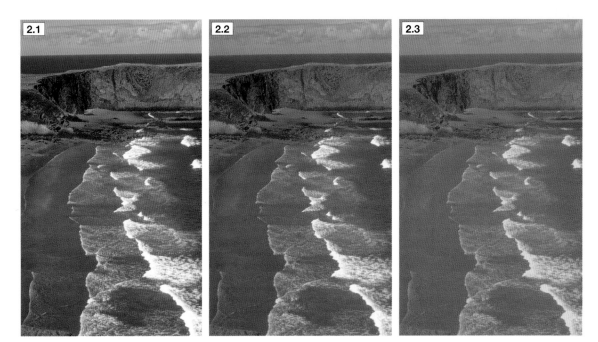

Shot with high-contrast option.

Shot with normal contrast option.

Shot with contrast option turned off.

Many digital cameras have contrast-adjusting settings to compensate for these naturally occurring situations. Yet, despite the usefulness of these, far greater control can be exercised using imaging software. Once a pre-set has been selected and imposed on an image file, there is no way of reversing it out; but with software-imposed adjustments, there is always the possibility of reverting back to the original file if mistakes are made.

Exposure Value 3

The exposure compensation function has been a feature of good-quality film cameras for many years and is much used by professionals in getting the best results from difficult film material such as color slides. This setting allows the user to deliberately override the exposure set by the camera in fixed increments. By setting a "+" value, images will be produced slightly brighter and by setting a "–" value, slightly darker images are created. If there are doubts as to the likelihood of an exposure working out, then a useful process is to shoot several identical images, each with

a different Exposure Value (EV). This process is called bracketing and is used by professional photographers to guarantee that they have at least one perfect result when faced with challenging circumstances.

Using pre-sets for direct printing

With the advent of cameras that have a direct printer connection, prints can be made without the need for computer transfer and enhancement. Pre-sets can be a very useful way of enhancing digital photographs, yet most printer software will allow the batch processing of a set of images using enhancement commands such as color, contrast correction and sharpness.

See also Exposure and how to measure it *pages 40–41* / Working with natural light *pages 50–51* / Seeing in monochrome *pages 60–61* /

Ideal camera settings for general-purpose photography

ISO: lowest (e.g. 200)
White balance: auto
File format: high-quality JPEG
Color space: RGB (or Adobe 1998)
Sharpening: off
Contrast: off
Image size: largest
+/–: set to zero or off

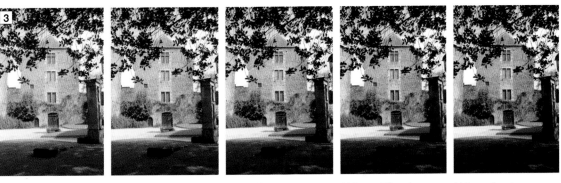

| Value: –1 less. | Value: –1/2 less. | Normal exposure. | Value: +1/2 extra. | Value: +1 extra. |

Point-and-shoot digital compact camera

Despite the low price tag and a restricted set of controls, the budget digital camera is a very useful tool indeed.

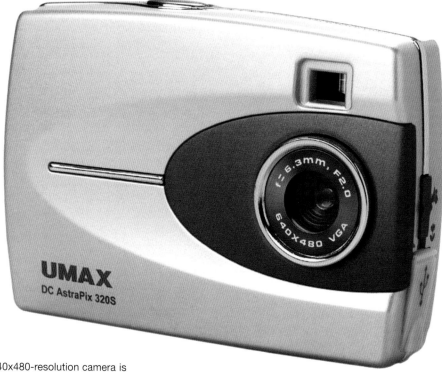

A simple 640x480-resolution camera is great for on-screen use.

Typical specifications

At this end of the market, cameras are said to be low-resolution devices and are generally capable of producing images containing only 300,000 pixels (0.3M) in a 640x480-pixel dimension. Images of this size are only suitable for on-screen or web-page use, or for very small and poor quality printout. Subject detail is not sharp, with fewer pixels making a bad job of describing curved or intricate shapes. Lenses are usually of a plastic construction and may prove poor at recording delicate subject detail and contrast extremes. Zoom lenses are unlikely in this price range, meaning the user has to move physically closer to or further away from a subject to achieve a pleasing composition. Lens-focusing controls are usually fixed, so there is no opportunity to pick a point of focus or experiment creatively with depth of field. Some devices are capable of low-quality webcam use, shooting very low-resolution images such 320x240 pixels every few seconds or so, which can then be transferred directly to a networked computer. Few cameras have cross-platform capability, favoring the universal Windows PC rather than the Apple computer user.

Practical uses

This kind of camera is sold as a general-purpose recording device for situations where any kind of image will suffice as long as it can show reasonable detail. Such images are destined for e-mail attachments and web-page use and will benefit from creative computer enhancement first. At their very low cost they are an ideal way for children to experience the fun of digital photography for the first time, rather than being a creative tool for aspiring photographers.

Typical camera features

Image storage

Many cameras have built-in memory, rather than a removable card. There is no way of increasing storage capacity and images need to be routinely transferred to a computer and the card cleared.

Previews

To keep costs low and battery usage to a minimum, few cameras of this kind have LCD preview screens, so there is no way of checking or editing results on location.

Creative controls

Exposure controls are usually entirely automatic with no option for setting creative shutter speeds or aperture values. These cameras are usually able to cope only with typical sunny-day photography. Subjects under extreme contrast or unusual lighting may not record as hoped.

Battery power

This is usually the throwaway alkaline type, rather than rechargeable, and rarely has an AC power option. Running costs can be high, especially when used in power intensive situations such as computer transfer.

Viewfinder information

Little feedback information is presented in the viewfinder window with the exception of a single light that indicates when there is too little light for a successful exposure.

Flash unit

If present, this will be a low-power unit, with little or no controls for half or quarter power, or red-eye reduction.

Camera settings

There are few options to choose from other than high-, medium- and low-image compression settings.

Software

Only basic browser software will be included with the package, if at all, so images cannot be selectively edited or transferred to a computer.

See also Anatomy of a digital camera *pages 10–11* / Connecting to a computer *pages 36–37* / Camera handling *pages 62–63* / Budget workstation *pages 112–113* /

Midprice compact camera

Falling costs and rising specifications make the midprice compact camera the ideal model to start with.

Typical specifications

With a better quality of construction for both body and lens, this type of device will support more creative play than a basic point-and-shoot camera. With a sensor capable of producing 2–3M pixels, print quality up to 8½ x 11 inches (21.5 x 28cm) will be excellent. These cameras usually have a zoom lens, varying from a semi-wide angle to a moderately long telephoto, giving much needed assistance to the photographer when shooting indoors and out on location, respectively. Different models also give value-added functions to tempt the potential buyer, such as Motion Picture Experts Group (MPEG) video clip creation, sound annotation, time-lapse controls or a weatherproof outer casing. There are sufficient models within this price range to meet the demands of most lifestyles and pastimes.

Styled with a handy grip and useful zoom lens, the Olympus Camedia can capture images with over 2M pixels.

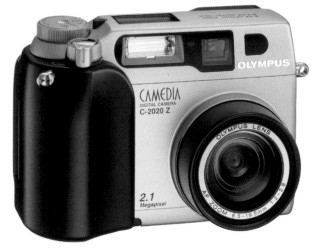

On its reverse is a clearly laid out set of mode dials and setting selections, plus a good-sized LCD preview screen.

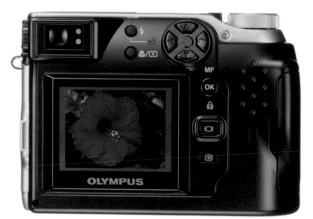

Practical uses

These cameras are excellent for producing high-quality images for in-house brochures and websites, assignment work for creative art and design projects and great photographs of family and friends. Results will be similar to those produced by a good-quality 35mm-film compact camera and computer-enhanced images will make ink-jet prints that are indistinguishable from conventional photographs.

Typical camera features

Image storage

Images are stored on removable memory cards and additional or higher capacity cards may be purchased to reduce the need to return home (or carry along a laptop) for computer transfer.

Previews

Images can be checked as soon as they have been shot using a small, color LCD preview screen on the reverse of the camera. Different playback modes allow images to be viewed as tiny thumbnails or as a rolling slide show. Individual images can be deleted from the memory card, making more space available to take better photographs.

Live composing

An added bonus is the ability to frame and compose a shot live by using the LCD screen. Just like the viewfinder of a video camera, the LCD preview gives a real-time display without having to bring the camera to your eye, allowing you to press the shutter at exactly the right moment.

Creative controls

Special shooting modes, including portrait, action, landscape or close-up, are offered, each with a pre-set combination of correct aperture and shutter speed to match the situation. Better cameras will have a manual exposure mode together with a limited number of aperture and shutter speed settings for photographers who have some previous experience with a 35mm SLR camera.

Camera settings

In addition to JPEG compression options these cameras offer exposure compensation and pre-sets such as sharpening, white balance and contrast compensation. On better cameras an uncompressed TIFF may be an alternative, but will take much longer to save and store. At around seven megabytes (MB) in size, a TIFF will rapidly occupy capacity on a memory card.

Lens control

With an autofocus system in place, specific points of focus can be selected by depressing halfway the shutter release. Focus points can also be held by keeping the shutter release half-depressed and recomposing the shot — a very useful tool when off-center compositions are required. Better cameras will also have a macro function for close-up photography of small objects or details, or creative shooting.

Playback information

The LCD playback screen will provide access to all camera settings chosen and set by use of a range of companion navigation buttons and dials. For users not accustomed to operating handheld electronic devices, navigating different levels of commands can take time to master. The best cameras are designed with intuitive navigation and very few levels, so all the commonly needed controls are at hand.

See also Anatomy of a digital camera *pages 10–11* / Connecting to a computer *pages 36–37* / Camera handling *pages 62–63* / Midprice workstation *pages 114–115* /

Top-price compact camera

Designed very much for the discerning and demanding photographer, the top-price compact camera offers almost all the same controls found on a traditional SLR.

Typical specifications

This kind of camera boasts a more rugged shell for taking the rough and tumble of repeated professional use. Together with a CCD sensor that can produce 4–6M pixels, this camera can make bigger and better images than a typical mid-price device — images that could easily be used for publication.

Practical uses

Very useful for professional photographers with complex and time-consuming commissions — and which could be simplified by avoiding the conventional film route — this kind of camera is an essential addition to any kit bag. Among the functions for technically demanding situations are full aperture and shutter speed controls, a greater

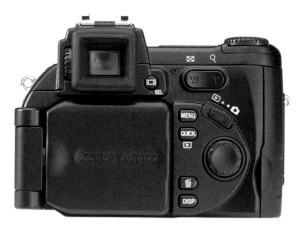

Ergonomically designed with the most important controls within easy reach, this camera also has a useful LCD.

The Nikon 5700 is built with a high specification and allows direct viewing through the lens.

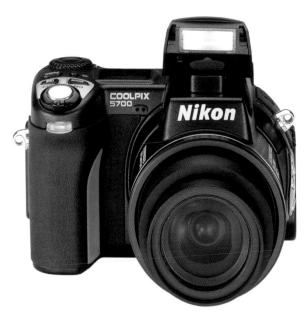

range of ISO, and white balance settings. Versatility is the key to this kind of camera, but a solid understanding of conventional photographic techniques is essential for making the most of it. Better cameras have a hot-shoe for adding more powerful external flash units and additional flash modes for creating great effects including rear curtain sync.

Typical camera features

Image storage
Many devices can utilize the high-capacity IBM Microdrive, providing up to one gigabyte (GB) of storage on one removable card, and have high-speed FireWire ports for fast computer transfer. In addition to JPEG and TIFF image formats, unique raw data files can also be created, such as the Nikon Electronic Format (NEF) common to Nikon cameras. Much like

a conventional computer, many cameras have additional onboard Random Access Memory (RAM) to help with processing and storing high-resolution images quickly, so several different images can be shot within the same second.

Previews

Preview functions extend to fully documented settings such as time and date of shooting. All pre-sets are recorded with each image, and the user can refer back to them at a later date.

Creative controls

Full aperture and shutter speed controls are common throughout the range, combined with fully manual operation — an essential option for photographers who want to create precise results and creative effects. The better cameras have the option of additional metering modes to complement the standard center-weighted system, such as multi-segment matrix mode and precision spot mode.

Camera settings

Instead of customized shooting modes — for example portrait — top-price cameras revert to standard film-camera mode descriptions such as aperture-priority and shutter speed-priority modes.

Lenses

In addition to a useful zoom, many cameras offer additional clip-on lens converters or a limited range of interchangeable lenses. Clip-on lenses are essentially filters that offer an opportunity to extend a camera's maximum wide-angle or telephoto range, albeit with a slight drop in image sharpness.

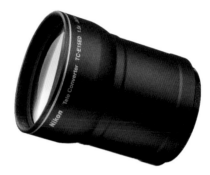

A slip-on telephoto lens.

Rotational lens

Found on one brand only — Nikon — the rotational lens offers a photographer the chance to try different viewpoints without compromising the visibility of the LCD preview screen. Unlike a conventional film camera, the rotational-lens digital compact camera allows the user to change position without, for example, squatting down or climbing up a stepladder.

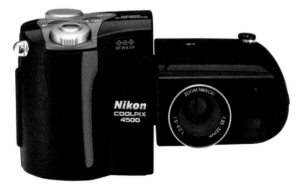

A rotating lens prevents awkward shooting posture.

See also Anatomy of a digital camera *pages 10–11* / Connecting to a computer *pages 36–37* / Camera handling *pages 62–63* / Professional workstation *pages 116–117* /

Multimedia features

Using the latest technology in video and sound compression, camera manufacturers have produced exciting features that offer great value for web designers and multimedia enthusiasts.

Compression techniques have not been applied just to digital photographs, but also to sound and video. As broadband Internet access increases across the world, web designers are offering a more interesting visitor experience through sound and video.

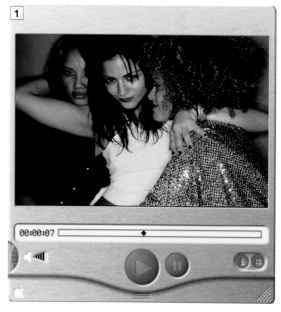

A desktop video clip viewed in Quicktime.

Desktop video

Many digital cameras offer the option of shooting a desktop video clip. These clips have a small pixel dimension — usually around 320x240 — and are only suitable for desktop computer use rather than television playback. This kind of video is not to be confused with camcorder capture, which is of a much higher resolution and quality. Many digital cameras can record 12 to 16 still images per second, which are then sequenced into the universal MPEG or Audio Video Interleave (AVI) movie file formats. There is a perceptible jarring in desktop video resulting from the limited frames shot per second. The length of video clip capture is determined by the capacity of a camera's memory card and, although data is compressed into efficient MPEG files, individual movies can run into many megabytes (MB) in size. Once transferred to a computer, desktop video files can be modified and even joined together using a basic video-editing software package.

Time lapse and webcam

Many digital cameras at the lower end of the market can also be used as webcams. Essentially, webcams capture a sequence of low-resolution images with a user-defined delay between each one. The images are then uploaded automatically to a web server where they immediately refresh a web page with the latest image. Time-lapse functions follow a similar pattern, but without the web upload. Time-lapse stills can be captured in high resolution, and sequenced into a slide show using any of the commonly available slide show shareware.

Sound annotation

Many digital cameras are fitted with built-in microphones, which can be used for adding sound to video clips or recording personal annotations when shooting still images. These verbal "memos" can be a very useful way of recording important reference detail, making later editing and cataloging a much easier process.

Wireless transfer

Some top-price digital compacts offer the ability to transfer images directly to a personal web server or through a compatible cellphone. This kind of image transfer can be slow and expensive when large numbers of images are involved, but it is a useful aid if speed is of the essence or in an urgent situation.

MP3 player · 2

The digital revolution is also affecting music, with the creation of data-efficient MP3 music files. MP3 players use removable media for storage and later playback — just like digital cameras — and for the media-hungry consumer, there are devices that will do both.

Panoramic shooting

Another great web invention is the digital panoramic image. A number of pictures taken in a 360-degree arc can be "stitched together" using special onboard software. When viewed on a desktop media player such as Quicktime, or within a web browser, the user is able to scroll left and right and even to zoom in

closer. More precise panoramic images can be made using still images stitched together into Quicktime Virtual Reality (QTVR) files. This facility is used when advertising products on the Internet and enables users to go on virtual tours of, for example, a house.

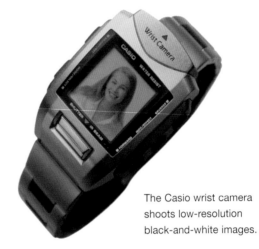

The Casio wrist camera shoots low-resolution black-and-white images.

See also Quicktime VR software *pages 160–161* / Slide-show software *pages 162–163* /

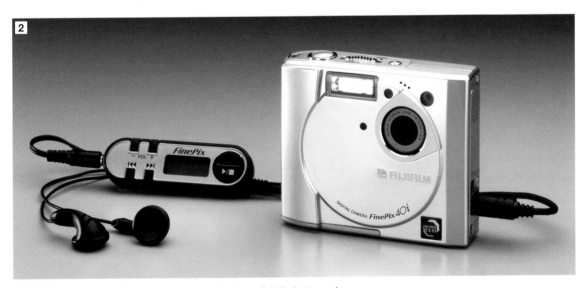

The Fuji FinePix 40i can play MP3 music and shoot digital photographs.

Digital SLR

At the top of the price range is the versatile single lens reflex (SLR) digital camera with interchangeable lenses and fully manual controls.

Typical specifications

The digital SLR is ergonomically designed to have all the important dials and switches within range of a roving thumb and index finger so that photography can continue with the camera pressed to the eye. The camera body is rugged enough to take repeated professional use and all lenses and accessories are of the highest specification.

Practical uses

This is an essential tool for the keen photographer who doesn't want to sacrifice creative control for convenience. Set at ten times the price of a basic digital point-and-shoot, this camera will easily pay for itself within the first year of commercial use. With a sensor creating a minimum of 6M pixels, there is sufficient image data to make high-quality printouts for most commercial purposes, including catalog photography, weddings, portraits and photojournalism.

Typical camera features [1]

Image storage

Most cameras use the CompactFlash or IBM Microdrive systems to store large image files, with older models favoring the PCMCIA mini hard drive. A large onboard memory affords minimum delay between exposures — an essential prerequisite for sports and reportage photography.

Previews

With an SLR, subject matter is viewed and composed through the lens rather than a separate viewfinder window, so what you see is what you get. The better

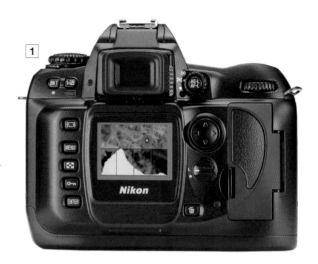

The Nikon D100 provides a histogram preview function.

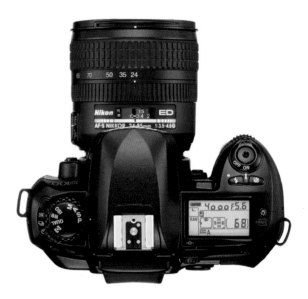

Nikon D100 SLR top.

cameras will have a dial-in diopter, so glasses-wearers can select a setting to match their prescription. On the LCD preview screen, in addition to a comprehensive assortment of playback styles and a useful zoom function for checking focus, the SLR will also display areas of overexposure and — invaluable for the professional user — offers a graphic representation of image tonality via a histogram. To an experienced user, the histogram depicts highlight, midtone and shadow values and can tell the photographer if another exposure needs to be taken.

Creative controls

As with a good-quality film SLR, all creative controls — aperture, shutter speed and exposure compensation — are available independently. There are usually three options for precise light metering: standard center-weighted mode, where a light reading is taken from a central part of the image; the more accurate matrix mode, which makes an average value from five or more segments across the whole image area; and spot metering. Spot readings should only be taken when tiny sections of an image are deemed important — a person's face in a location portrait, for example.

Camera settings

Precision controls are on hand to extend the ISO range into the super-sensitive ISO 1600 and beyond, and white balance settings can be customized to match exact color temperature values and light sources. Color space options may extend beyond the standard RGB to include other universal tags such as Adobe RGB (1998).

Lenses

Digital SLR camera bodies are based on existing Nikon or Canon film cameras and can use existing lenses in a photographer's kit. As the image sensor is smaller than 35mm film, lens focal lengths effectively increase, usually by a factor of 1.5. This has obvious advantages with telephotos, as 200mm increases to 300mm. To achieve the same effect as a film camera's 28mm wide angles, however, a new 17mm lens will need to be purchased. Autofocus controls are more advanced too, with many cameras offering five or more options, so the user can lock on to subjects off-center. The better cameras also offer a tracking autofocus mode for moving subjects.

Software

Additional software is available to control the camera directly from a computer — a particularly useful way of working on repetitive tabletop studio shoots.

Battery power

Large rechargeable packs are supplied and enable a good day of uninterrupted shooting. The better cameras have additional car chargers, essential for photographers on the move.

Flash connectors

Both studio and hot-shoe flash connections are present, allowing a wider range of commercial tasks to be undertaken.

See also Anatomy of a digital camera *pages 10–11* / Camera functions *pages 12–16* / Professional workstation *pages 116–117* / Location workstation *pages 118–119* /

Capture backs for medium-format cameras

The most exciting innovation for professional photographers is the digital capture back.

Medium-format cameras ⬚1

Unlike the small-format 35mm-film camera, the medium-format camera uses larger film stock and can produce highly detailed images capable of greater enlargement. Many medium-format camera systems have been developed along similar lines by Hasselblad, Mamiya and Bronica. They are typified by a wide range of interchangeable lenses, winders, viewers and removable film backs. The great advantage of removable film backs is the ability to change film type during a shoot, without the need for a separate camera or rewinding a half-used film.

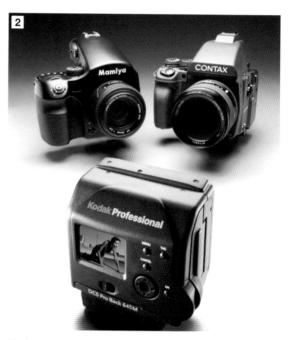

Kodak Pro Back supports a wide range of camera bodies.

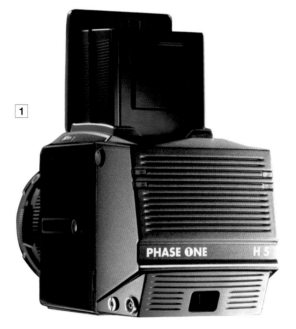

Phase One capture back for medium-format cameras.

Digital capture back ⬚2

The digital capture back has been designed to integrate within this well-established professional camera system, and fits onto the rear of the medium-format camera body just like any other film back. In addition to shooting color and black-and-white film options, therefore, the professional can shoot digital too. Most digital backs have been designed with interchangeable adaptors to fit onto most professional camera bodies, so the photographer can still use existing lenses and accessories. Unlike digital backs for large-format cameras, these backs are single shot and can be used on moving subject matter.

Tethered and handheld 3

Two different types of digital camera back are currently available: the tethered model, which has to be connected to a computer or storage unit with power supply; and the handheld model. The tethered device is fine for still-life studio subjects and even portraits, but may prove cumbersome if the photographer enjoys freedom of movement away from a tripod. It is also impractical on location. The more versatile handheld camera back has its own power source, removable memory, and permits the same shooting freedom as a medium-format camera fitted with a conventional film back.

Typical specifications

Better backs offer 8-bit RGB capture in excess of 48MB — well over twice the size of the nearest digital SLR rival and more than enough for most commercial assignments for lithographic reproduction. As with a good-quality digital compact camera, full LCD previews and functions are provided, together with a range of ISO speed and compression settings. CompactFlash removable media is standard and FireWire or SCSI II connectors are provided for fast computer transfer. Sophisticated color-management software is also provided for color-critical assignments and for working within a specific color space.

In use

With such large quantities of data to save and store, there will be a short delay between exposures. Better backs have onboard memory modules that act as buffers to enable repeated shooting for three to five exposures before writing to a permanent storage media. With all the flexibility of a top-quality digital SLR, the handheld digital back allows the photographer to shoot, review and package image data for a seamless integration into professional color-calibrated devices.

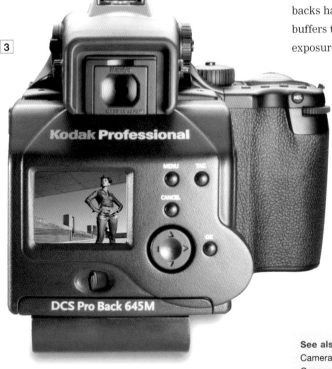

3

The Pro Back provides a useful LCD preview function.

See also Anatomy of a digital camera *pages 10–11* / Camera functions *pages 12–13* / Memory cards *pages 34–35* / Connecting to a computer *pages 36–37* /

Scanning backs for large-format cameras

Large-format film cameras are traditionally used for shooting highly detailed and precise images for commercial reproduction.

Large-format cameras

At the top end of the professional camera market is the large-format 4x5 film camera, so called because it uses film cut into 4x5-inch sheets rather than cassettes or rolls. Despite the high price tag the design of a 4x5 camera has changed little in the last 50 years. Essentially, the camera consists of a high-quality lens set into a front U-shaped standard, a set of extendable bellows and a film holder set into a rear U-shaped standard. All variable settings such as aperture and shutter speeds are placed on the lens, together with a wind-up clockwork shutter and a manual shutter release. The camera is still in great demand because both lens and film standards can be moved independently from each other and can manipulate an object's shape, focus and depth of field. All exposure measurements are made with a handheld light or flash meter and, with the exception of architectural subjects, the camera is designed primarily for studio use. Unlike different medium-format film backs, the film holder for a 4x5 is a universal shape, size and design.

Digital scanning back   1

The digital scanning back is designed to be the same size as a standard 4x5 film holder and inserts into the camera in exactly the same way. Like a desktop flatbed scanner, the scanning back has a linear rather than a grid-like CCD sensor. With a linear sensor, the thin CCD moves slowly along in a single pass, detecting continuous light along the way. Power and an external storage drive are essential, as data is collected and processed into enormous files of up to 550MB.

See also Connecting to a computer *pages 36–37* / Data management *pages 84–85* / Flatbed scanner interface *pages 124–125* /

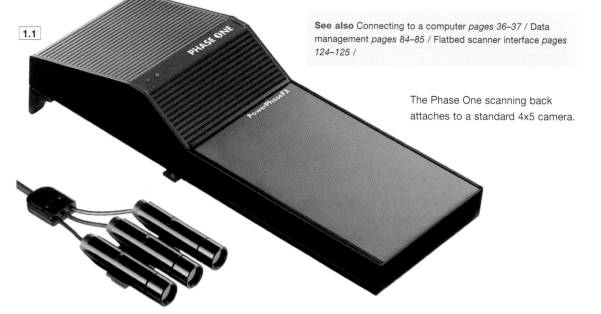

1.1

The Phase One scanning back attaches to a standard 4x5 camera.

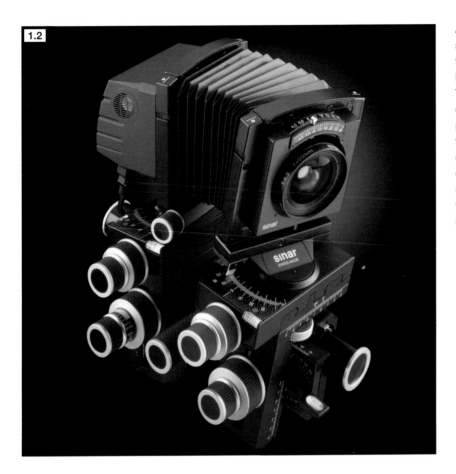

1.2

An alternative to the scanning back for a large-format camera is the matrix back such as this Sinar. Taking advantage of the camera's movement and perspective control functions, this kind of digital sensor offers high quality results, albeit with an effective increase in lens focal length due the small size of the sensor.

Typical specifications

Most scanning backs have precision software controls for color management and a wide range of file size, format and color-depth controls. Many devices allow the capture of 14-bit data per RGB color channel for producing flawless tonal gradations. Connection to a computer is usually via the fast SCSI II or IEEE 1394 FireWire ports. Like all digital sensors, the scanning back is smaller than a sheet of 4x5 film material, so existing lens focal lengths will be longer than normal. For most studio assignments, this does not pose a significant problem. Unlike traditional film, this type of digital sensor has an exceptional dynamic range and can produce detail across an enormous 11 f-stop range.

In use

Moving objects and those that cannot hold a fixed position for longer than a few seconds cannot be recorded, because the sensor can make sharp results from static subject matter only. The device can also work only under continuous lighting, rather than the rapid fire of a studio flash unit. Lighting can range from the hot and uncomfortable tungsten style to a bank of cooler daylight-corrected fluorescent tubes. In use, capture time will depend on the size of the image selected, with exposure times running into several minutes for capture at the highest resolution. When using a SCSI II cable to transfer data directly to a computer workstation, the scanning back can rarely be used further than 16 feet (5m) away.

Digital video cameras

The next few years will see a convergence between the technology used in mid-priced digital cameras and digital video camcorders.

D esigned for a totally different market and purpose, the superior digital camcorder can also shoot still images. The range of camcorders available runs into several platforms, recording media and levels of resolution. In the last couple of years, the digital camcorder has become the dominant tool, replacing analog Video Home System (VHS) and Superior Video Home System (SVHS) recorders. Digital video cameras record directly onto mini digital video (DV) tape cassettes and the better models can produce a near broadcast quality image. Camcorders work by shooting a sequence of images every second — up to 25 in most cases. Individual frames or scans do not have to be particularly high in resolution because they appear in quick succession during playback. This major functional difference between stills and movies explains why still images extracted from existing video footage — called video grabs — are always such poor quality.

Shooting stills

Each camcorder is marketed on its sensor size and a typical CCD can produce 0.8 to 1.3M pixels in still-shooting mode. Further to the high-capacity mini DV tape for recording stills and video footage, many camcorders have an additional storage card for stills only. Typical media are the Memory Stick in Sony devices and the Secure Digital (SD) card or the less frequently found MultiMedia cards. All can be connected to a PC using standard USB or FireWire cables, or removed and used in memory-card readers. Stills can be shot during normal video recording or during preview with the LCD screen. The better camcorders have mechanical shutters to prevent image blurring and can produce reasonably good-quality results in the universal JPEG format. Users should look for a camcorder that offers a range of different JPEG compression options, because a fixed

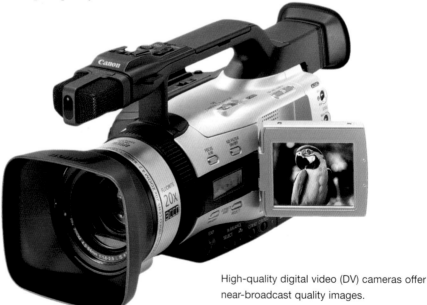

High-quality digital video (DV) cameras offer near-broadcast quality images.

JPEG routine may not work well for finely detailed images with many colors. Great care must be taken to steady the camera during shooting, as camcorders do not have the same ergonomics as a digital compact camera. With a more extensive zoom lens range than a typical stills camera, a camcorder also uses a digital zoom function for pulling in far-away subjects, but often at the expense of image quality. Don't expect pin-sharp results in stills shot with a digital zoom.

See also Memory cards *pages 34–35* / Compression *pages 88–89* / Packaging image files *pages 90–91* / Connections and ports *pages 104–105* /

Acceptable use

With images containing fewer than 1M pixels, print quality will be poor over a standard 6x4 size, but as camcorder specifications improve, image quality should rise. Camcorder stills are ideal for web and on-screen use, and will look even better when their pixel dimensions are reduced to fit within the size restrictions of a typical web page. Less ideal for recording sharp detail or intricate shapes, camcorder stills are fine for cataloging collections or product ranges. Saved in the universal JPEG format, the stills can also be enhanced in Photoshop and other imaging applications. Camcorders are better than digital stills cameras that can record desktop video, as high-quality video footage from a camcorder can be compressed in both data and physical dimensions for web or intranet use.

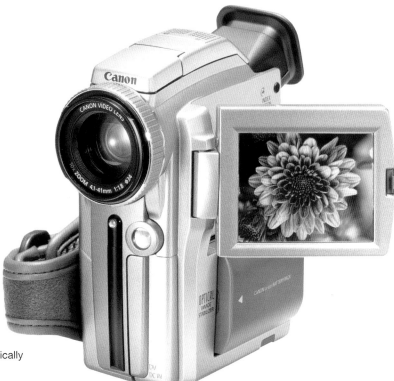

A compact DV camera is typically aimed at the family user.

Memory cards

There are several different types of media used for storing digital camera data and all have their advantages and limitations.

Buying a camera

Most cameras are bundled with at least one memory card, but these are usually of a small capacity such as 8 or 16MB. An additional higher-capacity card is an essential part of the photographer's kit and, with prices dropping all the time, extra media won't break the bank. Extra cards or extra storage space give users the chance to roam and shoot without needing to return to base and, with today's better digital cameras needing 1MB per image, it makes sense to invest in the largest affordable model. Cards can be vulnerable when carried outside the camera body and should only be transported in purpose-made antistatic containers.

SmartMedia 1

Found in Fuji, Ricoh and Olympus digital cameras, the SmartMedia looks like a thin black wafer with one corner missing. Less hardy than CompactFlash media, the SmartMedia card has a gold-covered contact area for linking with the camera. Available in most common capacities up to 128MB, earlier versions of the cards worked at a different voltage and are incompatible with newer cameras. Good brands to look out for are Fuji and Samsung.

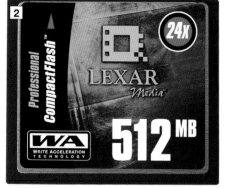

CompactFlash 2

Bigger and thicker than a SmartMedia card is the CompactFlash memory card. Establishing itself firmly as the dominant media type, these cards are used by Nikon, Kodak and Epson digital cameras. CompactFlash cards are square in shape and have 50 female plugs on one end, which slide easily into the camera card bay. Capacities range up to 512MB and recent developments have seen the introduction of cards with different read/write speeds. Like a computer compact disc (CD) writer, these latest cards can be bought with speeds like 4X, 16X and 24X and essentially allow users to shoot and save at a greater rate. Good brands to consider are Lexar and Kensington.

IBM Microdrive 3

The largest-capacity card is the IBM Microdrive, which is available in a 340, 512MB or gigantic one-gigabyte (GB) version. Unlike CompactFlash and SmartMedia cards, which are solid — that is with no internal moving parts — the Microdrive is essentially a mini computer hard drive. Microdrives can share the same 50-pin port as a CompactFlash card, but

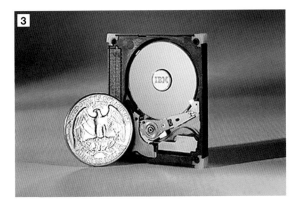

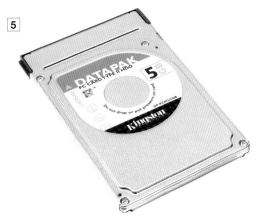

need a wider bay to cope with their increased thickness. Not all cameras that can use CompactFlash can support the Microdrive.

Memory Stick

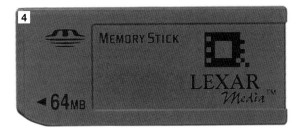

Found only in Sony digital cameras and digital video cameras, the Memory Stick is an entirely different shape to other media, but works in exactly the same way. Useful for storing low-resolution stills captured with superior digital video cameras, the Memory Stick can also be found in the Sony range of digital cameras. Special Memory Stick-compatible card readers are necessary for computer transfer, if direct camera-to-computer transfer is not available.

PCMCIA hard-drive

Technically the largest-capacity media and the standard in the first wave of professional digital cameras, the PCMCIA card is, in fact, a hard drive in miniature. Sold in a 240MB configuration, these cards can be inserted directly into any laptop fitted with a PCMCIA bay or into a PCMCIA card reader.

Mini CD-R

This is a revolutionary format which writes image data directly onto mini writable compact discs (CD-R). Only a handful of top-price cameras employ this technology, which is used by forensic and police photographers for capturing digital images that can be used as unequivocal evidence owing to the write-once nature of the discs and their original capture date.

3.5-inch floppy disk

Found in the Sony Mavica range of digital cameras, the floppy disk is a practical and efficient method of managing image data. The obvious drawback is the small capacity of the media and its slow transfer speed.

Disk errors

Although designed for repeated use, memory cards can develop errors. Reformatting the card in-camera is a sensible part of routine maintenance, and erasing and deleting images should not be carried out in third-party card readers. If catastrophic data loss occurs, special utility software can be used to rescue lost files.

See also Anatomy of a digital camera *pages 10–11* / Camera handling *pages 62–63* / What is a digital image? *pages 72–73* / Capture, storage and transfer *pages 74–75* /

Connecting to a computer

Before investing money in a camera, it is essential to check its computer compatibility beforehand.

Setting up and troubleshooting

A recent Windows PC or Apple Mac will have an essential USB port for connecting to a digital camera. The most unfortunate situation occurs when trying to connect a new camera to an older computer. Many older computers are not fitted with USB ports, but have slower and incompatible serial or parallel ports instead. If a computer has a vacant Peripheral Component Interconnect (PCI) slot, then the easiest and cheapest option is to install an internal USB card — an exercise that is no harder than wiring a home outlet. Before committing to a camera purchase, download its specifications from the maker's website and double check all hardware and software requirements.

Many cameras connect to computer hardware via the universal Toolkit Without An Interesting Name (TWAIN) software. TWAIN is like a software travel-plug adapter and allows many different hardware and standards to "talk" to each other. Other potential problems occur when camera connection software doesn't support older computer operating systems, such as Windows 95 and Mac OS 8.5. Such software updates are usually available for free download from the camera manufacturer's website. For business-orientated operating systems, such as Windows NT, USB is not supported. Once installed on a computer, camera software will start up as soon as the camera is connected.

Browser software 1

Many cameras are supplied with browser software that presents images as thumbnails, thereby allowing the user to decide which ones to upload. It is not essential to use browser software, as editing can be done using a more sophisticated imaging application. Once plugged into a computer, both the external card reader and the connected camera will appear on the desktop as icons, just as a CD or 3.5-inch floppy disk does. The contents can then be copied across to the hard drive without using the browser. Recent operating systems such as Apple OSX offer a built-in browser-like interface when viewing folders full of images.

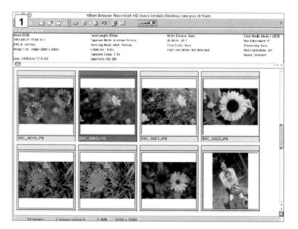

The Nikon View browser interface.

See also Memory cards *pages 34–35* / Computer basics *pages 96–97* / Connections and ports *pages 104–105* / Peripherals *pages 106–107* /

Download speed 2

The speed of data transfer can be a major factor when uploading images to a computer, with older serial port systems taking as long as half an hour to transfer the contents of a 32MB card. Precise comparisons between different kinds of computer connector are not easy to make, but as a general rule the fastest transfer occurs with FireWire, followed by USB and SCSI. Serial connectors are much slower, and slowest of all are the floppy-disk look-alike FlashPath converters. Wireless transfer using Bluetooth technology also sacrifices high-speed transfer for convenience.

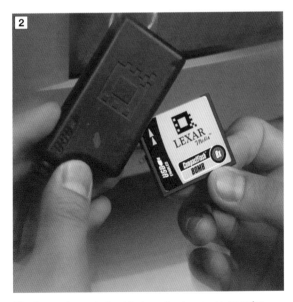

The Lexar Jumpshot cable is a simple way to transfer data from a CompactFlash card.

Dual-format card reader 3

A good accessory to add to a computer workstation is the dual-format card reader. Better models can accept all variations of SmartMedia, CompactFlash and IBM Microdrive media and can be left plugged into a computer for continual use. With most USB card readers drawing power from a computer's USB port, there is no need for additional power leads and no drain on a camera's batteries during download. Card readers can be an easy way to solve software incompatibilities between camera and computer.

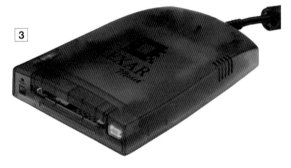

Docking station

An excellent invention is the docking station, which provides a digital camera with both a permanent connection to a computer and a power supply for topping up rechargeable batteries. Avoiding the need to keep plugging tiny USB plugs into tiny ports, the docking station is ideal for users who want to keep technology very much in the background and ready to use.

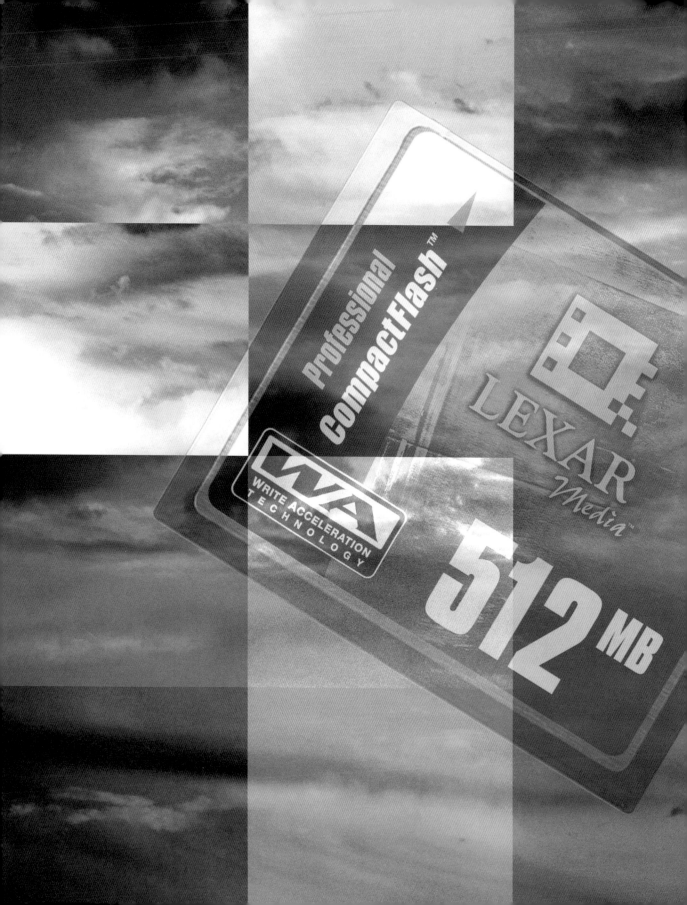

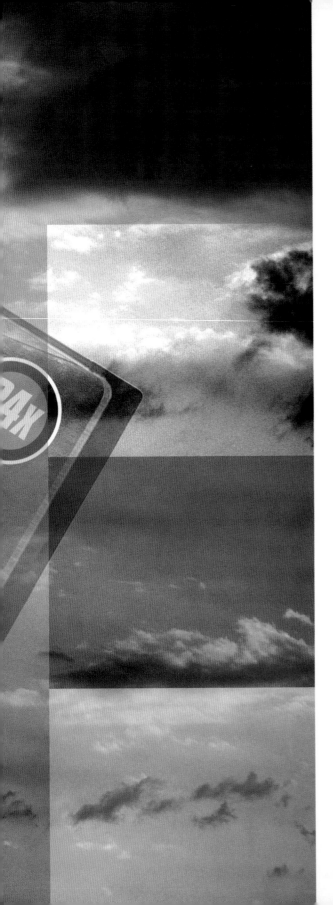

2 Taking Better Photos

Exposure and how to measure it

Correct exposure is the right combination of aperture f-number (f-stop) and shutter speed and makes all the difference to image quality.

Despite the many rescue tools found within digital imaging applications, there is no substitute for a good exposure. A perfect exposure will result in an even balance of highlight and shadow detail. Too much or too little light will have a profound effect on image detail, tone and color reproduction.

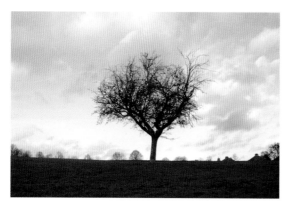

Shot without adjustment.

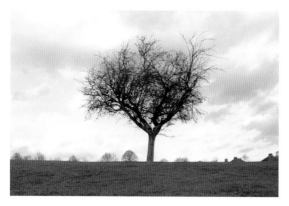

Shot at +1 stop over.

Camera metering systems   1

Every digital camera has a light-sensitive meter, which is used to regulate the automatic exposure functions and, on more advanced cameras, the manual exposure readout in the viewfinder. Light meters can only respond to the brightest values in a subject — regardless of size, shape or color — and consequently can be fooled by everyday situations. Bad exposures occur when a photographer wrongly presumes that the light meter knows the most important element of the picture, which of course it can't. Even a tiny lamp, taking up a small proportion of a composition, will be the dominant influence on the meter. Good photographers, therefore, are always aware of the bright highlight areas in their subjects.

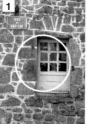 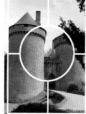 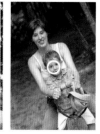

Three common metering systems (from left to right): center weighted, matrix and spot.

Overexposure and how to avoid it   2

Too much light makes pale and low-contrast images with burned-out details that cannot be rescued using software trickery. Although overexposure rarely occurs in digital cameras set to automatic exposure mode, it can still happen if too high an ISO value, such as ISO 800, is selected under bright lighting conditions. The most common cause of overexposure with digital compacts is when flash is used to light a nearby subject. Close-up flash can create too much light for a small aperture value to cope with and may cause image highlights to white out. On fully manual mode, overexposure is caused by selecting either a very slow shutter speed or a large aperture.

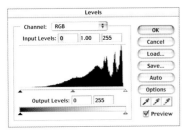

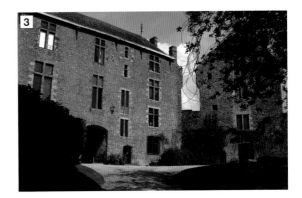

Overexposed images are washed out and show peaks in the highlight part of the histogram.

Underexposed images are dark and dull, with most pixels in the shadow part of the histogram.

Underexposure

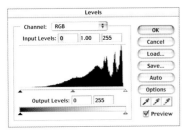

Underexposure occurs when too little light hits the camera sensor and creates dark images with muddy colors. Such images can be rescued using imaging software, but excessive changes will result in the sudden, random appearance of colored pixels and a general deterioration in image quality. Underexposure often results from shooting in low light on automatic exposure mode, because the camera's shutter speed range may not extend beyond a few seconds. Photographs taken using flash may be underexposed if the subject is further than 16 feet (5m) away, as the small burst of light is too weak to reach out to distant subjects.

The exposure compensation dial

Most good digital compact cameras and all SLRs have an additional exposure control called the exposure compensation switch. Identified by the "+/–" symbol, this can be used to counteract lighting situations that would otherwise fool the light meter. It works by allowing more or less light to reach the sensor as follows: the + settings increase exposure, for example +0.3, and the – settings decrease exposure, for example –0.6. Each whole number represents a difference of one aperture value, commonly referred to as a stop.

Bracketing

A sensible way to approach difficult exposure situations is to shoot a number of different variations of the same subject. Bracketing is really an insurance against failure and most situations are easily covered within a five-shot range where two versions are slightly over and two are slightly under. As a starting point users should try: normal (no exposure dial correction), +0.6, +1.0, –0.6, –1.0.

See also Camera functions *pages 16–17* / Aperture and depth of field *pages 42–43* / Shutter and movement *pages 44–45* / Capture, storage and transfer *pages 74–75* /

Aperture and depth of field

The aperture is the circular opening inside the camera lens, which controls the amount of light passing onto the CCD sensor. The aperture is primarily used to moderate light levels for a successful exposure, but it can also have a creative effect.

To enable photography under variable lighting conditions, lenses are manufactured with a built-in range of apertures, measured on an internationally recognized scale. Called f-numbers (or f-stop), the scale is as follows: f/2.8, f/4, f/5.6, f/8, f/11, f/16, f/22. At f/2.8, the aperture is at its largest and will let in the maximum amount of light possible. At the f/22 end of the scale, the aperture is at its smallest and lets in the minimum amount of light. In general, when available light levels are low, a large aperture should be selected and when light is too intense, a small aperture should be used.

Access to the aperture scale is usually found on one of the control buttons on the back of the camera, but only when manual or aperture-priority exposure mode is selected. In other modes such as automatic or shutter speed, the camera will decide on the right aperture value to make a correct exposure. Many point-and-shoot digital cameras only have a reduced aperture scale available, such as f/4 and f/11, while digital SLRs have the full range.

Aperture and light levels

The circular opening is manufactured precisely to allow an exact quantity of light to pass through. Moving one step up the scale halves the amount of light and moving one step down doubles it. This corresponds exactly to the fixed shutter speed scale, where the duration of light passing through the aperture is also halved or doubled.

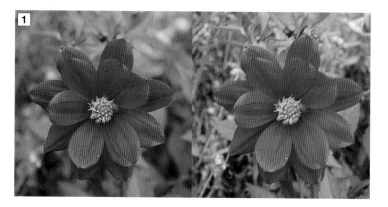

Depth of field [1]

Depth of field is a term used to describe the plane of sharp focus set between the nearest and furthest parts of a photographic subject. Depth of field is controlled by two factors: the aperture value selected on the lens and the user's distance to the subject. Small aperture values like f/22 will create a greater depth of field than larger aperture values like f/2.8.

Shallow depth of field [2]

This effect is used to blur out a distracting background and allow greater emphasis on the main subject. It is achieved by selecting a large aperture like f/2.4 or f/4 and framing the subject tightly in the viewfinder. It is used by wildlife and sports photographers to pick out a subject from a distance.

Deep depth of field [3]

Greater depth can be achieved by using smaller aperture values like f/16 and f/22. This is useful when a photograph needs to show sharp detail from foreground through to background, and is commonly used by landscape and architectural photographers.

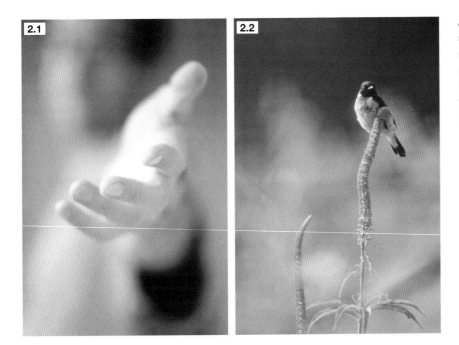

At close range, far left, a shallow depth of field can make you feel part of the picture. At a distance, near left, a shallow depth of field is used to blur out background details.

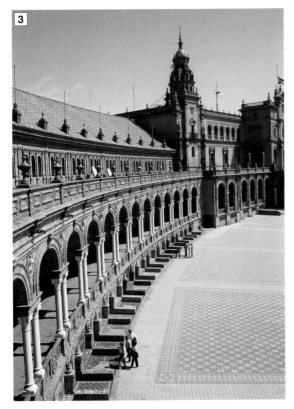

Subject detail

In addition to affecting the depth of field, aperture values also have a bearing on the amount of fine detail recorded. A lens records the sharpest detail when set to the middle value of its scale. On a lens that ranges from f/2.8 to f/22, therefore, the sharpest results will be produced at f/8.

See also Exposure and how to measure it *pages 40–41* / Shutter and movement *pages 44–45* / Working with natural light *pages 50–51* / Capture, storage and transfer *pages 74–75* /

Shutter and movement

Like aperture values, the shutter is an integral part of the exposure process, but it can also create stunning visual effects.

Shutter release button

The shutter release is the button to press down when taking a picture, and is so called because of the mechanical shutters on film cameras, which had to be opened at the moment of exposure. Digital cameras have electronic rather than mechanical shutters and do not produce the same satisfying clunk when released.

Shutter function

The shutter controls the length of time that the sensor is exposed to light. The shutter speeds are measured on a standard scale in fractions of a second. Unusually for an international measurement, shutter speeds are expressed in old-fashioned fractions, rather than decimal values, and are typically arranged as follows: $\frac{1}{1000}^{th}$, $\frac{1}{500}^{th}$, $\frac{1}{250}^{th}$, $\frac{1}{125}^{th}$, $\frac{1}{60}^{th}$, $\frac{1}{30}^{th}$, $\frac{1}{15}^{th}$, $\frac{1}{8}^{th}$, $\frac{1}{4}$, $\frac{1}{2}$ and 1. At the $\frac{1}{1000}^{th}$ end of the scale, the shutter remains open for a short time, while at $\frac{1}{2}$ second, the shutter remains open for longer. As with the aperture scale, one step along the scale will either double or halve the value.

Camera shake   1

Unintentionally blurred images are generally caused by camera shake. This happens when a slow shutter speed is selected, and there is slight body movement during exposure. Even a slight sway can cause the lens to move during exposure and the problem frequently occurs with telephoto lenses, or in low-light conditions. Setting a shutter speed of $\frac{1}{125}^{th}$ of a second or faster will solve the problem. If fast shutter speeds cannot be used, a tripod can be set up. Ultra-long telephoto lenses used on digital SLRs need a minimum $\frac{1}{250}^{th}$ to offset the increase in camera shake resulting from the extra weight and balance involved.

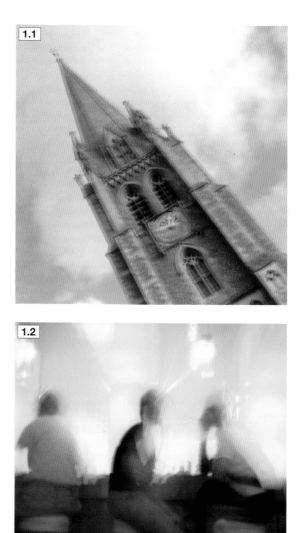

Excessive shake can actually be quite creative.

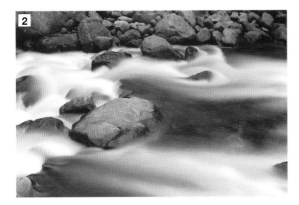

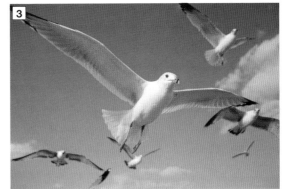

In order to create intentionally blurred effects, a slow shutter speed should be selected. Movement within photographic images can be used to create a sense of activity and action. Moving subjects, such as people for example, should be photographed side-on so that any movement trail is captured within the frame. Users can experiment with shutter speed settings from $^1/_2$ to $^1/_8$ of a second. Blurring can also be achieved by moving the camera itself during exposure. The better digital cameras allow users to keep the shutter held open on the B setting for an indefinite period of time. With this technique, moving bright lights record as streaks while static objects record as they appear.

Fast shutter speeds ||3|

For freezing sport and action subjects, fast shutter speeds are essential. Most running and jumping action will require $^1/_{250}{}^{th}$, while $^1/_{500}{}^{th}$ and above are needed for motor sports. Because fast shutter speeds allow light to hit the sensor for a very short time only, a large aperture value must be set to compensate. If little natural light at the scene prevents the selection of a fast shutter speed, an

See also Exposure and how to measure it *pages 40–41* / Aperture and depth of field *pages 42–43* / Working with flash *pages 52–53* / Capture, storage and transfer *pages 74–75* /

increase in ISO value from 200 to 800 will solve the problem.

Flash synchronization speed ||4|

Many digital cameras have a built-in flash unit which fires under fully automatic settings. If an external flash unit is used, the correct shutter speed must be set accordingly. All cameras have a minimum flash synchronization shutter speed, such as $^1/_{60}{}^{th}$ or $^1/_{125}{}^{th}$. If a faster shutter speed is selected, the resulting photograph will display a characteristic strip-like error. This is because the moving shutter curtain only reveals a portion of the sensor at any one time when set to faster speeds. Unless a dedicated flash program mode is available to match the external flash unit, the camera must be operated on fully manual mode.

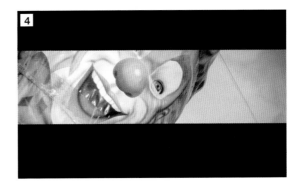

The lens and focusing

Effective control of a camera lens is the key to great photography.

Angle of view

The amount of subject that can be framed through an LCD or a viewfinder is determined by the focal length of the lens. Many digital cameras are sold with a zoom lens that has a variable focal length, such as 35–105mm. At the shorter end of this scale (35mm), the lens is said to be wide-angle and allows in the greatest amount of the subject. At the longer end of the scale (105mm), the lens is described as telephoto and lets in the least amount of subject.

Zoom lens 1

A zoom lens affords users the freedom to frame photographs from variable distances, enabling a photographer to carefully compose a subject from a fixed position. Many zooms have a maximum aperture, which is greater at the wide-angle end of the scale. Macro zooms are specialized lenses, offering an additional tool for close-up photography.

Wide-angle lens 2

Wide-angle lenses are best employed in confined spaces or where a photographer is very close to his subject. The wide angle appears to push a subject away from the camera and is a very useful tool. Its use should be avoided in everyday situations, where subjects will appear much smaller, and for portrait photography, where unflattering distortion will occur.

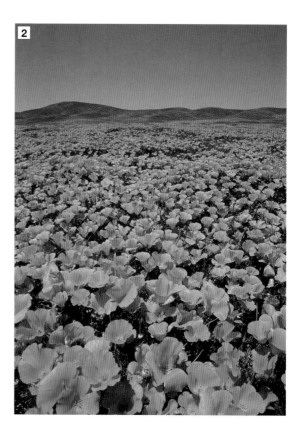

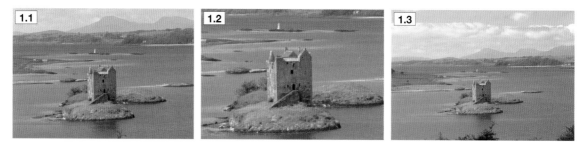

Three images to show the effect of a digital zoom. **1.1**: the middle of the zoom range; **1.2**: the telephoto end of the zoom lens; and **1.3**: at the widest zoom setting.

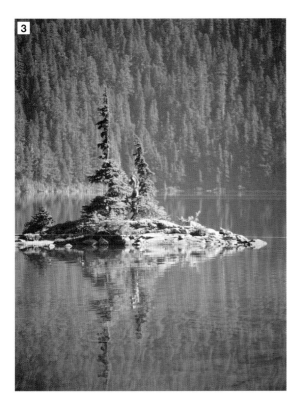

Every lens has a minimum focusing distance and will not be able to give sharp results on subjects that are too close. Superior digital compacts and SLRs have the option of manual focusing for more creative effects. Autofocus is also unable to focus on low-contrast subjects, such as large areas of flat color, and will track the lens back and forth in error focus. This problem can be resolved by focusing on the edge of the subject instead.

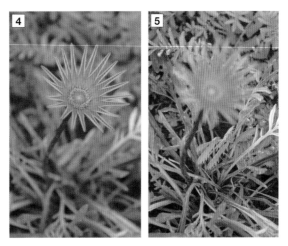

Autofocus can easily slip beyond your intended subject if it is not placed centrally.

Telephoto lens 3

A telephoto lens is useful for making distant subjects appear bigger in the viewfinder, and is well suited to travel photography. It is also very useful for portrait photography, as little distortion occurs. Most magazine cover images are taken with a telephoto lens, where foreshortening can create a flattering result. It is essential to hold the camera steady or use a tripod when using a zoom lens on its telephoto setting.

Autofocus 4

Digital cameras use autofocus to remove human error from picture taking. Users will find an autofocus target in the center of the viewfinder, which is best placed over the main subject. Depressing the shutter button halfway will activate the autofocus and a green confirmation light will appear in most cameras.

Autofocus problems 5

A common problem occurs when a subject falls outside the central portion of the frame and the camera sets the focus on another object in the distance by mistake. Most cameras allow pre-focusing to counter this problem, and this is achieved by depressing the shutter release halfway and holding it, or pressing an additional locking button, while recomposing the shot.

See also Seeing pattern close-up *pages 48–49* / Better composition *pages 54–55* / Framing in the viewfinder *pages 66–67* / Perspective control *pages 68–69* /

Seeing pattern close-up

Repeat pattern offers the photographer a chance to create a visual maze where shapes and colors collide together.

Shooting pattern [1]

Many similar lines or shapes arranged in one place can be composed to create effective abstract studies of pattern. These small detail images can be a very useful addition to a photo story, helping to set the story ambience.

Viewpoint [2]

Patterns are generally flat and look best when observed from above, so the position a photographer adopts will largely determine the success of a shot. Crouching above or standing well over the subject will help to make a flat field composition with little else than foreground. Different lens settings can be used to exaggerate pattern as well, with a close-up wide-angle lens making distorted shapes with receding depth. At the opposite end of the zoom lens, the telephoto setting will record shapes truthfully, while producing a subject lacking in spatial depth.

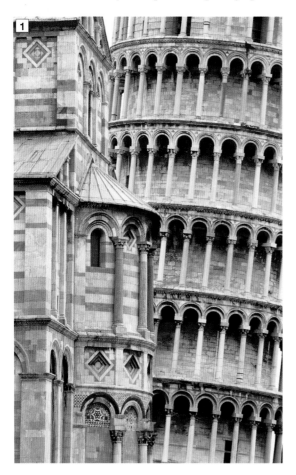

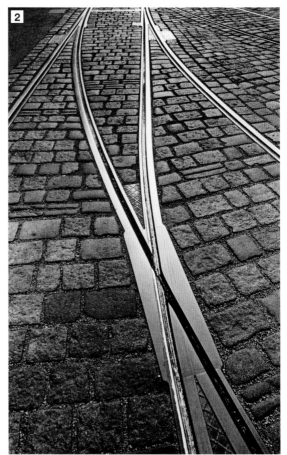

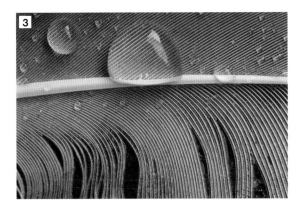

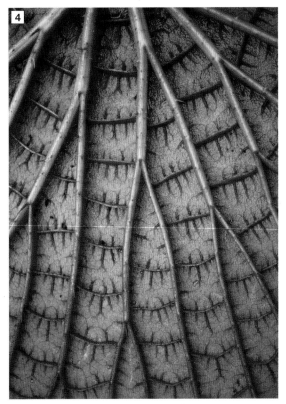

Close-up focusing [3]

All close-up photography is best achieved with a tripod, because light levels are generally lower and camera shake is more of a problem. A fixed camera position enables you to experiment with various compositions, where tiny changes in position can make a significant difference. The classic problem with close-up focusing is the diminishing depth of field, which leaves a zone of sharp focus, typically measured in just centimeters. Even when the lens is set to its minimum aperture, say f/22, little extra depth will be achieved. At the opposite end of the aperture scale, a wide aperture may only produce a few millimeters of depth. The best results are achieved when a focus point is carefully selected at one-third of the distance from the desirable foreground to background. The better SLR cameras have a depth of field preview button, which gives a preview of the likely result. For most users the LCD preview screen on the rear of a digital camera will perform exactly the same service. For subjects shot on location, another potential problem could be caused by the wind. At such close distances and small apertures, a photographer has to use slow shutter speeds to compensate for lower light levels, so any movement, even that of a gentle wind, will result in a blurred image. The practical answer to this is a makeshift windbreak using a piece of stiff card.

Patterns of nature [4]

Best shot in the great gardens and horticultural collections open to the public, close-ups of natural subjects can be as fascinating as an undiscovered world. Intricately structured tropical specimens or delicate and ephemeral flowers make intriguing subjects and users should choose only the most perfect examples to photograph. Plants can be architectural with complex interlocking structures or they can be part of a more complex overall pattern. If rules allow, photographers can rearrange slightly imperfect situations for the camera.

See also The lens and focusing *pages 46–47* / Better composition *pages 54–55* / Looking for shape *pages 56–57* / Graphic elements *pages 64–65* /

Working with natural light

This is a free, and very creative, tool to use, and the expert control of natural light separates the skilled photographer from the amateur.

Natural light and color reproduction 〔1〕

Daylight is infinitely variable in both brightness and color, and digital sensors have limitations to its reproduction. When shooting in the early morning, natural light casts a bluish color, giving cold results. At midday, with overhead sunlight, a more neutral but often harsh color is produced, while at the end of the day and in early evening, natural daylight becomes redder or warmer. The automatic white balance function on a digital camera will attempt to correct these differences, but it pays to understand light and experiment with different settings. Daylight can also be affected by a subject's immediate surroundings, with light bouncing off colored walls, for example, or passing through a translucent material like glass. The canopy created by tree foliage can result in an unpleasant green cast over portraits. Color casts can easily be removed using the color balance function in a digital imaging application.

Natural light for portraits 〔2〕

Natural light can produce sensitive, character-enhancing portraits, but can be difficult to control outdoors. Portraits can be shot indoors using natural light that is easily modified using a homemade reflector. The subject should sit near a window, and the image be composed so that the window remains out of view. Light from the window can be (bounced and) balanced by holding a sheet of newspaper close to the darker side of the subject, but not actually in the frame. This homemade reflector will soften the depth of any shadows and create a more flattering result. The flash should be turned off and a wide aperture such as f/4 selected to make the background blurred. Very bright window light can be softened or diffused by attaching a sheet of waxed paper to the window. This effect will create a softer light and much less shadow on the face of the subject.

Shooting in the summer months

The long hours of daylight make the summer months ideal for keen photographers, but there are plenty of pitfalls to avoid. Camera light meters are easily fooled into making results darker than expected and ultra-bright highlights can creep into a composition. Shiny and reflective surfaces, such as water, metal

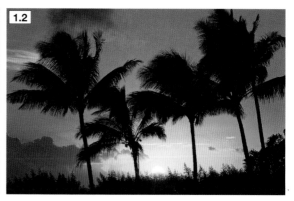

Early morning color is weak but very atmospheric.

Evening color is warmer and more vivid.

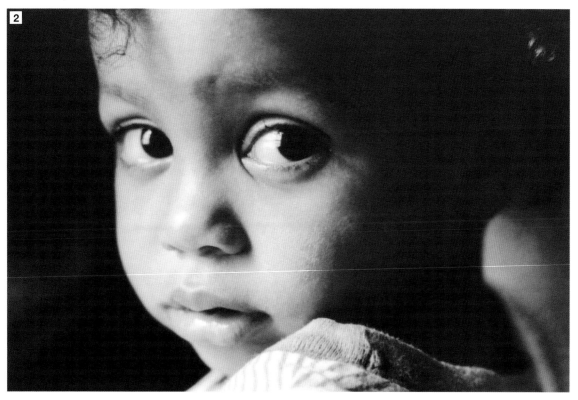

Natural light can create very evocative portraits.

and glass, produce bright hotspots that can trick a light meter into setting an exposure for a much brighter situation. To avoid this problem, try recomposing the image until the offending hotspot is out of the frame, then take and lock a light reading before returning to the original shot. Direct sunlight can also cause excessive contrast, producing large black shadows and empty white highlights. This can be counteracted by using fill flash for smaller subjects, or waiting for cloud cover.

Shooting in the winter 3

Winter light can be very atmospheric and offers the thinking photographer a different set of technical issues to overcome. With much less light available,

See also Camera functions *pages 14–17* / Aperture and depth of field *pages 42–43* / Working with flash *pages 52–53* /

location photography can be all but impossible after 3 p.m. and colder temperatures will drain battery power. Yet winter light is uniquely atmospheric, shining at low angles and creating long shadows. Landscape subjects will be drained of rich color, but the natural light will pick out texture and detail.

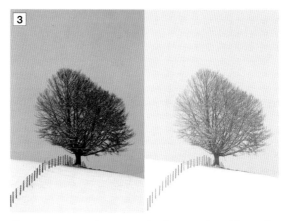

Snow scenes need overexposing to prevent muddy results.

Working with flash

A built-in flash is a very useful tool on a digital camera — and not just for low-light situations.

Most digital cameras have a built-in or pop-up flash unit that can be set to fire under different circumstances. Used indoors in low-light situations, flash adds a short burst of instant light, which overrides any existing ambient light, giving results that are often flat and lacking in atmosphere. Used outdoors, however, in conjunction with bright natural light, the fill-flash technique will give objects in the foreground more saturated colors.

How a flash works 1

A flash unit is usually self-regulating and switches itself off when light is bounced back to the camera from the first object it hits. For most situations, flash works perfectly well provided there are no obstacles between camera and subject. Flash fails when it hits a closer object, regardless of its size or position, and stops prematurely. Typical results from this situation are a subject darker than expected with a burned-out object in the foreground.

Avoiding simple mistakes 2

The two recurring problems with flash are red eye and hotspots. Red eye occurs when flash is used in low-light conditions, resulting in a solid red disc over a subject's eyes. This happens because the iris opens

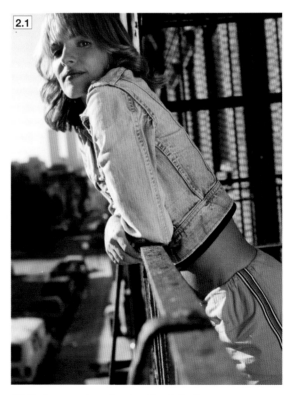

The hammerhead flashgun can be used to light objects at a great distance.

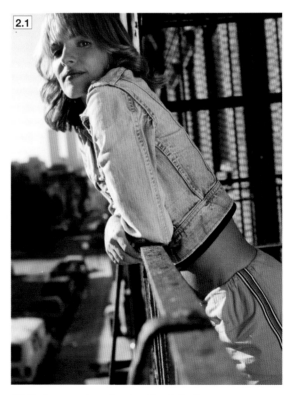2.1

Fill flash can reduce the density of shadow areas.

See also Anatomy of a digital camera *pages 10–11* / Digital SLR *pages 26–27* / Working with natural light *pages 50–51* /

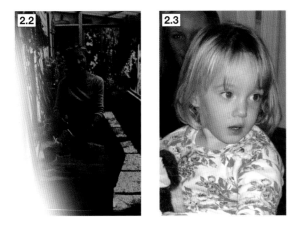

The most common flash errors are an object in the way of the flash (left) and red eye (right).

wide to compensate for the low light, in the same way that a wide aperture in a lens does. The red is created as the flash light bounces off the retina and returns to the camera in a straight line. This problem is easily solved by using the camera's red-eye reduction mode, which fires a tiny pre-flash first, causing the iris in the subject's eyes to narrow.

Hotspots

Very difficult to see at the time, and impossible to predict, hotspots are caused when flash reflects off a shiny surface. Windows in the background, glass in picture frames and even eyeglasses are all potential danger areas to look out for. Most problems can be avoided by positioning the camera at an angle to avoid shooting straight on. In a digital image, hotspots show up as pure white pixels with little or no detail and can be replaced with cloned pixels using the Rubber Stamp tool.

Connecting external flash units

The better digital cameras have a socket for connecting a more powerful flash unit. A universal hot-shoe is found on more advanced digital compacts and SLRs and allows the connection of a

hammerhead flash unit. An alternative connector, sometimes called the x-sync, can be found on professional SLR cameras and allows a connection to professional studio lighting equipment. External flash units are much more versatile and permit the photographer to change light direction and contrast.

Creative flash tips   3

Built-in flash units often produce a strong black shadow line around a subject, which can be softened by sticking a tiny piece of tracing paper or vellum over the flash. Professional photographers use a fabric or plastic diffuser on portable flash units to soften shadows and make the flash light look more like natural light.

3

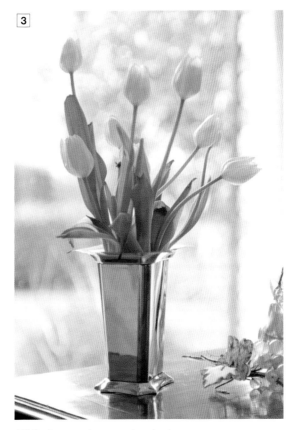

Fill flash prevents excessive shadows.

Better composition

Composition is the photographer's skill in organizing a subject, its background and foreground into a balanced and pleasing position in the camera viewfinder.

Practical positions

For immovable subjects, such as the natural landscape, composition is essentially influenced by the photographer's own shooting position and choice of lens. For more pliable subjects, for example people, composition may also be determined by the photographer's directing skills and organization.

Balance and weight 1

Experience only comes with shooting many different situations over time, until an intuitive understanding of visual balance is achieved. Each different element in a composition vies for visual attention by its shape, color, size and position. Cluttered compositions have too much emphasis in all areas of the image and lack a clear message. The best results tend to occur when fewer elements are involved. Strong colors and textures can dominate and swamp a main subject, as can intensely patterned backgrounds. "Visual weight" describes the effect of a color or tone pulling the viewer's eye in a particular direction and, if used effectively, can act as a counterbalance to the central subject.

Symmetry 2

The easiest composition to make is a symmetrical one. This is where near identical eye-catching elements sit on either side of an imaginary fold. A good starting point is to place the main elements of a composition in the center of the frame until a balance is achieved along the vertical or horizontal axis. This kind of approach works well with architectural and landscape subjects.

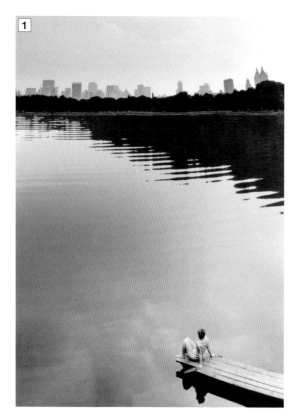

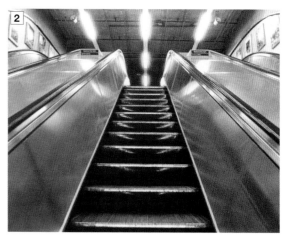

Asymmetry

Perhaps harder to define, owing to the inherent rule-breaking nature of the concept, is asymmetry, where the success of a composition relies on its non-conformity. Off-center compositions can work if balance is achieved by another part of the image. A good guide to remember is the "rule of thirds," where an image is divided up into a grid of nine equal but invisible sections. Used by painters throughout the history of Western art, this theory suggests that if elements are placed on the grid lines, or at their intersections, a pleasing result can be achieved.

Organizing people

It can be an ordeal to arrange large numbers of people into a good composition, and group shape is the issue to tackle first. Often a subject is simply the wrong shape to fit into the rectangle of a viewfinder. It is not essential to cram in every part of a person and it is more important to see facial expressions over feet and shoes.

Software rescue

Digital images can, of course, be cropped and recomposed in a digital imaging application. More useful perhaps is the ability to remove unwanted elements by using the Rubber Stamp tool, thereby painting out distracting parts of the image that went unnoticed at the time of capture.

See also The lens and focusing *pages 46–47* / Framing in the viewfinder *pages 66–67* / Perspective control *pages 68–69* /

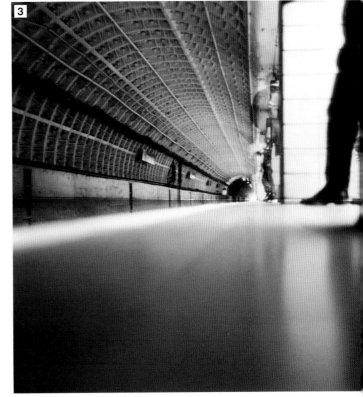

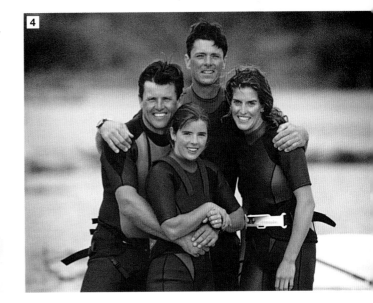

Looking for shape

Train your eye to see shapes rather than people, places or things and you will soon discover an abstract world to capture with your camera.

Shape is best defined as the perimeter edge of an object and as such forms the basis of many of the most skillful photographs. An object's shape is far from set in stone and, with the clever use of camera position and different lenses, shape can be manipulated until it sits attractively in the viewfinder frame. Deciding on the perfect camera angle when shooting on location is near impossible and even professional photographers shoot a few frames for choice. If a photograph is worth taking, then it pays to go to the effort of taking several variations.

Changing your own position   1

Most photographs are taken from the same predictable vantage point — that of an adult of average height. Rarely do we think about moving our own shooting position, except when stepping backward to cram a bit more subject into the viewfinder. In this example, a worm's-eye vantage point has distorted the shape of the columns, resulting in a photograph that suggests a stronger sense of their monumental size.

Plain backgrounds   2

Complex or subtle shapes are difficult to separate out visually from busy or patterned backgrounds. By changing shooting position, a photographer can easily discard unwanted background detail. If it is impossible to move, a wide aperture setting such as f/2.8 or f/4 will blur out the background very effectively, giving clear emphasis to the main subject of the photograph. If this is not done at the time of shooting, it is always possible to rectify the problem later on with image manipulation software. This delicate natural shape would have looked much less evocative with a highly detailed background.

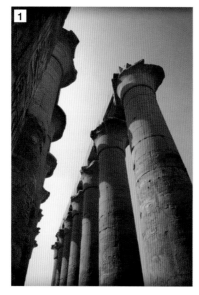

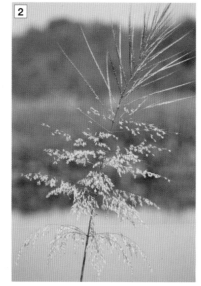

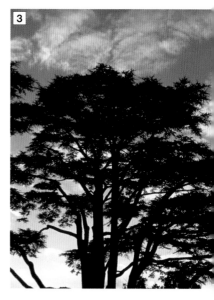

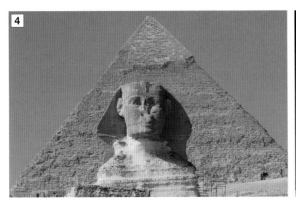

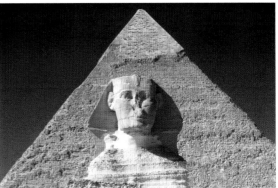

Slight imperfections...

...can be retouched easily using the Rubber Stamp tool.

Silhouettes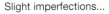

A good way to add an interesting twist to otherwise difficult lighting conditions is to shoot a silhouette. These shapes can be just as descriptive as the main subject in detail and can add a touch of mystery. Natural light at the end of the day is ideal, but it may be worth experimenting with exposure settings for a perfect result. To get rid of any unwanted detail in a silhouette, take an exposure reading from the sky, lock it and re-compose the shot. It is a good idea to shoot more variations than normal and rejected frames can easily be deleted in camera to preserve space on the memory card.

Contrasting shapes

Framing a combination of opposites — black and white, curved and straight or rough and smooth — makes a great photograph. This digital photograph was disappointing in its original color state, with unwanted scaffolding and tourists interrupting the two dominant shapes. The problems were solved simply using the Rubber Stamp tool to clone them away, making the remaining shapes visually stronger. When original color is washed out, or does nothing to enhance the subject, convert it to black and white for a more graphic effect, using a high-contrast conversion to monochrome with the Channel Mixer.

Eye direction

Photographers can dictate the way in which a photograph is "read" by arranging shapes and lines in the viewfinder before pressing the shutter. When looking at a photograph, the human eye follows lines and shapes, much in the same way as when planning a route with a road map. Photographs that engage a viewer in this way are considered to be more skilful than the snapshot type with clumsy and accidental placements. This example provides a clean line that links foreground to background.

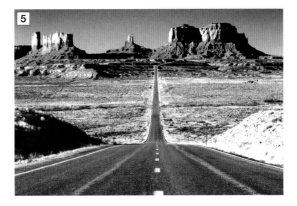

See also Seeing pattern close-up *pages 48–49* / Better composition *pages 54–55* / Graphic elements *pages 64–65* / Framing in the viewfinder *pages 66–67* /

Seeing in color

Successfully arranging color in a photograph is just like decorating a home, with close harmonies working best and all clashes avoided.

Color palettes

As with all visual art and design work, photography can make good use of well-established color palettes found in every book on painting, textiles and design. Grouping harmonious colors together gives a coherence and emphasis to an image and a photographer's skill lies first in recognizing these colors and then framing them pleasingly. Keeping a lookout for tiny islands of color amid the clutter of everyday life can take patience and practice and is best achieved by experimenting with different compositions in the viewfinder.

Highly saturated palette   [1]

Great for making bold statements and graphic shapes, saturated colors are those at their maximum intensity. A close-up or abstract shape with a strong color can be a subject in its own right. This is a situation where several variations need to be shot in order to be certain of the best result. When shooting outdoors, the most saturated color is achieved either under midday overcast light or early/late day front light. In the event that raw digital files lack the color saturation expected, they are easily enhanced using the saturation slider in Photoshop's Hue/Saturation software dialog box. However, excessive manipulation of color saturation will result in a crude and visible posterization where originally subtle colors merge into each other and authenticity is lost.

Low-saturated palette   [2]

A faded palette, with its lower color saturation, is subtle and subjective. The delicate colors of a faded

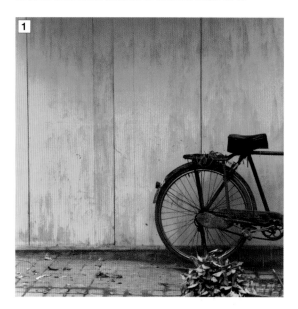

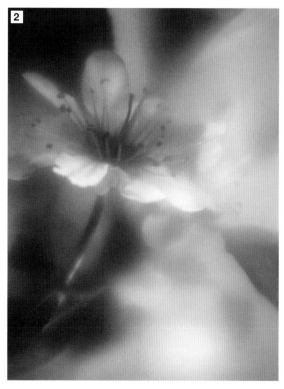

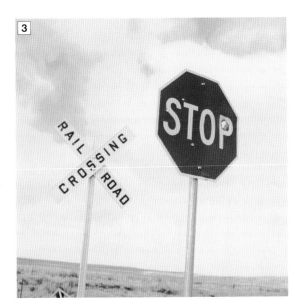

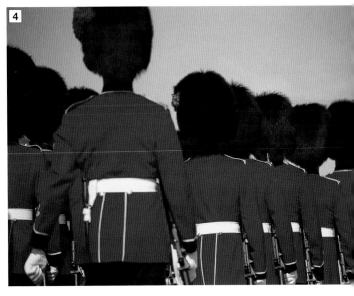

palette appeal because of the way they differ from the colors of everyday life. Low-saturated colors evoke the seasons and other ephemeral events, and are best found during the early morning hours. The effects of low color saturation can be applied to straight color images using the saturation slider in the Hue/Saturation software dialog box. Low-saturation colors print very well on ink-jet printers using handmade artist's paper.

Restricted color palette [3]

Following the universal "less is more" theory, a palette of very few colors can be effective when composing an image. Set within its own boundaries, a restricted palette offers a rare slice of life and can make the resulting photograph look jewel-like or precious. Single- or reduced-palette color images are often used in magazine publishing to attract a reader's attention.

Color combinations [4]

Great works often result from breaking every rule in the art and design handbook, and odd color combinations are often successful because of their novelty. Opposites — old and new, primary and secondary, natural and manmade — all offer the possibility of an effective combination. Colors also have cultural meanings that vary widely. Blue, for instance, is thought to be a calming and meditative color; red is traditionally the opposite.

See also Camera functions *pages 14–15* / Working with natural light *pages 50–51* / Seeing in monochrome *pages 60–61* /

Seeing in monochrome

Black-and-white photography has long been a favorite with creative photographers and in the digital era it has improved significantly.

With the opportunity to alter an image in the darkroom, black-and-white photography is more of a craft than merely a picture-taking process. Yet the real skill in black-and-white photography still lies in the shooting. When color is largely absent or subtle texture needs enhancing, this is an ideal moment to shoot black and white.

Shooting settings

With a comprehensive assortment of software processes available to convert color to black and white, there is no advantage in starting with a monochrome original. Users should avoid mono or sepia shooting modes and shoot in RGB color instead.

Looking for subjects

Many photographic situations do not present the photographer with a rich and varied selection of color and tend to look uninspiring. With a black-and-white interpretation, however, color is replaced with a more dramatic tonal range for more effective visual effect.

Contrast   1

The different shades of gray set between a photograph's black-and-white points are called "contrast" in traditional photography but are referred to as "brightness" in digital imaging. Pixel brightness can be made darker and lighter very simply, allowing skillful users to separate and enhance different areas of an image, creating a totally different visual balance at a whim. Unlike straight color photography, where little tonal manipulation can occur without looking invented, black-and-white interpretation can be highly individualistic. In addition to correcting low- and high-contrast images, software tools also give users an opportunity to express their own creative ideas through to the printed end product.

High contrast   2

When strong whites and blacks are present with very few accompanying gray tones, the result is said to be "high contrast." Best suited to strongly shaped

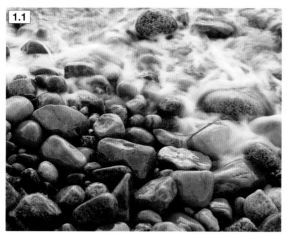

This example shows a flat-contrast image.

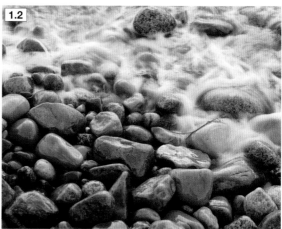

A much better result is achieved with higher contrast.

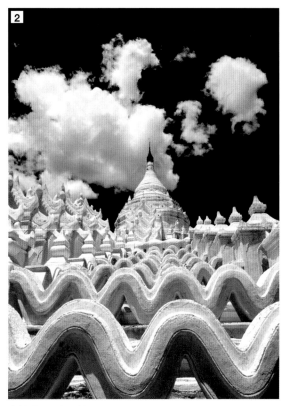

A high-contrast image.

subjects, high-contrast effects will enhance graceful lines and edges. The end result is usually a strong graphic image, which is different to the way we normally see the world. As a by-product of high contrast, any finer detail found in midtone gray areas will disappear. Excessive high contrast can be difficult to print out, with dark gray areas merging into black.

Normal contrast

With a good mixture of pure black and white and a full range of grays in between, the normal-contrast image presents a seamless jump from highlights to shadows. Software controls like Levels and Curves are ideal for putting black-and-white points into a low-contrast image and can also be used to shift the balance of the midtone grays.

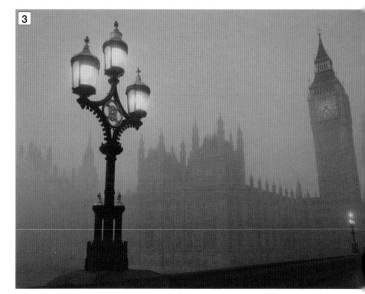

A low-contrast image.

Low contrast 3

With no black or white tone, the low-contrast image is derived from an expanded range of grays and can also be an expressive and atmospheric way to interpret a subject. With a softness associated with vintage photographs, the low-contrast effect works very well on portraits and flower subjects.

Toning

Any black-and-white image can be further enhanced by toning — a process that adds a delicate single color wash over the entire image. Adapted from the chemical toners of conventional photography, sepia, selenium and copper tones can add an enriching layer of interest to any work.

See also Camera functions *pages 16–17* / Seeing in color *pages 58–59* / Contrast correction with Levels *pages 178–179* / Contrast with Curves *pages 180–181* /

Camera handling

In addition to using creative controls, it is essential for a photographer to know how to handle a camera properly.

Holding the camera

If a digital camera isn't held properly, no amount of software trickery will rescue a problem picture. For the new user, it is surprisingly simple to make childlike errors such as draping a stray finger over the lens or causing camera shake because of bad posture. Digital compact cameras are small and lightweight and can be just as difficult to hold as a bulky professional SLR. Few compact cameras are designed ergonomically and don't offer many options for placing redundant fingers. The first thing to do is find a comfortable place for each finger. It is not essential to have a white-knuckle grip, as the main aim is to prevent fingers straying over the lens. Digital compact cameras with a window-like viewfinder don't let users view directly through the lens, so straying fingers will go unnoticed anyway. Holding the camera in one hand, a photographer will use the remaining hand to steady its base, draw both elbows toward the body and shoot.

Using a tripod 1

A tripod is a very useful tool for both amateurs and professionals. They are available in many sizes and weights — from a useful tabletop model that will fit in a camera bag to a lightweight telescopic version for travelers. The better ones have a pan-and-tilt head, useful for making precise compositions or linked panoramic shots. Useful for keeping the camera steady under slow shutter speeds, a tripod prevents blurred and out-of-focus results. An excellent variation on the tripod is the single-stem monopod with a ball-and-socket head, useful for extra support and steadiness when composing.

Cleaning the camera lens 2

To help the sensor record more saturated colors, digital camera lenses have a multicoated top layer that needs regular cleaning. Transparent grease from a photographer's fingers will quickly mark a lens and cause an instant decrease in image sharpness, contrast and color saturation. These greasy smears are best removed using alcohol-free eyeglass cleaner, gently applied to the lens in a smooth circular fashion. Other problems can be caused by dust, which is best removed using an antistatic cloth — an essential part of a photographer's kit. The most serious problems are caused by sand, which can

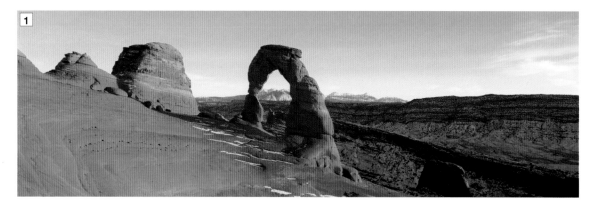

1

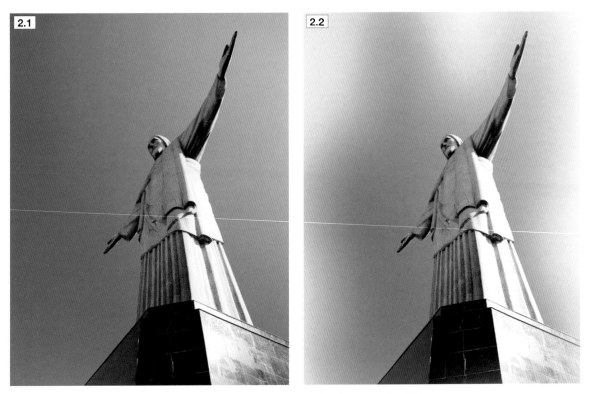

2.1 **2.2**

A greasy smear on the lens can create white blotches, as seen in the picture on the right.

interfere with camera mechanics and may even scratch the lens. Sand should only be removed using a photographer's blower brush or a soft watercolor paintbrush.

Electrical problems ▢3

Memory cards are vulnerable to static electricity and, in extreme cases, can accidentally be corrupted. To reduce potential risk, never place a card close to a television set or computer monitor. If it must be removed from the camera, ensure the card is kept in a protective purpose-designed case. Other media like PCMCIA cards, IBM Microdrive and the 3.5-inch floppy disk can also be vulnerable to magnetic fields. Strong magnetic fields, found near stereo speakers, electrified railroad tracks and electricity pylons, can cause irreparable damage to digital-image data.

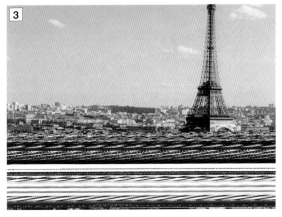

A corrupted image file.

See also Anatomy of a digital camera *pages 10–11* / Memory cards *pages 34–35* /

Graphic elements

There are many tools and techniques that can be used to give photographs greater visual punch.

It is no coincidence that signs and symbols designed for our public highways use clean colors and bold shapes to convey their messages. Graphic elements such as lines, squares, arrows and lettering, together with primary colors, form the essential ingredients of an attention-grabbing photograph.

Straight lines [1]

We live in a world where straight lines dominate: straight-edged vertical buildings and straight lines on the sidewalk. Diagonals are rarer, however, and so are much more likely to grab the attention. Diagonals can be produced in an image by moving position or using a longer lens. This example was taken with a zoom lens, so any unwanted foreground detail was easily omitted. If initial attempts are less than perfect, use the cropping tool to remove unwanted sections to make a more dynamic photograph.

Primary colors [2]

The primary colors — red, yellow and blue — are so-called because they cannot be mixed from any other color ingredients. Primaries are visually striking and always make great photographs. Complex and interlocking graphic elements demand all of a photographer's skill to obtain a good end result. This example is broken into many color compartments, like a puzzle, and took several attempts before the right composition was found. Even a slight repositioning of the camera to the left or right would have resulted in a radically different image.

Signs and symbols [3]

We are surrounded by a host of signs vying for our attention. Turned into an abstract or simple color study, even the most mundane item can make a worthy shot.

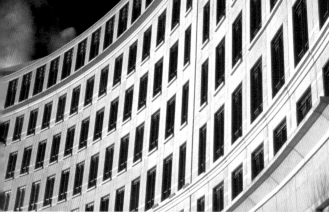

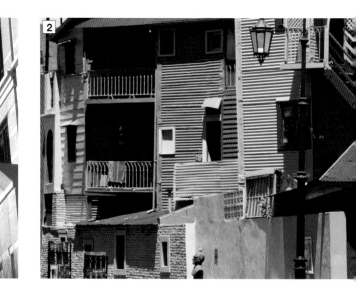

See also Seeing pattern close-up *pages 48–49* / Looking for shape *pages 56–57* / Seeing in color *pages 58–59* / Perspective control *pages 68–69* /

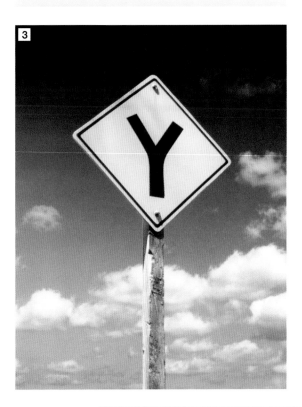

Tilting [4]

Tilting the camera is a good technique to use for creating a diagonal where none exists, though it can easily be overdone. The same effect can be achieved with a Rotate tool in a software application, although this will mean cropping the photograph and a number of original pixels. This example was carefully composed until all the lines in a glass roof formed a dynamic shape.

Shooting tips

Viewfinder cropping
Compact cameras that have a rangefinder window for composing a photograph can show deceptively more than will end up in the shot. Be wary of framing a photograph too tightly to the edges of the viewfinder, as peripheral details may not be recorded. It is much better to step back a bit or set the lens to a slightly wider angle, leaving a visible but non-essential space at the edges.

Long lens
For far-off subjects, try using the lens on its longest zoom setting. This will help to crop out any unwanted elements that would create a visual distraction. It also produces a very exciting effect called "foreshortening," where the actual physical distance between objects appears reduced.

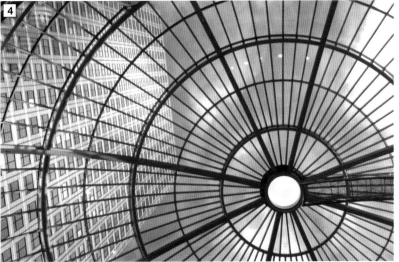

Framing in the viewfinder

Great photographs are made not at the moment the shutter release is pressed but beforehand, by virtue of critical judgment of what is in the viewfinder.

The viewfinder is the preview window in a camera. In addition to the image, most cameras also provide information in the viewfinder, such as focus and exposure. Large viewfinders are easier to use, especially if the user wears eyeglasses or finds it hard to see through a tiny window.

Big is best

Many photographs of people taken by amateurs are not taken closely enough to the subject because the photographer is worried about chopping off the heads and feet of portraits. A tall person doesn't easily fit into an 8x10 print, so rather than attempt to fit the whole person in the frame, the photographer should zoom in closer to bring forward important elements, like the face, and crop out unnecessary details like a busy background. Moving in also blurs the background, futher reducing its distractability.

Parallax error   1

In some older film cameras, the optics were not always very sophisticated and often led to a risk of cropping peoples' heads off by mistake. The only alternative was to stand well back from the subject and hope for the best. Also, with the viewfinder window set slightly to the left of the camera lens, unexpected crops occurred when focusing on something close. This is known as parallax error and has been responsible for many a disappointing family snapshot. Digital SLR cameras use a clever series of mirrors — a pentaprism — that allow the photographer to compose directly through the lens. Top-priced digital compacts also offer a direct LCD preview via the lens and so do not suffer from parallax error at all. If in doubt, however, make use of the LCD preview screen to confirm the composition by framing the subject looking at the LCD instead of through the camera's viewfinder.

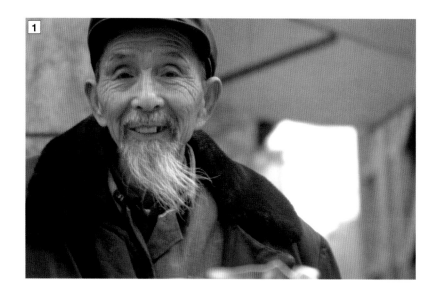

Tight crops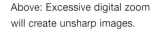

Just to compound the issue further, an LCD preview, a viewfinder and an SLR pentaprism do not necessarily display the end result in its entirety. SLRs can show marginally less around the perimeter edge than will appear in the final image files and viewfinder compacts can show deceptively more than they should. To counteract potential disappointment it is a good idea to avoid framing subjects too closely to the edge.

Suprises in the background

The hardest skill for an amateur photographer to learn is to keep an eye on distracting background detail. Caught up in the excitement of composing and arranging the central subject, a photographer may easily overlook the background detail. Common mistakes include telephone poles emerging from peoples' heads and signs with inappropriate wording. Small details can always be removed later in an imaging application, but it only takes a second to recompose another shot or to choose a wider aperture in order to blur out the unwanted background.

Digital zoom setting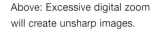

Many digital cameras have an additional function called a digital zoom, which works very differently to a conventional telephoto lens. Rather than pulling a subject closer, like a telescope, a digital zoom works by enlarging a small central section of pixels to make a far-off subject look bigger than it really is. The process is called interpolation and works by mixing new pixels of estimated color values with original pixels. The resulting images can be less sharp and of much lower quality than those shot with a conventional long lens.

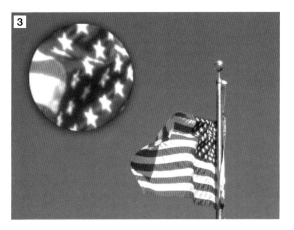

Above: Excessive digital zoom will create unsharp images.

Left: Avoid framing your subjects too tightly to prevent the edge of the image being cut off.

See also Anatomy of a digital camera *pages 10–11* / The lens and focusing *pages 46–47* / Better composition *pages 54–55* /

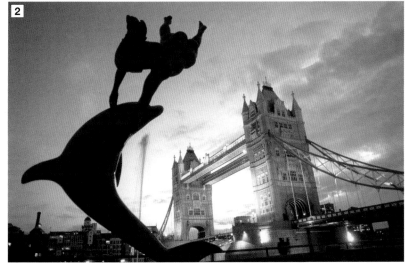

Perspective control

By experimenting with perspective control, a photographer can create photographs that look provocatively different than the world we see with the naked eye.

Viewpoint tips and ideas

Viewpoint can be defined as the vantage point and position of a camera. Most photographs are taken from the same viewpoint: a standing position. Changing the viewpoint creates a very different result and epitomizes the core purpose of photography: to see the world in a new and different way. Viewpoint can greatly influence the shape of an object, which then can be manipulated to fit in with a photographer's creative intentions. A low vantage point is easily set by squatting or kneeling down to a child's eye-level and will make ordinary

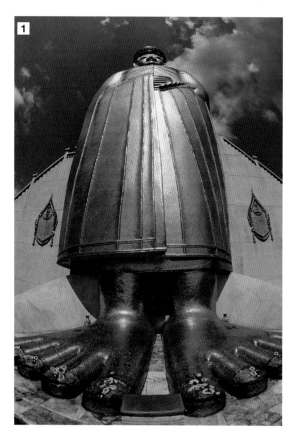

and everyday items seem surreal. A worm's-eye view is created by lying low, with the camera placed firmly on the ground or on a mini tripod. This can be an unexpected way to convey the drama of a surrounding landscape, an effect increased when combined with a wide-angle lens. Shooting downward from a high vantage point with a telephoto lens can make subjects small and impersonal.

Wide-angle lens distortion [1]

A curious by-product of the wide-angle lens is the extreme level of distortion it creates when the camera is tilted backward or forward. Nearby objects will start to taper away with very exaggerated lines and the relative sizes of shapes will also start to change dramatically. Wide angles can create a dramatic sense of space and volume, particularly useful in architectural or landscape settings, but always at the expense of straight lines. In order to achieve a perfectly level camera position, users should consider buying a photographic spirit level, designed to clip into a hot-shoe or tripod. Poor quality optics in some wide-angle lenses may also create barrel distortion, which is most evident when parallel lines start to get closer at the edges of the frame. Wide angles are not suitable for close portraits — unless a sense of location or setting is important — as they exaggerate features and proportions like a circus hall of mirrors does.

See also The lens and focusing *pages 46–47* / Framing in the viewfinder *pages 66–67* /

Telephoto lens distortion

2

At the opposite end of perspective control is the telephoto lens. Excellent for picking out faraway detail, the telephoto is an essential tool for keeping vertical lines straight and preserving original subject shape. Particularly useful when shooting subjects above eye-level, the long telephoto lens can be used from a distance to avoid vertical line convergence. Widely used in architectural photography for emphasizing an architect's original vision, the foreshortening effect of a telephoto lens creates a compressed space where objects perhaps 100 yards apart can seem much closer together. Much harder to use than a wide-angle lens, it can take time for a new user to start seeing potential long-lens photographs on location.

Software correction

3

With the benefit of software trickery, most perspective errors can be put right using the simple Transform tool. After making a careful selection of the element, the Transform/Perspective command allows the user to pull converged verticals apart again, filling in the new image areas with interpolated pixels. However, as we are all conditioned to seeing tall buildings from ground level, perspective-corrected images can look unnatural.

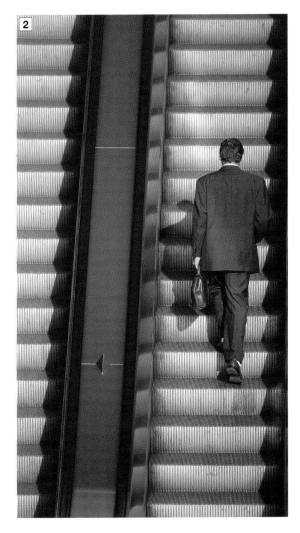

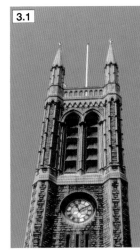

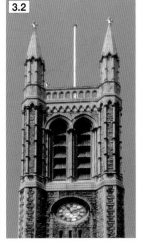

Uncorrected distortion.   Perspective correction.

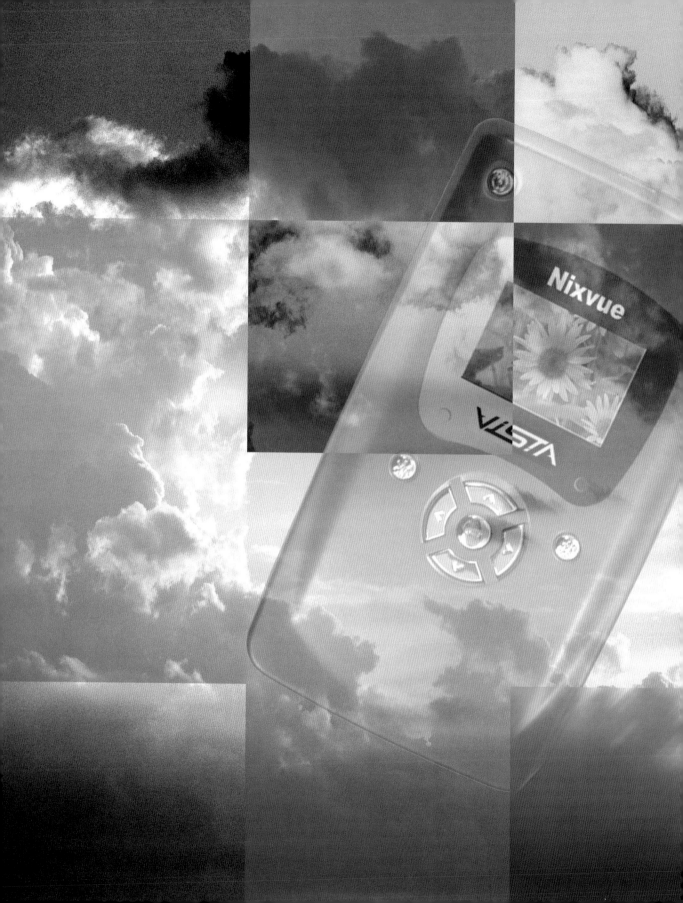

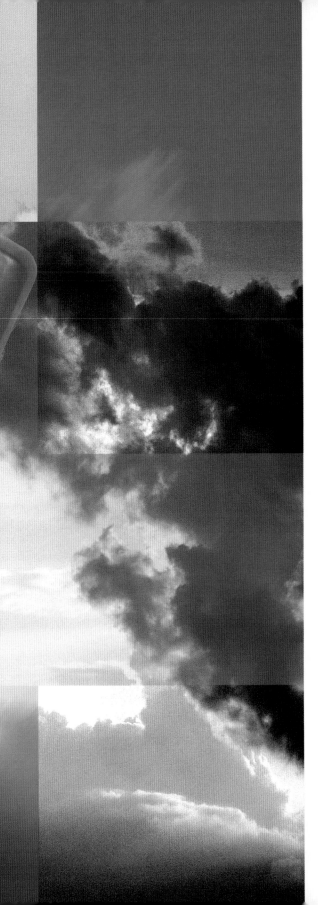

3 Essentials of a Digital Image

What is a digital image?

Digital images are mixed from an exact set of colors — each one defined by a precise array of numbers.

Every digital photograph is assembled from millions of tiny, square-shaped blocks called pixels. These blocks are arranged in a grid-like form called a bitmap — like a very fine mosaic. There is no mystery to the construction of a digital image, as each pixel is created from its own original color code, akin to a recipe. When light waves fall on each individual cell in a digital camera sensor, the CCD, the outcome is one individual pixel per cell.

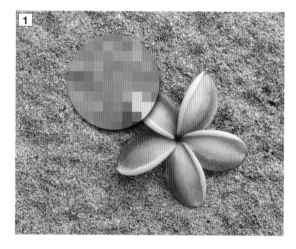

Pixel bitmap

The pixel bitmap is a way of describing a digital image by the number of pixels along the horizontal and vertical axes. Many digital cameras and scanners are sold with a description of the maximum size image they can create, such as 1200x1800. This figure refers to the actual number of pixels created in the bitmap. High-resolution images are made from millions of pixels and are able to describe curved shapes and fine details with clarity. Low-resolution images are made from far fewer pixels and cannot reproduce the same level of quality. The more pixels an image contains, the bigger and better a printout will be.

Color recipes

Each different ray of colored light is converted in a camera to a color code number which is created using only three color ingredients: red, green and blue. This number is then used to create pixel colors each and every time an image is opened on a computer. This recipe also can recreate an identical pixel at any size, be it 3 feet (1 m) or ¹⁄₁₆th of an inch (1 mm) square. In binary code such a number may look like this: 01011011+01111001+111011010.0.

Bit depth

Most digital sensors today are able to create a minimum number of colors. In computer terminology, the binary number scale is used to describe different colors. Every input and output device uses a minimum 8-bit scale to describe each RGB color channel. This allows 256 color states to be described for each color or 24-bit overall. Many devices can create colors using a much higher scale such as 42-bit or 14 bits per color channel. There is no advantage in having too much data, as most printers and image manipulation software can only operate with 24-bit data.

See also Camera functions *pages 12–15* / Color depth *pages 76–77* / Resolution *pages 78–79* / Pixels and print size *pages 82–83* / Compression *pages 88–89* /

2 **11001101**1001110100110110

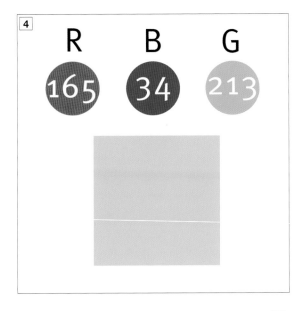

Color depth 4

Each one of the red, green and blue color ingredients in a digital image has the same range of brightness variations, fixed on a 0 – 255 scale. When each pixel is created, the color recipe looks something like this: R:121, G:234, B:176. The number of different combinations possible with these three scales is 16.7 million, enough to provide a virtually continuous palette of colors to the human eye.

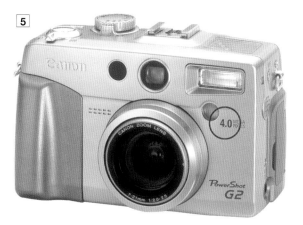

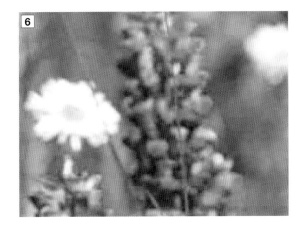

Digital data 5

Relatively speaking, the standard terminology for measuring, estimating and describing digital images is still in its infancy. Many digital cameras are promoted with the sensor size described in megapixels, which can be calculated simply by multiplying the vertical and horizontal values of the bitmap: For example, a 1200x1800 sensor makes a 2.1 megapixel camera. Scanners, however, are usually promoted on the basis of their resolution or, put simply, the maximum number of pixels — often confusingly referred to as "dots" — possibly created per linear inch; for example, 2400dpi.

Data and storage 6

Of course, all of this data needs to be stored in the camera each time a photograph is taken, so camera manufacturers have used clever mathematical routines to shrink down data to allow more images to be stored on the memory card. There are many innovative methods for compressing data, such as the JPEG routine (see pages 88–89), but all have some bearing on overall image quality. A good rule of thumb is to remember that the greater the compression, the lower the image quality will be. This example shows the block damage created by an over-compressed JPEG.

Capture, storage and transfer

Understanding how to successfully capture, store and transfer digital-image files from your digital camera to a computer.

Image sensor [1]

Instead of using light-sensitive film, a digital camera has a built-in sensor called a charged coupled device, or CCD for short. The sensor is constructed from millions of tiny light-sensitive cells arranged in a gridlike pattern. Each cell is responsible for creating one square pixel in a digital image. When light passes through the camera lens and hits an individual sensor cell, minutely different voltages are created. The sensor converts these signals into different brightness values, using a digital scale. After each photographic image is taken, the sensor assembles all the individual cell values into pixels, which are then arranged in a mosaic-like grid.

See also Anatomy of a digital camera *pages 10–11 /* Memory cards *pages 34–35 /* Connecting to a computer *pages 36–37 /* Peripherals *pages 106–107 /*

Sensor size

In digital photography the more pixels there are in an image file, the bigger and better quality print the user can make. Digital cameras, therefore, are sold with CCD sensors that have a different number of pixel-making light-sensitive cells. The standard measurement used for describing the pixel dimension of an image is called the megapixel value. A megapixel is one million pixels (M); the value is calculated by multiplying the number of pixels across the horizontal and vertical axes of a digital image. A camera with a 2.1M sensor, for example, creates images with a pixel dimension of 1800x1200. At the bottom end of the market are cameras with sensors capable of producing fewer than a million pixels, typically 300,000, which make 640x480 images — suitable only for web or on-screen use. At the top end of the scale, and at ten times the price, are cameras capable of producing in excess of 6M pixels and very high-quality results.

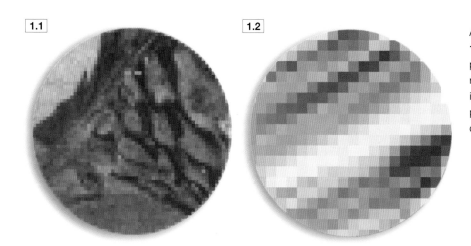

1.1 **1.2**

A high resolution image, **1.1**, has more pixels and produces better quality results. A low resolution image, **1.2**, has fewer pixels and can't describe complex shapes.

Megapixel size	Pixel dimensions (approx)	Print size at 200ppi	Print size at 300ppi	Print size at 400ppi
0.3M	640x480	3.2 x 2.4" (8.1 x 6.1cm)	2.1 x 1.6" (5.3 x 4cm)	1.6 x 1.2" (4.3cm)
1.3M	1350x1000	6.75 x 5" (17.1 x 12.7cm)	4.5 x 3.3" (11.4 x 8.4cm)	3.3 x 2.5" (8.4 x 6cm)
2.1M	1800x1200	9 x 6" (22 x 15cm)	6 x 4" (15 x 9.75cm)	4.5 x 3" (11.4 x 8cm)
3.3M	2100x1440	10.5 x 7.2" (26.7 x 18.3cm)	7 x 4.8" (17.8 x 12.1cm)	5.25 x 3.6" (13.3 x 9.1cm)
4M	2400x1700	12 x 8.5" (30 x 22.4cm)	8 x 5.6" (20 x 14.2cm)	6 x 4.25" (15 x 10.8cm)
5M	2750x1900	13.75 x 9.5" (34.9 x 24.1cm)	9.1 x 6.3" (23.1 x 16cm)	6.8 x 4.75" (17.2 x 12cm)
6M	3000x2000	15 x 10" (38.1 x 25.4cm)	10 x 6.6" (25.4 x 16.75cm)	7.5 x 5" (19 x 12.7cm)

Data storage

Digital-image files are very large in comparison to most computer data files created in an office environment and, in order to store the large volume of digital data created each time a photograph is produced, digital cameras use removable memory cards. These cards are available in different data capacities such as 8MB and 64MB, with larger capacities costing more. The bigger the capacity, the more images a card will take. There are two types of memory card in universal use, the SmartMedia card and the CompactFlash; neither are interchangeable. Only the most expensive cameras are able to use both and many budget cameras have their own built-in data storage, rather than a removable card.

Computer transfer

Once captured and stored, digital-image data files need to be transferred to a computer for enhancement and printing. There are two common ways to transfer files to a computer: The first is by using an external card reader; and the second by using a high-speed cable that connects the camera directly to a computer. The latter method is more convenient, as there is no need to remove the memory card, but driver software will need to be installed on the computer first. Dual-format card readers — those able to read both CompactFlash and SmartMedia cards — can remain plugged into a computer and are especially useful if different types of memory card are to be used, or if there is a software incompatibility between camera and computer.

Color depth

Color or bit depth is a term that refers to the size of color palette used to construct a digital image.

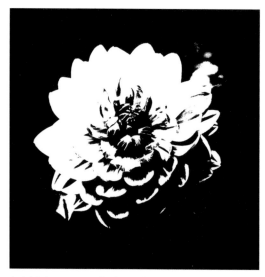

A 1-bit image can display only two different tones. This example uses black or white. Bitmap mode images are 1-bit and have a tiny file size.

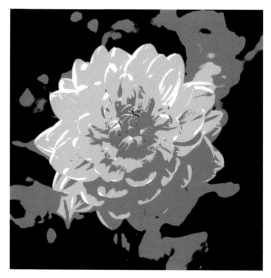

A 2-bit image can reproduce a maximum of four different tones. The image starts to make a better job at describing three-dimensional subject matter.

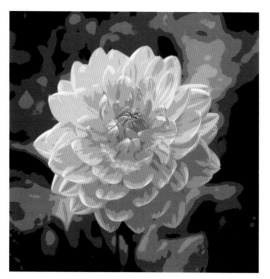

A 3-bit image increases to eight tones and greatly improves the illusion but with posterization still clearly visible.

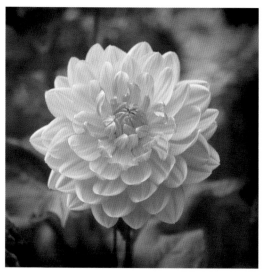

8-bit is the standard palette for a grayscale image. Human vision is unable to detect any sudden steps in a monochrome palette with a minimum of 256 tones.

See also Camera functions *pages 14–15* / Seeing in color *pages 58–59* / What is a digital image? *pages 72–73* / File formats *pages 86–87* /

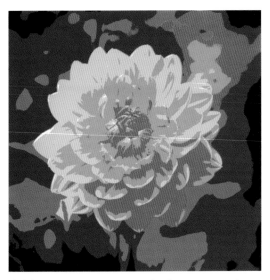

GIF-format color images can also be constructed with an 8-bit, 256-value palette, but the outcome is far from photographic quality.

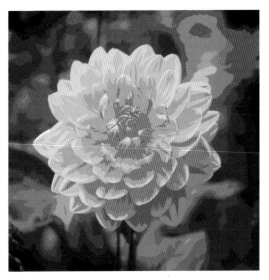

Compressed GIF image using a 16-bit palette. With 16 colors, subtle tones are destroyed.

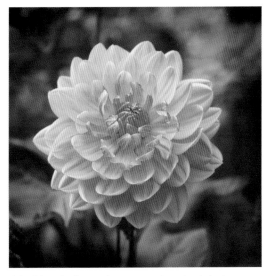

A 24-bit color image is common in output devices such as ink-jet printers and computer monitors.

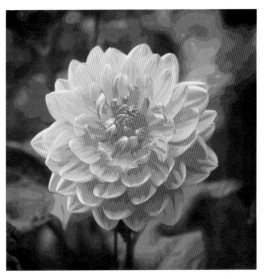

Compressed GIF image using a 32-bit palette. With 32 colors, the result is nearly photographic quality.

Resolution

To a new user of digital technology, understanding resolution — the physical relationship between pixels and print size — can be confusing.

Resolution is a curious term and describes both the spatial dimensions and the size of the color palette used to create a digital image. With additional terms such as megabytes and megapixels, it is reassuring to know that they all essentially tell us the same thing: how big and how good a printout can be.

It is useful to remember that a 12MB image file is sufficient to make a high-quality, photo-realistic 8½ x 11-inch ink-jet printout. Bigger files will take longer to process and the result will have no obvious visible advantage.

Pixel size 1

Astonishingly, pixels are not created with a fixed size. Instead, the three-color RGB recipe can re-create the same colored pixel be it 1 inch (2.5cm) or 3 feet (1m) square. The user is responsible for setting the pixel size to match the intended output. Using Adobe Photoshop's Image Size dialog box, pixel size (dpi) can be set at, for example, 72 per inch or 200 per inch. The number of pixels in the image remains the same, but they can be made physically bigger or smaller. At an inch square (2.5cm²), pixels will look like tiles from a giant mosaic and would be a poor photographic illusion. The smaller the pixels are, the more invisible they become and the more realistic a printout will be. All digital cameras create images with pixels set at 72 per inch. If the pixel size is reduced to 200 per inch, the printout is physically smaller but of a much higher quality. Some devices, for example a flatbed scanner, may not indicate the pixel dimension in the control panel, in which case users should go to Image>Image Size.

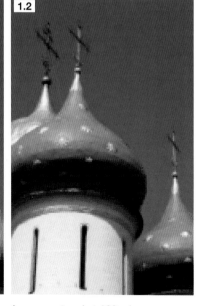 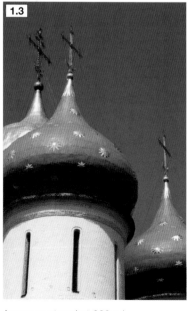

Image captured at 50ppi.

Image captured at 100ppi.

Image captured at 200ppi.

Super-sampling and 36-bit and 48-bit color images 2

Many new scanners and professional cameras are able to use a wider color palette to capture images using billions rather than millions of colors. The 36-bit and 48-bit image file is gigantic compared to the standard 24-bit and can be difficult to manage on older computers. Many professional repro houses advocate manipulating color and contrast on 48-bit files before they are scaled down to 24-bit just before output. Yet, with most digital photographers using ink-jet printers for output, little or no advantage will be visible. A more important quality factor in digital capture is the extent of its dynamic range, or its ability to record detail across an extensive tonal range. Devices with a range of 3.5 – 4.0 density (d) or thereabouts will give excellent results.

Enlarging and reducing pixel dimensions

New pixels can always be added to make a print bigger using a process called interpolation. New pixels are invented and inserted between original ones, with a color estimated from nearby pixels. The process of reducing deletes pixels from the bitmap to make the print smaller. In both situations, the resulting image will lose sharpness, but this can be re-established with the Unsharp Mask (USM) filter.

See also Camera functions *pages 14–15* / What is a digital image? *pages 72–73* / Pixels and print size *pages 82–83* / Printer types *pages 242–243* /

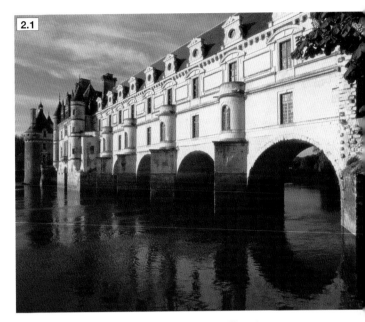

A good scanner with a large dynamic range will capture detail in the deepest shadows.

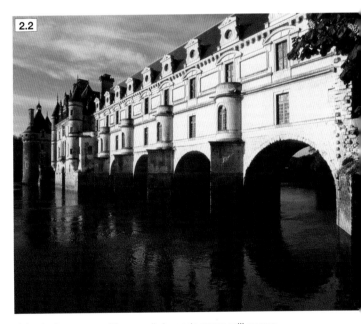

A budget scanner with a small dynamic range will merge dark grays and black shadows together.

Image modes

The individual characteristics of conventional photographic films run parallel to the broad range of different image modes that can be found in Adobe Photoshop.

There is no reason to change from RGB color to CMYK if the intention is to print images out on a desktop ink-jet printer, or to e-mail image attachments to friends. However, there are other image modes that can be used to meet specific output criteria.

RGB color mode [1]

Red Green Blue (RGB) color mode is the standard for image capture on digital cameras and scanners. An RGB image can be tagged with a color profile for greater color accuracy and displayed accurately and without too much variance on an RGB color monitor. Unlike less universal modes the RGB mode can use the entire range of commands and controls in Adobe Photoshop. The RGB image is subdivided into three separate color channels, which can all be edited independently and ink-jet printer software does an excellent job converting RGB pixels into Cyan, Magenta, Yellow and Black (CMYK) inks. The 8-bit per channel or 24-bit RGB file is a universal standard for output.

Grayscale mode [2]

The grayscale mode is similar to standard black-and-white film, but is in a positive rather than negative state. Created by scanners and some digital cameras, a grayscale image has a single black channel with 0 – 255 brightness steps. Grayscale images cannot be manipulated with commands relating to color, but can easily be converted to RGB prior to manipulation. The 8-bit grayscale is the standard for output, but many capture devices can create super-smooth 12-bit grayscales. Grayscale image data is only a third as large as a similar RGB file.

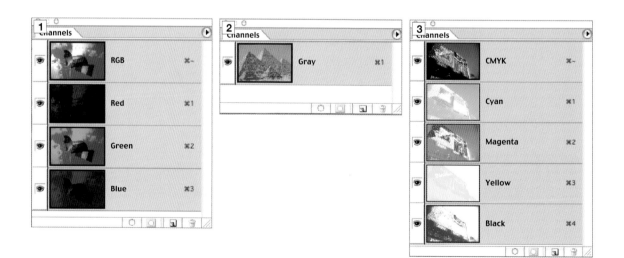

Cyan, Magenta, Yellow and Black mode [3]

The Cyan, Magenta, Yellow and Black (CMYK) mode is used for images destined for commercial lithographic output only, and there are no other advantages to working in this mode. Not all of Photoshop's commands and manipulation sequences work on CMYK images. The CMYK color palette is much smaller than RGB and, as a consequence, certain colors do not translate well on a RGB monitor. A good alternative is to edit in RGB mode with the CMYK Preview function selected by View>Proof colors. This gives a visual indication of the CMYK outcome while still working in RGB mode.

LAB mode [4]

LAB mode is an abstract and theoretical color space and is not used by any input or output device. LAB images are split into three channels, one for lightness and two for color and are made simply by converting from RGB. This mode is frequently used for making brighter monochrome conversions as an alternative to the normal grayscale made from RGB.

Bitmap mode [5]

This is not to be confused with Windows Bitmap mode, and is used purely for storing single-color line art such as black ink on white paper. Bitmaps are only 1-bit with two possible states, white or black, and therefore have the smallest file size of all. Once opened in a drawing or image-editing application, bitmaps can be scaled up to current working resolution without a significant loss of detail.

Multichannel mode [6]

This is used in the final preparation of lithographic printing plates for specific color separations, such as duotones. Once split into component colors, a duotone can be viewed but not edited.

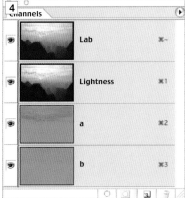

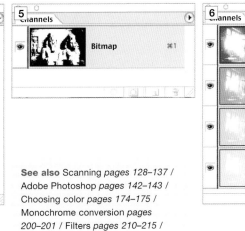

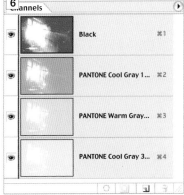

See also Scanning *pages 128–137* / Adobe Photoshop *pages 142–143* / Choosing color *pages 174–175* / Monochrome conversion *pages 200–201* / Filters *pages 210–215* /

Pixels and print size

A photographer armed with the knowledge of how pixels convert into ink droplets will find it nearly impossible to produce a bad-quality print.

Ink-jet resolution and image resolution [1]

Despite the claims of manufacturers regarding the ultra-high resolution of their printers, it is not essential to change image resolution settings in Photoshop to match a printer's 1440 or 2880 pixels per inch (ppi) capacity. Makers are justified in their claims that their printing devices do indeed drop these numbers of ink droplets, but it is important to understand how the drops fall. Essentially, ink droplets are produced by each individual color reservoir and are sprayed onto the paper on top of each other, rather than each on their own untouched area. For a 1440-ppi printer with six colors, therefore, the actual number of drops per inch is calculated by dividing 1440 by six — which makes 240. Some ink-jet printers have doubled their resolution to 2880ppi, but this is only because these newly designed ink heads are able to produce ink drops in two sizes rather than just one. For ink-jet printing, prepare your files at 200 dots per inch (dpi).

Output to other devices

Digital images for reproduction in a magazine or book publication, need to be prepared at a higher resolution of 300 pixels per inch if sharp results are to be guaranteed. For other photographic output devices, such as the super-high resolution Fuji Pictrography system, images need to be prepared at an even higher 400 pixels per inch.

Resolution

As with all visual material, photographic prints are generally viewed at a certain distance. When held close to the eye, only the finest-quality photographic prints will still look flawless and without grain or ink particles. Yet when viewed at a greater distance — in excess of arm's length — the human eye is unable to perceive a lower-quality print. This is because distance blurs the boundaries between individual ink droplets and pixels, making them merge together optically. Unlike the kind of high-quality photographic reproduction that occurs in glossy lifestyle magazines, large-scale ink-jet prints or billboard posters are not output to the same pin-sharp quality. Made to be viewed from a considerable distance away, a billboard image will be printed with coarse dots which go unnoticed unless viewed close-up.

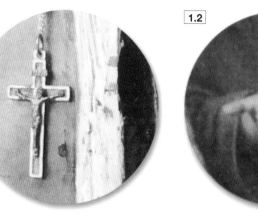

1.1 **1.2**

Images printed without re-sizing will retain sharp detail as shown on left. If over-enlarged, prints will look blurred and unsharp, as shown on right.

See also Capture *pages 74–75* / Resolution *pages 78–79* / Printer types *pages 242–243* /

Image mode	Data size	Mega pixel size	Pixel dimensions	Ink-jet print size (200ppi)	Dye-sub print size (300ppi)
RGB Color (standard 24-bit)	24MB	8M	3450x2450	12.5 x 15" (31 x 44cm or A3+)	11.5 x 8" (21 x 29cm or A4)
	12MB	4.1M	2350x1770	12 x 8.5" (30 x 22.4cm or A4+)	8 x 6" (20 x 15cm or A5)
	6MB	2.1M	1800x1200	9 x 6" (22 x 15cm or A5+)	6 x 4" (15 x 10cm or A6)
	2.25MB	n/a	1024x768	5 x 4" (13 x 9.75cm)	3.5 x 2.5" (8.6 x 6.5cm)
	900K	n/a	640x480	3 x 2.5" (8 x 6cm)	2 x 1.5" (5.4 x 4cm)
Grayscale (standard 8-bit)	8MB	n/a	3450x 2450	12.5 x 15" (31 x 44cm or A3+)	11.5 x 8" (21 x 29cm or A4)
	4MB	n/a	2350x1770	12 x 8.5" (30 x 22.4cm or A4+)	8 x 6" (20 x 15cm or A5)
	2MB	n/a	1800x1200	9 x 6" (22 x 15cm or A5+)	6 x 4" (15 x 10cm or A6)
	750K	n/a	1024x768	5 x 4" (13 x 9.75cm)	3.5 x 2.5" (8.6 x 6.5cm)
	300K	n/a	640x480	3 x 2.5" (8 x 6cm)	2 x 1.5" (5.4 x 4cm)

With large-format ink-jet print output for posters and point-of-sale displays, the same viewing distance theory applies and images can be printed at a much lower resolution than normal. For a typical ink-jet poster print, image resolution can be dropped to as low as 150ppi, which offers the added benefit of allowing an increase in the document size without the need to resample or add new pixels.

Super-sampled resolutions

When faced with an increased file size as a result of scanning an enhanced 48-bit color or 14-bit grayscale mode image, it is important to realize that this will not allow an increase in print size. After converting back to 24-bit and 8-bit, respectively, the pixel dimension will remain the same, but a smaller color palette will be used to draw the image.

Data management

Once uncompressed, digital photographs can place a heavy strain on a computer's limited hard disk.

Good housekeeping

It is not advisable to save multiple stages of any work in progress because unfinished and layered images will generate vast amounts of data. It is much better to get into the habit of keeping an unmanipulated or raw file in a write-protected volume to open and work on each time, just as conventional photographers work on original film negatives in the darkroom. Use simple and logical names to label files. Don't rely on your memory; a simple system will mean files are easily retrieved, even after some time has passed. Label versions or alternatives with a simple ascending number scale, such as tree1.tif.

Hard disk storage

The latest computers have hard drives with enormous memory capacities, yet there is still every reason to store original image files on write-protected removable media like CD-Rs. The hard drive (HD) storage area is often needed as emergency RAM during complex processes involving lots of data. Virtual memory, as it is called, still permits the process to go ahead but at a slower pace and only if there is enough free space on the HD in the first place. If a hard disk is filled to capacity, then virtual memory will not work and a user's complex Photoshop rendering will stop.

Storing on removable media [1]

Large image files are best stored on high-capacity and reliable media, such as CD-Rs. More dependable than rewritable CD-RWs, CD-Rs are both good value for money and universally accepted. A useful addition to a computer workstation is an internal

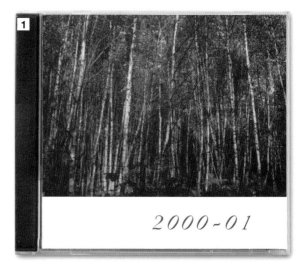

CD writer. With higher capacity Digital Versatile Disk Recordable (DVDR) and Digital Versatile Disk Random Access Memory (DVDRAM) disks going down in price, even greater economy and convenience is not far off.

Additional hard disks [2]

A good alternative to using removable media is to install an additional hard disk on a computer. Most new PCs are designed with space for at least one extra hard drive. With new products emerging every year, high-capacity drives up to 60GB in size can be installed for much less than an external drive of the same capacity. This extra disk space can be reserved solely for an image library and does not need to be associated with virtual memory functions. Hard disks are sold with different spin speeds, such as 7200 revolutions per minute (rpm), and the faster it revolves, the faster image data can be pulled off

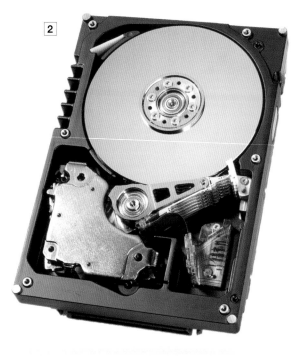

2

that. Another possibility is to revamp an older computer with new high-capacity hard disks and connect it up like a LAN server.

Backing up **3**

A sensible precaution for all photographers is to back up work on a regular basis with a back-up device and software like Retrospect. Unlike constantly saving and managing image files, the process of backing up can be scheduled to occur automatically at any time. There are many different kinds of high-capacity back-up drives on the market, such as Digital Linear Tape (DLT), Digital Audio Tape (DAT) or Advanced Intelligent Tape (AIT). Professional photographers should also keep a back-up on media that should be rotated on a regular basis with one copy held off-site. Data is often compressed in these devices and subsequent retrieval is often a slow process.

See also Storage media *pages 92–93* / Computer basics *pages 96–97* / Internal components *pages 98–99* / Configuring a workstation *pages 102–103* /

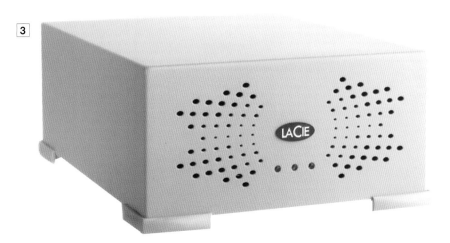

3

File formats

It is vital to prepare and save digital images in the correct format for integration with other programs and to store originals in perfect condition.

Image files can be packaged for a wide variety of end products, including commercial reproduction, the Internet or simple ink-jet output. An increasing number of unique file types, called formats, have been designed so that image data is prepared precisely for use in specific professional applications, such as QuarkXpress or InDesign. Not to be confused with the formatting process of blank disks, file formats are identified by a unique file extension that appears as a three-digit code at the end of its file name. For example "portrait.tif," which describes a TIFF file, and "bigdog.jpg," which describes a JPEG file. Many commonly used file formats are not restricted by copyright and can therefore be found in a wide variety of applications as alternatives in the Save As menu. Specialized file formats that were developed by a single application, however, such as the multi-layered Photoshop .psd format, are restricted to the original

application and a few other applications under license.

Swapping files between Apple and Windows PCs [1]

For those users who need to transfer files between Windows and Apple computers, the process is very simple provided a few basic rules are applied first. First and foremost is the need for a file extension like .jpg at the end of the filename. Unlike most PCs, Apple computers do not automatically add a file extension to a document name unless the application in use has this option as its preference settings. Removable media must be formatted specifically if swapping from Apple to PC, for Windows PC use only. Apple computers can read both Windows- and Apple-formatted media, but Windows can only read its own.

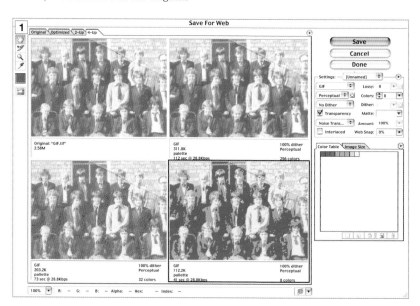

Common image file formats

CompuServe GIF

GIF stands for Graphic Interchanged Format and was developed by CompuServe for network use only. GIFs were never intended for printout, but for monitor display, since they have a much-reduced palette of colors. To make a GIF image, open a high-resolution image in a professional imaging application and then save it in the GIF format, where millions of colors are somehow squeezed into a palette of 256 or fewer. With colors reduced to 8-bit, file sizes drop dramatically. To retain some vestige of a photographic image, gradient colors are dithered, or converted into dots. GIFs are generally used for hard-edged graphic images, such as logos and banners, rather than photographic images containing subtle tones and colors.

TIFF

The Tagged Image File Format (TIFF) is the best file format for archiving digital images. TIFF is generally accepted by all desktop publishing applications such as QuarkXpress and InDesign. It is best to save a TIFF without selecting any of the three optional compression techniques, LZW, JPEG and ZIP, although LZW works without any visible loss of image quality and can reduce a document to two thirds of its original size. Compressed TIFFs are much less compatible with older applications and may not even open.

See also Camera functions *pages 12–13* / Compression *pages 88–89* / Packaging image files *pages 90–91* / Computer platforms and operating systems *pages 100–101* /

File formats are selected using the Save As menu.

Compression

Compression is the "downsizing" of digital data so that it takes less disk space, and is designed for faster network transmission and fewer demands on storage media.

There are two kinds of compression: lossy and lossless. Lossy compression is used when saving in the JPEG format and causes a significant loss of image detail and sharpness each time the file is resaved. The file size, however, is greatly reduced. This familiar damage has the appearance of a crude pattern of disjointed blocks appearing in previously detailed areas of the image. Lossless compression uses a different mathematical mechanism to discard data without causing visible damage to the image. The space savings are not as great as afforded by low-quality JPEG files, but sharp detail is preserved.

To visualize this mathematical routine, imagine a compressed TIFF file as a rolled-up photographic print, and a JPEG as a folded photographic print. Once opened, the "rolled" TIFF will show no signs of damage, while the lossy JPEG format will bear all the "crease" marks of the cruder method of compression. With cheap and plentiful high-capacity data storage available, there is no reason to compress images for storage unless they are destined for network end use.

Save as JPEG   1

To maximize the saving potential of a JPEG file for Internet use, the Save for Web command in Adobe Photoshop offers a wide range of tools. Images can be viewed in a two- or four-up window, so that different routines can be compared to each other. Current document sizes are displayed at the base of each image together with the estimated time it would take to download the image over a range of different bandwidths. Sophisticated applications like Photoshop present the JPEG scale as 0 – 100, rather than 0 – 10. With most data savings produced at the zero end — but better image quality preserved at the

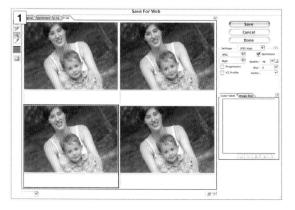

100 end — the slider is best started at 100 and moved toward zero until a noticeable deterioration appears. All images will compress differently and the greatest savings will be made on blurred images of only few colors. Sharply detailed images with lots of different colors will not compress as much and result in data saving, even if they had the same pixel dimensions as the blurry image. Extra functions can be added to the JPEG file, including the Progressive option which enables the file to download in multiple passes in a web-browser window. To maintain some control over color accuracy, the ICC Profile option allows the JPEG to be tagged with a standard color profile.

Digital camera compression   2

On a digital camera, there are usually three or more JPEG quality settings, which are primarily there to allow storage of more images onto a memory card. The lowest-quality JPEGs will not be good enough for fine printing or creative enhancement. A much better option is to select a high-quality JPEG setting and buy a bigger or additional memory card. Never save exceptional photographs as low-quality JPEGs as the quality cannot be recaptured at a later stage.

A blurred original saved using low-quality compression.

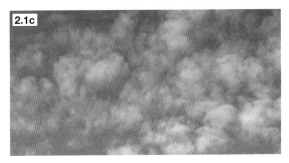

A blurred original saved using mid-quality compression.

A blurred original saved using high-quality compression.

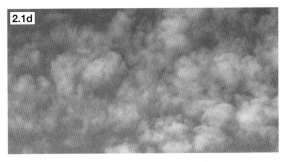

A blurred original saved without compression.

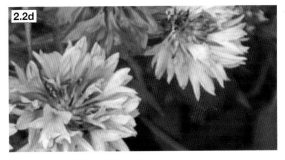

A sharp original saved using low-quality compression.

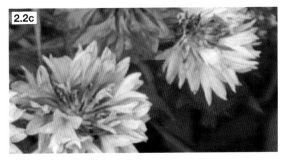

A sharp original saved using mid-quality compression.

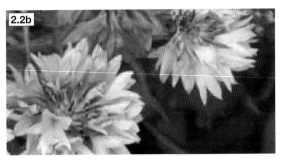

A sharp original saved using high-quality compression.

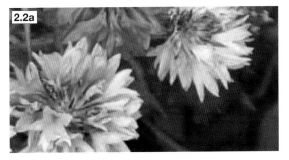

A sharp original saved without compression.

See also Camera functions *pages 12–13* / File formats *pages 86–87* / Packaging image files *pages 90–91* /

Packaging image files

Image files can be saved in various different formats for a range of specific future applications.

JPEG and JPEG 2000

Invented by a team of imaging scientists called the Joint Photographic Experts Group, the JPEG format is perhaps the most universal of all image formats and is commonly used in digital cameras. JPEG was invented to reduce the amount of image data without compromising photographic quality. It achieves this by sharing data between blocks of pixels, reducing the need for a discrete recipe for each and every pixel. The drawback with this method is a loss of image quality in return for space savings, and the greater the saving, the bigger the drop in quality. Photographic images on the Internet are usually JPEGs, since their small file sizes create little or no download delay. Most digital cameras allow for a JPEG format, with at least three different quality options, which are really different levels of JPEG compression. A recent development is the JPEG 2000 format which offers the chance to determine different levels of compression in different areas of an image. This clever application could be used for maximizing image quality on the most important area of an image while allowing less important areas to be compressed. The JPEG 2000 format has, at present, only emerging support from web browsers and imaging applications.

EPS [1]

The lesser-used Encapsulated Postscript (EPS) file format is for exclusive use in desktop-publishing (DTP) applications. EPS files can be created with a unique additional element called a clipping path, which is used to define the perimeter edges of irregularly shaped images destined to be used as cutouts in magazine page layouts. EPS files can

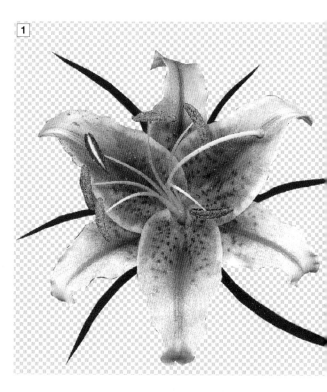

be created in a professional application like Adobe Photoshop.

PSD [2]

The versatile Photoshop (PSD) format allows supplementary image data to be saved, including layers, channels, paths and even captions. The PSD format is useful for storing work in progress, since the important decisions can be returned to at a later date. Once an image project is completed, layered Photoshop files can be flattened into a single layer for faster printout. If additional versions of the image need to be prepared as JPEGs or TIFFs, then the image must always be flattened first. Application-specific formats can cause compatibility issues when new software updates arrive on the market. For example, Photoshop version 7.0 files may lose data if opened in older versions of the application.

PDF

The innovative Portable Document Format (PDF) invented by Adobe brought desktop publishing into the Internet era. Once documents are laid out in a standard DTP application, such as QuarkXpress, they can be converted to the PDF format using an application like Acrobat Distiller. The PDF is a unique format which can be transmitted easily over networks and is read with freely available reader software called Adobe Acrobat. PDF files are cross-platform, have a very small file size and have become the standard way to distribute high-quality documents for download and desktop printout.

Photo CD

The Photo-CD format is owned by Kodak who have decided not to license the technology to any third party software company. As such, most professional imaging applications can open Photo-CD images, but none can save in the Photo-CD format. Conventional photographic film can be processed, scanned and saved in a Photo-CD package through most photo labs. Kodak's lesser-quality Picture CD is an alternative package aimed exclusively at the amateur market, and uses a low-quality JPEG format.

Archiving image files

Once image files have been scanned or transferred from a digital camera, it is important to store them in a stable file format. They should be saved as a TIFF in the RGB color mode, rather than CMYK. If CMYK images are required, an RGB version should be kept in reserve. When the three-channel RGB is converted into the four-channel CMYK, the new black channel is largely invented. Subsequent problems can happen if the process is reversed and CMYK is squeezed back into RGB, making a bad job of generating shadow areas.

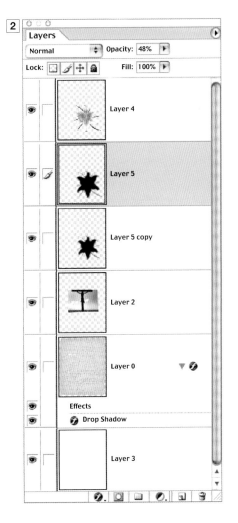

See also Camera functions *pages 12–13* / File formats *pages 86–87* / Compression *pages 88–89* / Lab services *pages 138–139* /

Storage media

The wide range of different storage media on the market can be confusing for new users.

CD-R and CD-RW disks [1]

Compact disk recordable media are cheap and high capacity, with products ranging from 640 to 740MB. Easily available, some even in supermarkets, the CD-R has become as popular as the music compact cassette. Three types are available: the cheaper blue-backed kind, the better-quality silver-backed, and the more expensive variant with a gold reverse. The latter is said to be more stable for archiving, but the cheaper disks do a very good job too. Disks can only be written once, but data can be added gradually to a disk until its capacity is reached using the Multi-Session recording option. Single-session disks are written to and effectively closed to further additions and are more compatible between Windows and Apple computers. CD-RW disks offer the same features but in a rewritable format. They are much more prone to disk errors and incompatibility problems. All but ancient computers have a CD-ROM drive, so disks are accepted worldwide, but a special CD writer is necessary to author disks. Extra care should be taken when handling CD media, in particular avoiding water, strong sunlight and adhesives. Labels should only be written on using the manufacturer's recommended products and on no account should ballpoint pens or pencils be used, as they will scrape off the reflective coating and render a disk unusable.

Iomega Zip disks [2]

Zip disks were for a long time the favorite media of the graphics professional. Cheap and rewritable, they offered a more flexible solution to the cumbersome and, now outdated, Syquest disks. Zips are still extremely useful and can be bought in two capacities: 100MB and 250MB. Like the old-fashioned

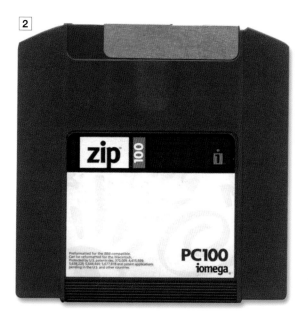

[1]

[2]

3.5-inch floppy, a Zip features a disk of magnetic media inside a protective outer case. And like floppies, they can be prepared or formatted for use in either Windows PCs or Apple computers and can be well maintained for an indefinite lifespan using a disk-utility application such as Norton. Zip disks need a special Zip drive attached to a computer in order to work, fitted either internally or externally. External drives can be purchased with a variety of connecting leads to suit most computers, such as USB, SCSI and even the largely defunct parallel port. 100MB Zip drives cannot read and write to newer 250MB disks but 250MB Zip drives can read both. Special care should be taken when handling this kind of media to avoid all sources of magnetic fields. Never pull back the protective metal shutter at the top of the ZIP disk and touch the exposed disk.

Pocket drives and digital wallets   3

The latest innovation is the portable digital wallet, which can be used to download digital camera images on location. With its built-in power supply stored in an internal battery and capacities of up to 20GB, these are ideal for shooting on location for long periods of time. The pocket hard drive is a similar device that is portable enough to carry in a camera bag. It draws its power from a computer's Universal Serial Bus (USB) or FireWire port. Without the need for driver software, this device is recognized by a host computer as an additional drive. The most versatile product is the USB personal storage device, which is small enough to fit on a key ring. It works by simply plugging into any USB port. It is an expensive way to buy rewritable storage and capacity is limited to around 256MB.

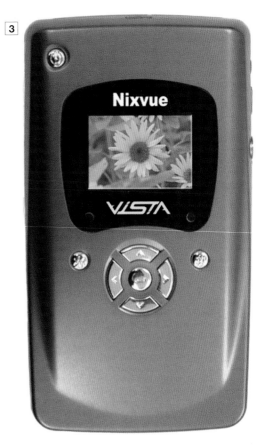

A digital wallet offers convenient storage when shooting on location.

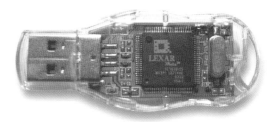

The USB key offers a high-priced but very convenient way of carrying digital data.

See also Data management *pages 84–85* / Connections and ports *pages 104–105* / Peripherals *pages 106–107* /

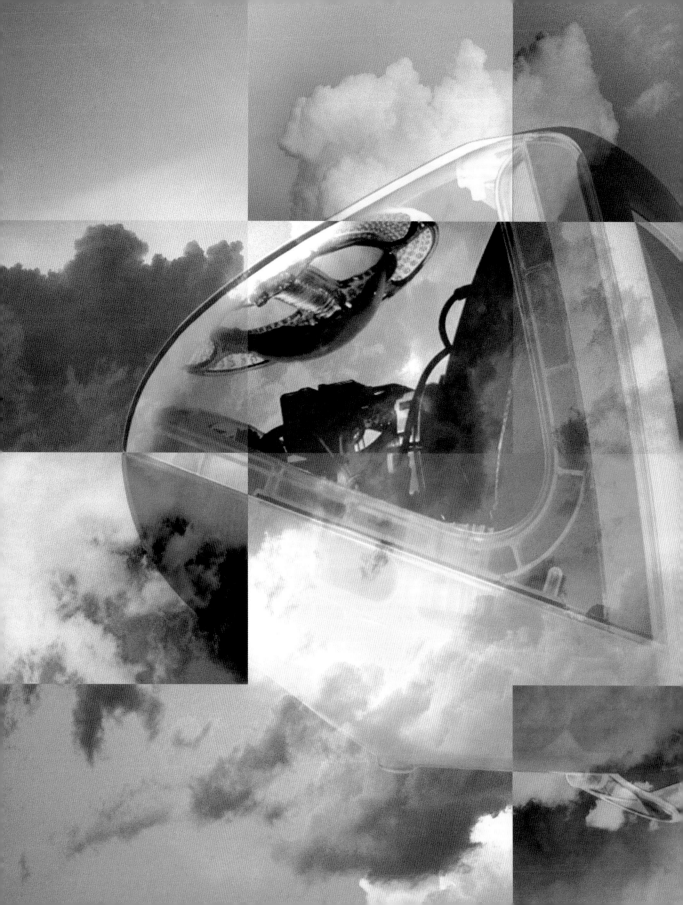

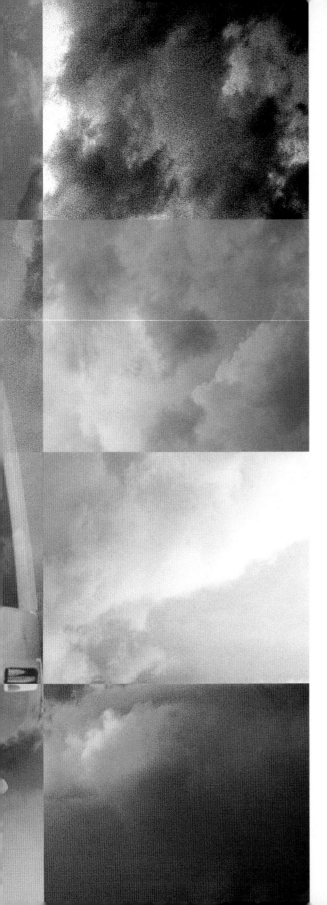

4 Computer Hardware

Computer basics

It is essential to understand the basic principles of a computer before pressing it into active service.

Operation

Contrary to popular belief, a computer does not have a mind of its own and will not develop strange personality defects. Instead, from the very first time it is switched on, a computer's responses are determined by the individual actions of the user alone. Like an automobile, a PC needs to be driven with care and needs regular maintenance to keep it working properly. Computers are operated by a combination of keyboard, mouse or stylus — three input devices that convey instructions to the machine. Despite a myriad of automatic tricks and timesaving gadgets that can be applied to raw data — be they digital photos or word-processed essays — there is simply no substitute for good quality input.

Hardware

The term hardware simply refers to the physical components of a PC — hard disk, keyboard and memory chip. Hardware largely determines the performance of a computer, and it is driven by the operating system and application software. As computer technology develops, most hardware items can be replaced easily with better and faster components, enabling users to get at least five years' service out of a PC. As with an automobile, most hardware is modular, allowing manufacturers and end users choice between different makes, models and prices. It is worth remembering that a cheap PC will be assembled with budget hardware compared to a more expensive model from a well-known manufacturer.

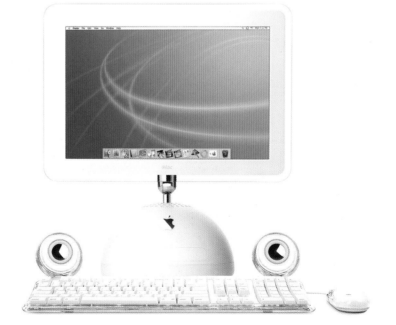

The all-in-one Apple imac is built for digital photography enthusiasts.

Software

The words software, program and application all mean the same thing: the interactive environments used to process and package data into a useful outcome. Even the start-up screen that appears on a PC is an application like Windows XP or Apple OSX, and it is part of the computer's operating system (OS). Applications generally are manufactured for specific tasks, such as accounting, image processing or web browsing, but all are designed to enable the user to manipulate and develop original material into a desired format. Like hardware, there is software available to suit all budgets, but good-quality results are difficult to produce from the cheaper products. Bundled software — an endless list of useful-sounding applications sold with off-the-shelf PCs — is rarely worth having for image processing.

Housekeeping

A computer will stay in top condition so long as from the very outset the user adopts a sensible routine for naming and storing work and a cautious approach to installing or removing new software. Most problems are caused by incompatibilities between products from different manufacturers or from using versions of applications that were not designed to work on older operating systems. An Internet connection is essential from the start and will provide users with all the necessary advice from a manufacturer's website, as well as help you solve rudimentary problems at little or no cost.

See also Internal components *pages 98–99* / Computer platforms and operating systems *pages 100–101* / Configuring a workstation *pages 102–103* /

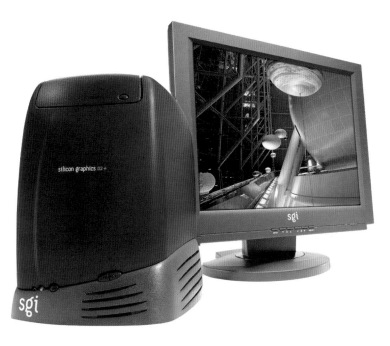

High-powered Silicon Graphics workstations offer lightning-speed processing.

Internal components

The technical jargon used by computer retailers can be baffling: the first thing to learn is the difference between a Pentium and a peripheral.

Processor   1

The processor resides in the computer's motherboard and is the engine of a computer. It works by making calculations at top speed. Common processor types are the Intel Pentium, Athlon and Apple G4 and their speeds are described in megahertz (MHz) or gigahertz (GHz), meaning one million or one billion calculations per second. The latest computers are sold with gigahertz processors. The fastest speeds are less of an issue for image processing and aimed more at users demanding gaming. Some computers have two processors that rip their way through tasks.

See also Data management *pages 84–85* / Computer basics *pages 96–97* / Configuring a workstation *pages 102–103* /

RAM and memory   2

RAM, or Random Access Memory, is a physical memory module slotted into the motherboard of a PC. A PC uses RAM to store working data when applications are up and running and documents are open. RAM is essentially a temporary storage facility — sometimes referred to as memory — and all data held in RAM is lost when a computer is switched off, rather than shut down, or crashes. The data used to create a digital image file can be enormous, running into many megabytes, and compared to an office PC an imaging workstation needs a large amount of RAM. If the budget permits, installing 256MB of RAM will make a significant difference. Even if a PC is fitted with the fastest processor, too little RAM will still slow it down.

1

The Apple G4 offers an easy way to upgrade system components with its drop-down side panel.

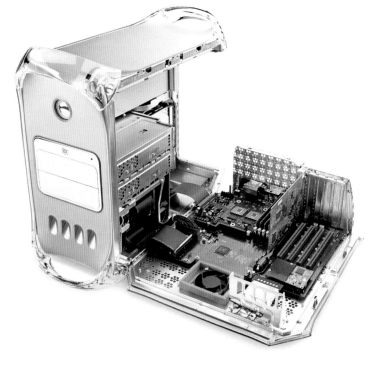

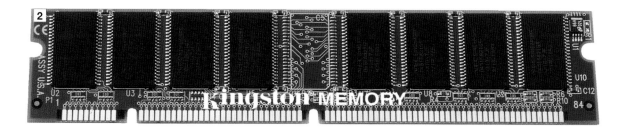

VRAM (Video Random Access Memory) or graphics card   3

How a PC displays color has less to do with the actual monitor than with a component referred to as a graphics card or Video Random Access Memory (VRAM). This device is designed essentially to allow users to see photos displayed in millions of colors at high resolution. A large monitor requires a better display card to cope with the increased area of the image displayed. For the best-quality results and ease of working with them, digital images should be displayed in millions of colors and at a screen resolution of 1024 or greater. Most modern PCs are fitted with a 32MB graphics card, which is more than adequate for quality imaging.

Hard disk or drive

The hard disk, or hard drive, is used to store unused documents and applications. A hard disk is like a library full of books, and should be organized sensibly. Hard disks are manufactured with enormous storage capacities, for example 120GB, and variable speeds, such as 7200rpm. The faster-spinning disks allow users to store and retrieve data quickly, leaving more time to get on with creative work. Most PCs have an additional internal space which can be used for adding a second hard disk for extra storage or dedicated use.

Internal bus

All components of a PC are connected by an internal network of wires that impacts on the speeds at which data can be passed from one component to another. Data travels along a cable much like a automobile travels along a highway, where the wider and straighter the road, the faster the possible speed. Just like a connection to the Internet, the bandwidth of a computer's internal connections also is responsible for the speed at which it will work.

3

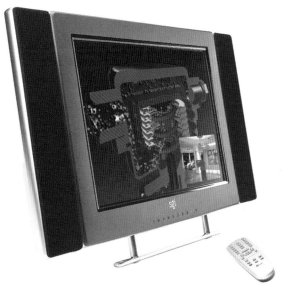

Computer platforms and operating systems

Now that Windows and Apple platforms are less mutually exclusive, it is difficult to make a bad decision when buying a computer.

Kit car or Mercedes-Benz? 　1

In the world of digital photography there are two computer platforms to pick from, the more aesthetically appealing Apple Mac and the ubiquitous, utilitarian Windows PC. Apple Macs are the standard tool for creative industries. Windows PCs, however, still dominate the home consumer marketplace and are used in offices worldwide. Apple's success is built on a tradition of technical innovation, including working hand-in-hand with many of the leading software giants, such as Adobe. The cheaper Windows PCs are assembled by thousands of different companies from an assortment of internal components and there is frequently no way to foresee a compatibility issue until everything grinds to a halt. All Apple computers are constructed from standard components and this drives other companies to conform to the Apple's set of standards. There is much less likelihood of new add-ons not working.

The better Windows PCs can be bought from recognized manufacturers such as Toshiba, HP and Sony. On a final note, hardly any destructive computer viruses target the Mac, since most malicious attention is directed at the ubiquitous Windows PC.

Operating systems

Windows 95, 98, 2000, NT, XP, Mac OS 9, OSX, Linux and Unix are all types of operating system software. The purpose of an operating system is to enable hardware components and software applications to communicate with each other. Operating systems determine the look and feel of a computer's desktop and are constantly redesigned to give a simpler working environment and to keep abreast of the latest technological developments. Both Microsoft and Apple create significant updates on a yearly basis, together with smaller revisions every few months or so. These smaller updates are usually responses

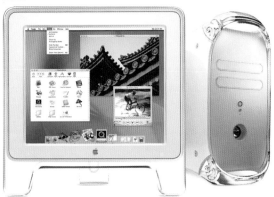

1.1

An Apple Mac computer.

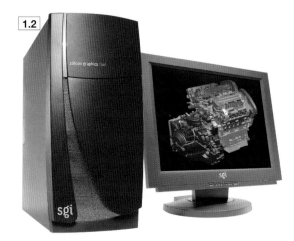

1.2

A Windows-compatible Silicon Graphics workstation.

to unforeseen glitches and are freely available as downloads from the manufacturers' websites. External hardware, such as ink-jet printers and film scanners, are designed to work with a specific OS and version, and free updates are easily available.

Applications for both platforms 2

There are very few applications that have been designed for Mac or Windows PC only, and most industry-standard tools like Adobe Photoshop are designed for both. Off-the-shelf software is purchased for one platform or the other and license agreements do not usually extend across platforms. Once installed, however, sharing files between the two platforms is simple. Users with a Windows PC at work and a Mac at home, for example, can transfer files from one to the other provided they use PC-formatted removable media, together with an essential file extension at the end of a document's file name.

The use of removable media can be bypassed by e-mailing files as attachments from one platform to another. Again, the necessary file extension must be used. The golden rule for preparing removable media for use on both platforms is to ensure it is PC-formatted. Zip or floppy disks can be created in the Windows compatible Disk Operating System (DOS) format and CD-R and CD-RWs can be created in the universal ISO 9660 format. All Apple computers can read and write to both Mac- and Windows-formatted media, while Windows can only recognize DOS- and ISO 9660-formatted media. A PC will not recognize an Apple-formatted disk. However, both Apple and Windows PCs can share a common network, which makes file transfer even easier.

See also Data management *pages 84–85* / File formats *pages 86–87* / Computer basics *pages 96–97* / Configuring a workstation *pages 102–103* /

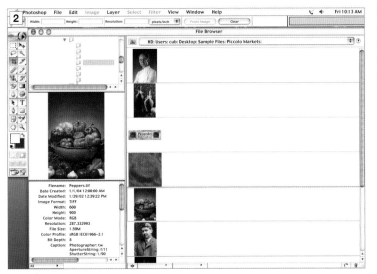

Photoshop is designed to work on both Mac OS and Windows platforms.

Configuring a workstation

Setting up a computer properly ensures that all components are used to their maximum potential.

Good housekeeping

It is essential to determine a coherent and organized system for storing files and applications right from the outset. A brand new computer is prepared with a pre-set arrangement of folders which should be adhered to at all times. For Windows PCs, all applications should be installed in the C>Program Files folder and in the Macintosh HD>Applications folder for Apple users. Digital images should be kept in two newly created folders called "masters" and "work in progress." Within these folders, finished or manipulated images are best kept separate from the raw unprocessed versions.

Software performance · 1

Once installed, imaging software may need simple tweaking to maximize its performance. This does not need to be more complicated than running through an application's preference settings. The two primary concerns with a memory-hungry application, such as Adobe Photoshop, are to set both the scratch disk and its memory allocation. A PC will have a fixed quantity of RAM installed, which is shared by the operating system and any other open applications. The user is responsible for allocating the size of a slice of RAM to each application, much like dividing an apple pie between several hungry children. For Adobe Photoshop it is recommended that the memory allocation be set to five times the size of the largest likely image document. If this is 30MB, for example, the memory allocation should be set to 150MB.

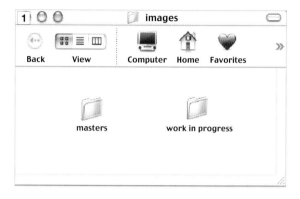

Memory allocation in Windows

With Adobe Photoshop or Photoshop Elements open, choose Edit>Preferences>Memory>Image Cache. Move the Memory Usage slider to the right until you achieve the desired figure.

Memory allocation in Apple OSX · 2

With Adobe Photoshop or Photoshop Elements open, choose Photoshop (or Photoshop Elements) >Preferences>Memory>Image Cache. Move the Memory Usage slider to the right until you achieve the desired figure.

Memory allocation in Apple OS 8-9

For earlier Mac OS, the memory preferences can only be set when the application is unopened. Click on the application icon — the one normally used to

See also Data management *pages 84–85* / Computer basics *pages 96–97* / Internal components *pages 98–99* / Workstations *pages 112–119* /

Preferences (panel 2)

2 | Preferences

Memory & Image Cache

OK | Cancel | Prev | Next

Cache Settings
Cache Levels: 4
☐ Use cache for histograms

Memory Usage
Available RAM: 221MB
Maximum Used by Photoshop: 70 ▸ % = 154MB

Note: Changes will take effect the next time you start Photoshop

launch it — then go to File>Get Info>Memory. Reset the memory and close, then launch the application.

Using other applications at the same time

Running other programs at the same time as an imaging application will make further demands on the RAM pie. Check that allocated totals (including the OS) don't go beyond the limit of the RAM. If they do, buy an extra RAM chip or reduce each application's total accordingly.

Scratch disk

When Photoshop runs out of available RAM space, it writes data to an overflow storage area called a scratch disk. In reality this is not an additional piece of hardware, but an area of the hard drive kept specifically for this purpose. It is a good idea to partition off a portion of the hard drive, so it is kept clear of any other demands or, if the budget will stretch to fit, install a second hard drive. Photoshop needs to be pointed to a scratch disk in order for it to work properly.

Setting the scratch disk in Windows

With Adobe Photoshop or Photoshop Elements open, choose Edit>Preferences>Plug-ins & Scratch Disk. Next pick the "C" drive (or your partition if you have created one) as the First disk.

Setting the scratch disk in Apple OSX 3

With Adobe Photoshop or Photoshop Elements open, choose Photoshop (or Photoshop Elements>Plug-ins & Scratch Disk.) Next pick the "Macintosh HD" drive (or your partition if you have created one) as the First disk.

3 | Preferences

Plug-Ins & Scratch Disks

OK | Cancel | Prev | Next

☐ Additional Plug-Ins Folder
<None>   Choose

Legacy Photoshop Serial Number:

Scratch Disks
First: Macintosh HD
Second: None
Third: None
Fourth: None

Note: Scratch disks will remain in use until you quit Photoshop.

Setting the scratch disk in Apple OS 8-9

With Adobe Photoshop or Photoshop Elements open, choose File or Edit>Preferences>Plug-ins>Scratch Disk. Next pick the "Macintosh HD" drive (or your partition if you have created one) as the First disk.

Connections and ports

Set at the back of a PC, ports are used to plug in a wide range of peripheral devices. They also determine the speed at which data to or from these devices is loaded.

Essential connectors 1

All the important hardware components, such as the monitor, keyboard and mouse, have their own dedicated port on the back side of a PC. Additional sockets are provided for sound in and out to external speakers, video out to a data projector, a second monitor and a printer port. Both Windows and Apple computers use their own types of connector, but adaptors can be easily purchased.

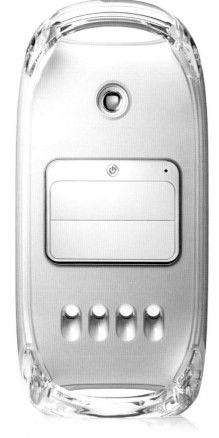

Data transfer

As digital cameras get better and digital video editing becomes more popular, fast data transfer becomes essential. Many digital cameras can produce files in excess of 20MB, so the speed at which data is uploaded to a PC becomes a critical issue. Three commonly used connecting systems are available for Apple and Windows platforms and all have different rates of transfer: SCSI, USB and FireWire.

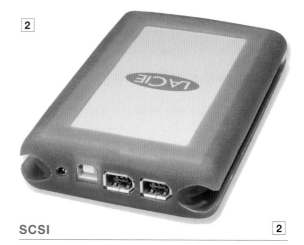

SCSI 2

Short for Small Computer System Interface and pronounced "scuzzi," this is the oldest system and is currently available in four different speeds: SCSI-1, SCSI-2, SCSI-3 and, the fastest of them all, Wide Ultra SCSI-II. SCSI leads have a rectangular plug of tiny pins and sockets and cannot be unplugged unless the PC is switched off first. Individual SCSI devices, such as scanners and external drives, can be connected to each other, or daisy chained, but they must first be assigned an identity number. In ideal situations, the faster SCSI variants can deliver between 10–40 megabits (Mbps) of data per second.

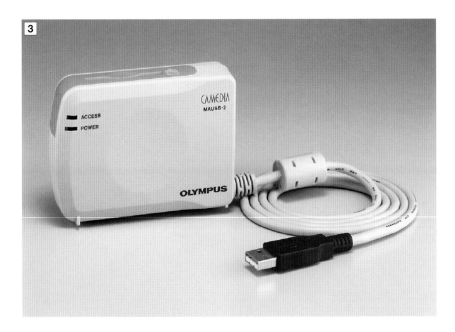

3

USB is a common interface between digital cameras, scanners, printers and computers.

See also Anatomy of a digital camera *pages 10–11* / Connecting to a computer *pages 36–37* / Peripherals *pages 106–107* /

Universal Serial Bus   3

The Universal Serial Bus (USB) has revolutionized the world of creative computing. Found on most digital cameras and scanners, USB is essentially a one-plug-fits-all system. Less fiddly to connect and hot-swappable, USB devices can be plugged into a PC without switching it off. All recent Apple computers have two USB ports on the keyboard, so there is no need to reach around to the back of the machine to plug in a peripheral. Useful connecting hubs can also be used for easier access, and for increasing the number of devices that can be connected at any one time. Most innovative is the power supply, which can be delivered through a USB port, so that some scanners do not need to be plugged into the power supply. Most USB devices are based on the original USB 1.1 standard and deliver data at 12Mbps, while the latest, and still largely rare, USB 2.0 can reach speeds of up to 480Mbps.

FireWire

Also referred to as IEEE1394, FireWire offers data transfer at the speed of light. With rates of up to 400Mbps, this type of connecting system is used with high-end digital cameras, scanners and digital video camcorders. Like USB, it provides power to external devices, but at a much greater rate of 15 watts. FireWire ports are standard on all recent Apple computers, but are found only on Windows PCs from the top manufacturers, such as Sony, HP and Compaq.

Upgrade cards

It is not impossible to fit an additional USB or FireWire port to a computer in order to connect the latest devices, and prices for an upgrade card are very competitive. All desktop computers are sold with vacant PCI slots, so that extras can be added later on. These upgrade cards are easy to install and are a much better idea than buying external cable adaptors or connectors.

Peripherals

A useful creative workstation allows easy access to a range of additional input, output and storage devices called peripherals.

The flatbed scanner [1]

With specifications rising all the time, even a budget flatbed scanner will capture far more data than is really needed to make great prints with an ink-jet printer. Flatbed scanners work by converting two-dimensional original artwork, such as photographs, paintings or even magazine pages, into pixel images. The better scanners are those made by manufacturers who also make professional cameras or scanners, and include the Umax, Epson and Heidelberg brands. Combination devices, such as a scanner/fax/printer or even a dual flatbed and film scanner, will give much lower-quality results.

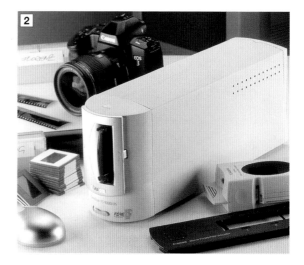

The film scanner [2]

A dedicated film scanner is used to capture data from individual color and black-and-white negatives and slides. They cost about six times the price of a basic flatbed. Even a midprice 35mm scanner will capture enough data from a 35mm original to make a very high-quality $8\frac{1}{2}$ x 11-inch (21.5 x 28cm) printout. Higher quality results are achieved in scans from film compared to scans taken from photographic prints — especially machine-processed prints from a professional lab. Film scanners are a great way to "restore" old family negatives or slides.

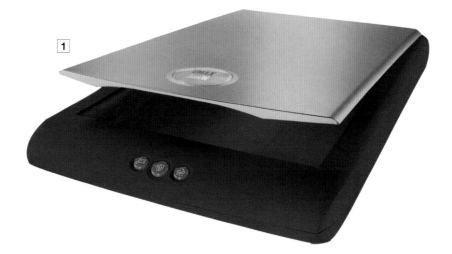

Ink-jet printer [3]

Very good ink-jet printers now cost less than twenty rolls of conventional film, and are the most common kind of printing device. They are cheap to run, easy to use and sold with four, five, six or seven color ink cartridges. Generally, the more colors, the better quality the printouts. Ink-jets spray tiny drops of ink onto special printing paper, and produce results that look indistinguishable from conventional photographs when viewed from a handheld distance. Newer printers can be hooked up directly to a digital camera or will accept removable memory cards without the need for a computer.

See also Data management *pages 84–85* / Storage media *pages 92–93* / Connections and ports *pages 104–105* / Scanners *pages 124–127* / Printer types *pages 242–243* /

[3]

Digital camera card reader

A digital memory card reader greatly speeds up data transfer and preserves camera batteries. Card readers appear on a PC's desktop like an external drive, eliminating the need for browser software for previewing digital camera images before upload. The better card readers use USB or FireWire ports, while the floppy disk look-alike FlashPath adaptor is extremely slow.

External storage

It is a good idea to have an external storage drive connected to a PC. External drives can be used to back up important data or to hold a large library of images that need to be accessed only occasionally. The best models are FireWire hard drives with gigantic capacities above and beyond a PC's. Keeping less-frequently used data off a main computer's drive will help it to run smoothly and efficiently. An alternative to the external drive is to network an older computer and use its hard drive as storage space.

Internet connection

Most modern computers are fitted with 56K internal modems for connecting to the Internet. More important is the kind of service bought from an Internet provider. As the price of high-speed or broadband Internet connection drops, more users will be able to send high-resolution image files to clients and services without the need for compression.

Monitors

The hardware most critical to making high-quality printouts is the computer monitor.

The human eye is very complex, capable of sensing subtle variation within an enormous range of different colors, but a computer monitor is much more limited. Monitors are available in two types — the traditional, bulbous cathode ray tube (CRT) model, and the recently introduced thin film transistor (TFT) or flat panel model, sometimes also called an LCD monitor. Just like a good quality photographic camera lens, a good monitor lets the user view sharp, color-correct images.

All images reproduced on paper or on a computer screen are defined by the inherent limitations of the display medium and will never be equal to the original version. This means that an image displayed by a monitor will never look the same printed out and it is a good idea to accept this fact before starting. Monitors have a much smaller dynamic range, and cannot display the deepest of shadows or brightest highlights in the way that a top-quality print can.

Size and make [1]

A large-screen monitor is essential for creative work. Applications like Photoshop spread more and more menus and windows across the screen, leaving little desktop space for an image window. Effective retouching and montage projects are difficult on smaller monitors and, if you are on a limited budget, money is best spent on a good 19 inch (48cm) monitor rather than a computer with the fastest processor. Best buys are from reputable international companies like Sony, Mitsubishi or La Cie and, with a little research, other brands using the excellent Diamondtron or Trinitron tube can be found at lower cost. For a little bit more money, a monitor with a flatter tube will render less distortion at the edges. TFT monitors cost about three times more than CRT monitors and take up much less tabletop space, but they must be placed carefully to avoid unwanted reflections. TFTs also suffer less from the, sometimes

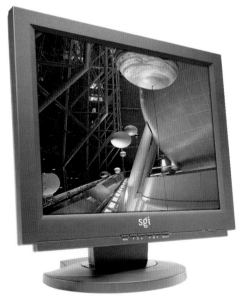

1.1
An ultra-high-resolution TFT made by Silicon Graphics.

misleading, "actual viewing area" measurement quoted on CRT models, with 15-inch (38cm) displays showing nearly as much as a 17-inch (43cm) CRT.

Setting up

Take time to position a monitor at a comfortable height to avoid straining the eyes. Place a workstation away from strong light sources, which could be reflected onto the monitor surface, reducing your ability to correct color and brightness defects. Many professional monitors, such as those manufactured by La Cie, come equipped with an additional hood, which prevents stray light from hitting the screen. Professional repro houses take great care with color-corrected, low-level ambient room lighting, to avoid creating an environment that is difficult to work in. A dark room is better than a bright one.

Monitor care

Like a camera lens, a monitor will display color less effectively if it is smeared with greasy fingerprints. Never touch the surface of a CRT monitor, as its delicate coating is easily damaged resulting in a much less satisfactory display. If greasy prints do appear, remove them only with a lens cleaning tissue or antistatic cloth and never use detergents or household polishes. All CRT monitors have a fixed shelf life and, once certain phosphors have lost their effectiveness, a truly color-correct display may be impossible. LCD monitors are vulnerable to surface damage and are very easily scratched.

See also Configuring a workstation *pages 102–103* / Monitor calibration *pages 110–111* / Workstations *pages 112–117* /

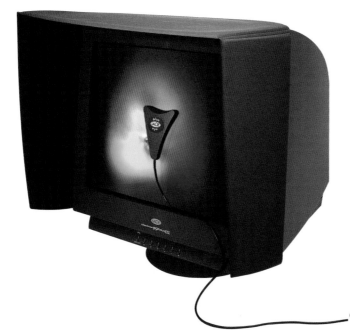

1.2
A top-quality CRT monitor, such as one made by La Cie, offers excellent color reproduction.

Monitor calibration

Before use, a monitor needs careful calibration appropriate to how it will be used.

Color [1]

A monitor can be set up to display a fixed number of different colors, regardless of the actual color depth of the displayed image, and in most cases there is a choice of three levels: 256 colors, thousands of colors, and millions of colors. It is a bad idea to view digital images on anything less than thousands of colors, but it is not necessary to view in millions of colors mode, as such a high degree of subtlety will not be reproduced when printing.

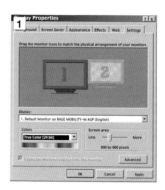

See also Monitors pages 108–109 / Using profiles and color management pages 248–249 /

Monitor resolution [2]

Depending on the display card installed on a PC, there are usually several screen resolutions to choose from. These resolutions are measured in pixels and are commonly described as 640x480/VGA, 800x600/SVGA, or 1024x800/XGA and beyond. High-resolution settings prevent less scrolling, but menu type and tool icons can become difficult to see. For best results, try 1024x800 to start with.

Setting up directions

Apple OS 8-9: Apple menu>Control Panels>Monitors.
Apple OS X: Apple menu>System Preferences>Displays.
Windows PC: Start>Settings>Monitor.

Desktop colors and working environment

Never use highly patterned or saturated-color desktop designs. Strong colors will always influence color judgment and errors are likely. Situate a monitor away from strongly colored walls and bright lights — especially fluorescent tubes.

Screen savers and sleep mode

The screen saver is a useful device that prevents a stationary desktop image from burning a permanent mark on the monitor. Many computers are left unattended for long periods of time and the screen saver is used to kick in automatically after a user-determined time, such as five minutes. Despite the novelty value of many screen savers, their purpose is to "exercise" the monitor with a moving slide show, movie or graphic. Sleep mode is an alternative to the screen saver and works by temporarily switching the monitor off until the user is ready to return to work

Color calibration [3]

All monitors should be color-calibrated using purpose-built software tools rather than the basic front panel switches and controls. The best tool to use is Adobe Gamma, supplied for free with most OS and imaging applications. Adobe Gamma works by taking the user through a simple step-by-step process in order to set brightness, contrast and color balance, after which the results are saved as a special file called a "profile." This profile is then called into play each time the computer is switched on, bypassing the

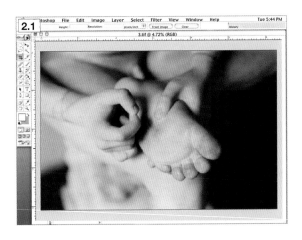

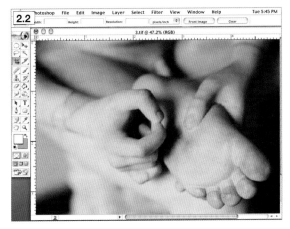

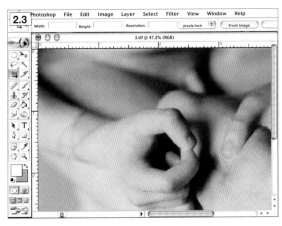

The same monitor is shown in all three photos above, but in three different resolution settings. Top: SVGA; Middle: VGA; Bottom: XGA.

physical controls on the outside of the monitor case. Profiles are a useful way to create a fixed environment where color consistency can be managed and maintained when working with images. When preparing digital images for a professional repro house or for publication, it is a good idea to work on a system that has been calibrated to match the common profiles used in that industry. Universal color profiles have been established by a group of leading hardware and software manufacturers called the International Color Consortium, or ICC for short. An ICC-compatible profile, such as the much-used Adobe RGB (1998), maintains color integrity when an image is transferred from one system to another.

The Adobe Gamma dialog box (top) and the three color calibrating patches (bottom).

Budget workstation

It is possible to create dynamic digital images on a shoestring budget.

PC and monitor [1]

Most manufacturers sell their previous year's product range at a heavy discount, and users can buy a high-specification computer for a good price. All but the most complex filtering processes will work instantaneously on a computer fitted with a lowly 450Mhz processor. There is little advantage in a superfast processor if working on digital files captured from a modest scanner, as there won't be any significant difference in the original material. Minimum memory must be 128MB, and additional RAM can be bought when the budget allows. Look for a computer with a good-size hard disk, such as 10 or 20GB, and one that is fitted with a SCSI or USB port, so that external disk drives can be added at a later stage. A CD-ROM drive is essential for importing digital files from disk and for loading applications. A monitor should be at least 17 inches (43 cm) and bought from a recognized manufacturer. Users

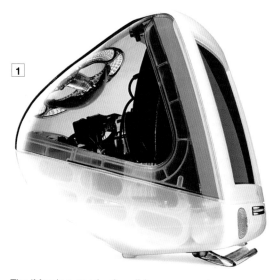

[1]

The iMac is a good-value all-in-one computer.

should never consider buying secondhand: as monitors age, their effectiveness becomes reduced, so it is never worth taking the risk. A very good buy is the all-in-one computer such as the Apple iMac, which comes with its own monitor.

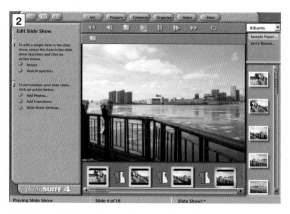

MGI PhotoSuite software is a good starting point for a new user.

Software [2]

It is not essential to buy into the latest version of Adobe Photoshop right away, but makes better sense to spend six months learning the basics in the reduced LE version or Photoshop Elements. Photoshop LE is frequently bundled with scanners and digital cameras and works in a fashion identical to the full version, with a few of the high-end functions removed. Another bundled image-processing package worth considering is the more accessible MGI Photosuite, with an interface based on a web browser. This has little similarity to professional applications, so users will need to start from scratch when ready to try more advanced applications. Obscure image-processing applications should be avoided.

Input and output 3

A basic flatbed scanner is an essential part of a workstation and offers a cost-effective way to create digital files from existing photographic prints and artwork. Good quality devices for a small budget can be bought from Umax and Canon. For printing, a four-color ink-jet printer from Epson or Canon is preferable to the cheaper generic ink cartridges available, and mass-produced copier paper is no match for proper ink-jet media.

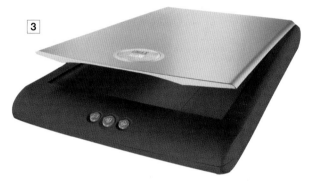

3

A basic flatbed scanner.

Services 4

For top-quality printouts, it is worth sending digital files to an Internet-based photo lab. If you are working with a point-and-shoot compact digital camera, consider getting a Kodak Photo CD each time a conventional film is processed at the local lab. This disk will provide high-quality scans at a fraction of the cost of a film scanner.

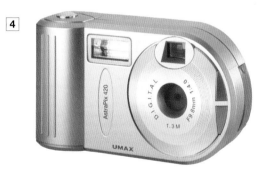

4

A low-resolution digital camera.

Future upgrades

Users should look out for bargains in extra memory cards and a CD writer. The slower external CD writers can be bought cheaply and allow users to dump master images onto cheap CD-R disks.

See also Flatbed scanner interface *pages 124–125* / Lab services *pages 138–139* / Software applications *pages 144–149* / Printer types *pages 242–243* /

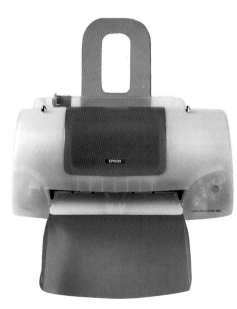

A four-color ink-jet printer.

Midprice workstation

A midprice workstation offers the convenience of a dedicated system with little compromise on speed, quality or ease of use.

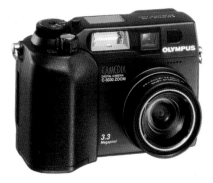

A midprice digital compact.

PC and monitor

The best option here is for a higher-specification computer from one of the leading manufacturers rather than a hardware bundle that might also include a scanner, printer and digital camera. Spending the extra money on a better computer will mean that good quality peripherals can be added when they are needed. The option to upgrade in the future is the key to this model, so users should look for three or more vacant PCI slots, three RAM slots and space for an additional hard drive. A mid-range processor is preferable to the fastest Pentium or G4 on the market, with additional RAM making 256MB a minimum if necessary. Having a single RAM chip installed instead of two smaller ones will leave more slots for upgrading later on. An internal CD writer should be standard on this kind of machine, together with a good-sized hard disk of 40GB or more. In order to add a range of different input devices possible in the future, users should look for a model with FireWire ports. A good monitor needs to be a branded name, 19 inches (48cm), preferably with a Trinitron tube, and definitely not secondhand.

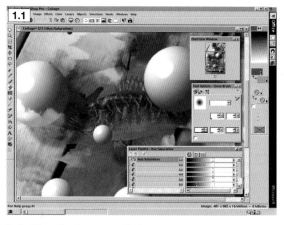

PaintShop Pro is a versatile image-editing package.

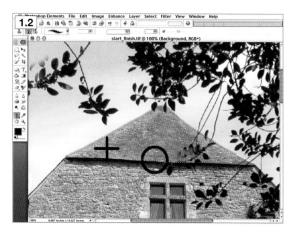

Adobe Photoshop Elements offers a user-friendly service.

Software

Adobe Photoshop Elements is a very good package, and shares many of the professional features of the full Photoshop application, but is designed with a kinder interface and much more "hands on" help. PaintShop Pro is a sophisticated package for Windows PC users only and is very good value for the money. Both packages are available from any good

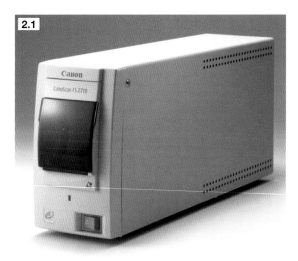

2.1

A purpose-made film scanner offers better results than those produced from scanning print originals.

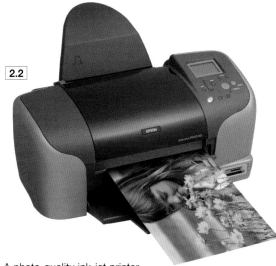

2.2

A photo-quality ink-jet printer.

retailer and a comprehensive manual will be included in the price.

Input and output   2

A good flatbed scanner should have a minimum resolution of 1200dpi and be capable of working with TWAIN compatible software or as a Photoshop plug-in. In addition to this, users should consider adding a dedicated film scanner to a workstation for extra flexibility. Good brands to try are Minolta, Canon and Nikon. Entry-level models are capable of scanning 35mm film in both cut lengths and mounted slide holders. Former Advanced Photo System (APS) users can usually buy a special holder as an extra. Film scanners pull out detail that may not be evident in a photo print and produce vast image files, typically between 20–30MB in size, so it's essential to have a fast USB or SCSI port. For printout, a photo-quality ink-jet with a minimum of six colors is preferable. At twice the price of a basic ink-jet, results will be top quality and less prone to rapid fading. The better printers from Epson and Canon can also print onto special media, such as plastic film, CD-Rs and ink-jet canvas. No workstation is complete without a good-quality midprice digital compact camera, capable of producing big enough files to output photo-quality images at $8\frac{1}{2}$ x 11-inch size, complete with a direct USB transfer cable, rechargeable batteries and an electrical adaptor.

Future additions and upgrades

At a later date, and if budget permits, users should aim to buy the full version of Adobe Photoshop and install additional RAM. If it isn't included already, a good maintenance utility application like Norton will keep the workstation in top condition, particularly with virus-vulnerable PCs.

See also Flatbed scanner interface *pages 124–125* / Film scanner interface *pages 126–127* / Software applications *pages 142–147* / Printer types *pages 242–243* /

Professional workstation

A professional-quality workstation makes perfect sense for anyone already committed to digital photography.

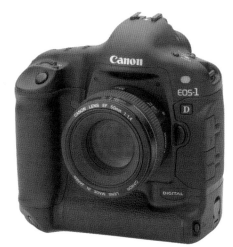

Professional Canon EOS-1 SLR.

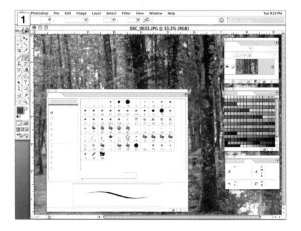

PC and monitor

The best quality workstations for the dedicated graphics professional are made by Apple, and are purpose-built to run the most memory-intensive applications, such as Adobe Photoshop. With the option of a dual processor for crunching large image files, the top-speed Apple Mac will outperform even the fastest Pentium-processor machine. Built-in support for sophisticated color-management tools like ColorSync, and fast FireWire ports for connecting high-end scanners, make the Apple Mac a good choice. Users should install 512MB RAM or more, and an additional hard drive can be used as an independent scratch disk. A high-speed internal CD-RW is essential for burning files and a good option is

an internal 250MB Zip drive, useful for dealing with source images from suppliers. Users should look for a top-quality monitor from La Cie or Mitsubishi that comes with a hardware color-calibration device to ensure that work is always viewed in optimum condition. For the die-hard anti-Apple brigade, the ultra-sleek Silicon Graphics workstation offers a system built on raw processing power.

Software

Adobe Photoshop is the only option here, as users will need to keep a tight rein over color-management issues — unsupported by lesser packages. For creating sophisticated content for the Internet, the partner Image Ready application provides all the necessary tools for compression, animation and image slicing. Useful Photoshop plug-in software, such as PhotoFrame and Mask Pro, provide extra functionality to the more challenging creative briefs, and Portfolio — from the same software stable, Extensis — is a very useful tool for cataloging image files.

See also Digital SLR *pages 26–27* / Scanners *pages 124–127* / Adobe Photoshop *pages 142–143* / Printer types *pages 242–243* /

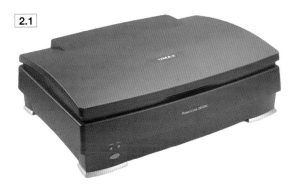

2.1

High-spec flatbed scanner.

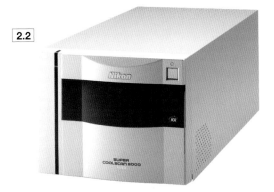

2.2

Medium-format film scanner.

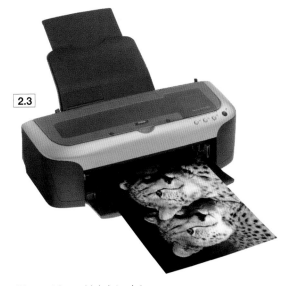

2.3

Pigment-based ink-jet printer.

A top-price film scanner from Nikon — capable of handling medium-format film originals — may cost the same as the entire computer workstation, but it is a worthwhile investment for anyone undertaking commercial assignments. Built with a high-resolution sensor, this type of scanner can create files in excess of 80MB in size and can be used to scan all sorts of non-standard sized originals. For flatbed scanning, users should look for a midprice model from Heidelberg or Umax, both of which have sophisticated built-in Silverfast scanning software and a higher-than-average dynamic range for coping with difficult originals. For printout, the best option is a professional pigment-based ink-jet printer equipped with six or more colors for photo-quality output on archival media. For sending and receiving high-resolution images via the Internet, a broadband service from an Internet or cable television provider is essential. When it comes to the camera, a top-of-the-range digital SLR from Nikon or Canon fitted with a high-capacity MicroDrive and a good assortment of lenses is ideal for the highest quality image capture.

Future additions and upgrades

None of this equipment will become obsolete and all will remain useful for as long as users keep active. Good hardware additions are a high-capacity external drive for backing up important work, together with back-up software to fully automate the process on a regular basis. For critical environments, an uninterrupted power supply unit, or UPS, will buy time to shut the system down properly in the face of a power cut, avoiding loss of critical files.

Location workstation

A special portable workstation allows location photographers to work on location without having to return to home base.

Laptop PC　1

A good-quality laptop is a prerequisite for shooting digital on location, and good models are those from Apple, Sony or Compaq. Large displays are worth the extra cost and help users to inspect work for sharp focus at close quarters. Laptops are vulnerable to rechargeable batteries losing their power in the cold, so a good investment is a power adaptor for charging the laptop battery between locations. Laptops are a great way to involve a client in a shoot, as they can make instant edits or amendments to a brief based on immediate high-resolution results. A laptop with a video-out port also allows users to display images on a larger monitor or present them on a data projector. Although not essential as an internal device, a portable USB-powered CD-RW drive enables users to burn back-up copies of valuable files on disk, just in case there is an unforeseen accident on location or on the road.

Traveling abroad

It is essential to have all the necessary plug adaptors to enable charging in a foreign country. There are also special kits for converting a conventional telephone jack into the many different plugs used across the world. A good way to manage data abroad is to use an Internet-based storage system, so you can upload raw compressed files from a hotel bedroom and retrieve them on return to the studio.

1.1

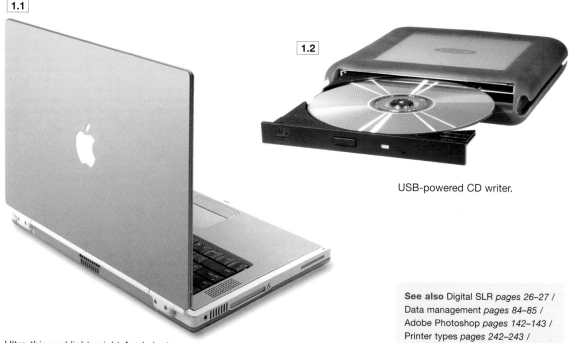

1.2

USB-powered CD writer.

Ultra-thin and lightweight Apple laptop.

See also Digital SLR *pages 26–27* / Data management *pages 84–85* / Adobe Photoshop *pages 142–143* / Printer types *pages 242–243* /

Software

It is unlikely you will prepare images for final reproduction on a laptop on location, but raw material may need color management for later use. Full Adobe Photoshop keeps tight control over original color and has useful batch-processing functions for applying automatic commands to a group of images in one run. The better image browsers that come with good-quality digital cameras offer most basic functions, such as rotate, zoom in and out and crop, and use less memory resources than a full application.

Input and output

In addition to a good-quality digital SLR, users should opt for a USB-powered card reader to prevent any other power demands on the camera during download. If printouts are needed on location, a small $8\frac{1}{2}$ x 11-inch photo-quality ink-jet is the best option, and is easily transported in a flight case. Before printing, users should make sure the printer heads are aligned using the self-correcting printer head utility. Finally, if proof-quality prints are all that are needed, the printer can be operated at a lower output resolution, such as 720dpi, rather than the finer and much slower to print 1440 or 2880dpi.

Future additions and upgrades

Hardware components for laptops are always slightly more expensive than corresponding items for desktop PCs, so consider adding extra memory at a later stage. For truly portable connectivity, many laptops can be connected to a cellphone so that images can be transmitted from the middle of nowhere!

2.1

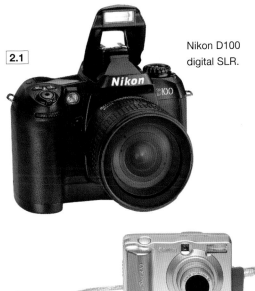

Nikon D100 digital SLR.

2.2

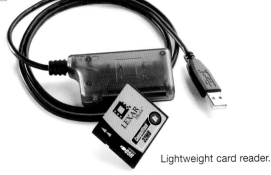

Portable digital printer.

2.3

Lightweight card reader.

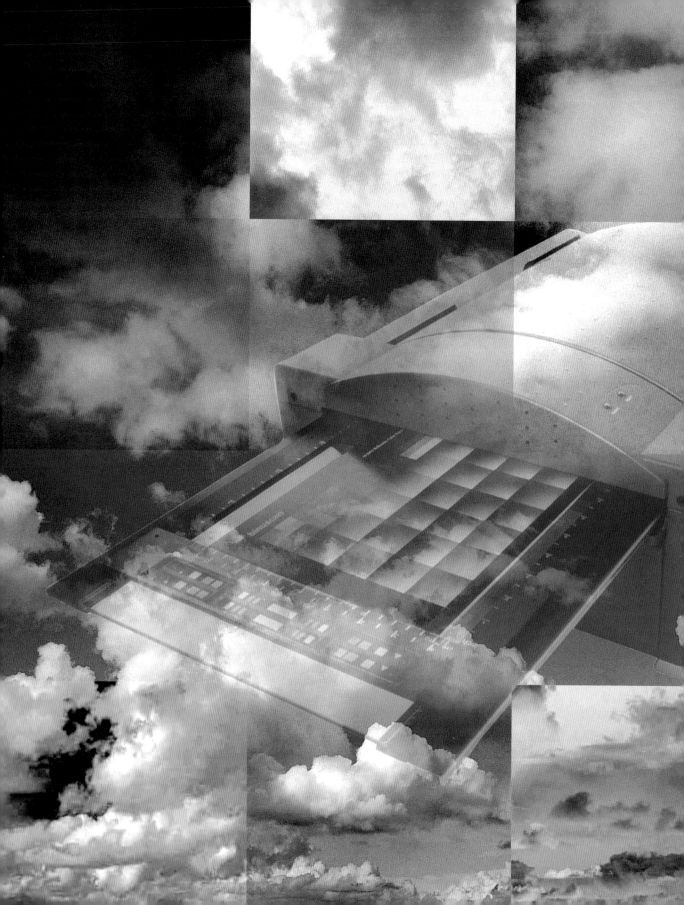

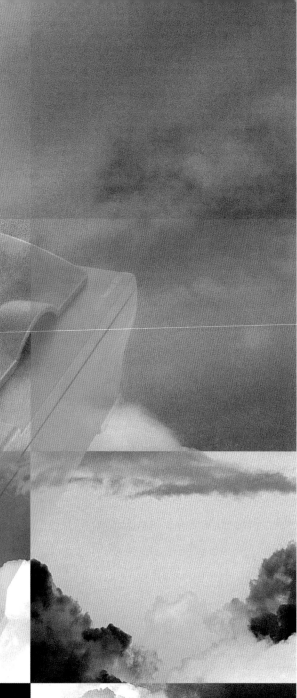

5 Scanning and Other Output

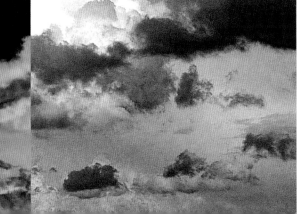

How scanners work

A good scanner is an integral part of any workstation, and is used for converting original film material and photographic prints into digital images.

How flatbed scanners work   1

Just like digital cameras, most flatbeds use light-detecting CCD sensors, although they are arranged in a thin movable strip rather than a fixed rectangular matrix. The scanner looks like a mini photocopier with the sensor attached underneath the glass to two tracking rods that move along the glass platen in a smooth pass. Illumination is provided by a strip light, which turns on and off during the scan. As the CCD moves along the original, each sensor cell creates an individual pixel in the resulting digital image. Surprisingly, three-dimensional objects can be scanned, too, provided the scanner lid is removable. Scanners are connected to a PC by a USB or FireWire lead and many models draw power directly through this port rather than from a separate power connection.

Flatbed scanner quality

Flatbeds are sold on the basis of their resolution, where the term "resolution" is just another way of describing potential image quality. Unlike digital cameras, scanner quality is not described in megapixels or in pixel dimensions, but by the ability to capture pixels across one linear inch (2.5cm). In other words a 600-pixel-per-inch or ppi scanner will create a 2400x3600 digital image from a 4 x 6 inch photo print. If this kind of calculation brings an unwanted element of mathematics to the creative workflow, users should fear not, as the scanning software is much less technical. Even budget-priced 1200ppi scanners create more data than is really needed; anything over 2400ppi is overkill for desktop photo printing. Flatbed scanners generate more digital data than does a professional digital SLR camera and so are still the most accessible and cost-effective route into digital photography.

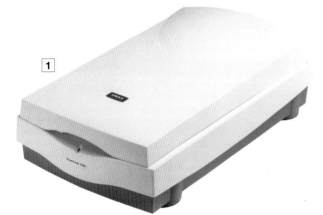

1

General purpose flatbed scanner.

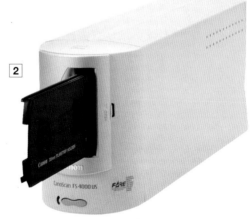

2

35mm film scanner.

How film scanners work   [2]

Film scanners are designed to capture data from much smaller originals, typically individual 24x36mm film frames. This type of scanner has a line of CCD sensors set inside a closed unit — either fixed in position for original material to be passed over, or sliding along tracking rods across film frames held in position. Film scanners are sold in three formats: 35mm and APS, 35mm and 120, and professional repro models that can scan up to 4x5-inch film material. All types are supplied with film holders for uncut filmstrips or mounted slides and universal glass carriers with removable masks for dealing with the 4$\frac{1}{2}$x6, 6x6, 6x7, 6x8, 6x9 variations in medium-format film. Film scanners can capture negative and positive material in color and black and white. Once the film holder is inserted in the unit, the scanner pulls it in, in preparation for scanning.

Film scanner quality   [3]

As with flatbed scanners, film-scanner quality is described by a linear resolution measurement such as 2800ppi. Compared to flatbeds, resolution on a film scanner is very high, but this is entirely owing to the tiny nature of the original material. A good scanner has a resolution of 2500ppi and above, and easily will produce enough data for a pin-sharp 11 x 17-inch print. With such varying densities found in film material, or in the way light is transmitted through deepest black shadows and clear highlights, film scanners need to work across a wider dynamic range than flatbeds. Users should look for a device that scans across a 3.6D range or more.

See also Anatomy of a digital camera *pages 10–11* / Flatbed scanner interface *pages 124–125* / Film scanner interface *pages 126–127* /

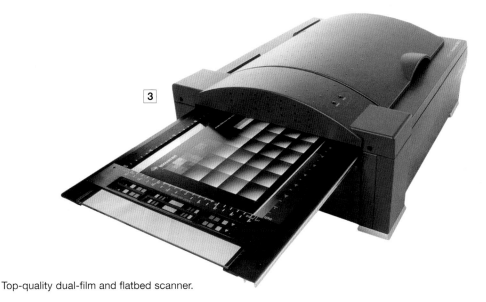

Top-quality dual-film and flatbed scanner.

Flatbed scanner interface

Flatbed scanners and their software work in much the same way as a photocopier does.

Scanner operation

Most flatbed scanners will operate using their own stand-alone scanning software or from within a chosen imaging application. The former option places less of a strain on computer memory, and the application is launched simply by pushing a button on the front of the scanner itself. The downside with this method is that image files need to be saved, closed, then re-opened in the scanning software. By acquiring the scanner as a plug-in device accessible from within Photoshop, the same scanning software will appear on the desktop, and after each image has been scanned it is left open in Photoshop, ready for editing.

Scanner software interface

All scanner software is operable in either basic or advanced mode. Basic mode offers few or no hands-on controls, with target output devices such as e-mail, ink-jet print or fax as the only options. Much better results are gained when the scanner is operated in advanced mode, where the exact quality and image mode of a soon-to-be digital original can be determined.

Software tools

Following are the basic options available to select, or not, when preparing to scan an original.

The Marquee tool

This is used to crop around an original artwork, so that additional white space is not scanned by mistake.

See also Workstations *pages 112–119* / How scanners work *pages 122–123* / Scanning *pages 128–137* /

Image modes

Unlike the standard terminology used in imaging applications for image modes, such as RGB, CMYK and grayscale, scanner manufacturers use different words to describe these modes. Within this drop-down menu are RGB color, Bitmap (or line art), Grayscale (or mono) and Web color (or 256 colors).

Resolution

This describes the pixel count per inch (2.5 cm) of the intended scan. Interpolated values are usually shown in a different color or type style in the scanner menu.

Scale

Just like the enlarge/reduce button on a photocopier, this option allows the user to determine the new size of a scan. It is important to remember, however, that pin-sharp posters from postcard-sized originals are not possible.

Automatic exposure button

Many scanners offer excellent results using the auto exposure function, provided all non-essential areas are cropped off first using the Marquee tool.

Device or profile matcher

This smart-sounding option offers an automatic scan to match the idiosyncrasies of a particular printer or output device, but rarely produces top-quality results because all workstations are set up differently. This is best left unselected.

Dropper tools

Three tools are designed for the user to hand select shadow, midtone and highlight points on an

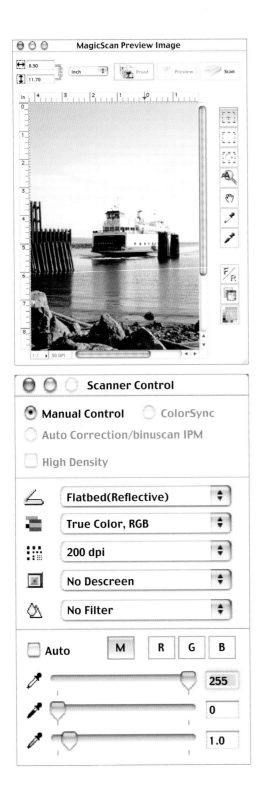

original. This is essential only if the original presents an unusual tonal range that cannot be captured accurately using the auto exposure mode.

Brightness and contrast scales

Rudimentary changes can be made to a scan using these two primitive sliders. Finer contrast control, however, is best attempted in Photoshop at a later stage.

Preview

All originals should have a scan preview made before the final scan, as this helps the scanning software to determine the right settings, or "exposure" for the artwork and allows you to make any further adjustments.

Scan

Once the results of a preview scan prove satisfactory, the final scan is launched from this button. The scanner software interface will close when the scan is complete.

Menu items

Many scanners have additional controls hidden away in drop-down menus or panels, including filters and preset processing routines. Common filters are the Unsharp Mask (USM), Descreen and Auto Contrast.

Dialogs

Good scanning software offers additional tools for the more experienced user, such as Levels and Curves — both universal, industry-standard methods for correcting contrast, brightness and color. Although these options are offered in Photoshop and PaintShop Pro, high- or low-contrast originals that are corrected using Levels or Curves in the scanning stage — called "on the fly" — are much less prone to later posterization.

Film scanner interface

The film scanner interface offers a similar set of controls to the flatbed, but with additional tools for correcting imperfect film originals.

Scanner operation

Film scanners are supplied with their own dedicated software that works as a stand-alone application or Photoshop plug-in. With the likelihood of very high-resolution scans being made one after the other, it is a good idea to operate the device via the stand-alone software to prevent unnecessary use of the computer's limited RAM resources. As huge amounts of data will reside in RAM with each scan, it is essential to install as much RAM as possible. All film scanners need to self-initialize or self-calibrate at the start of each session, and film holders should not be placed inside until this has occurred. After launching the scanning software, most devices have a batch-preview function, which creates a quick low-resolution scan of all the frames in the film holder. Once complete, each preview can be adjusted individually before final scanning takes place. Film scanners are still sold with a variety of connecting leads, such as SCSI, USB and FireWire; for the fastest operation, opt for a FireWire model.

Scanner software interface   [1]

The Nikon scanner interface presents a clear and coherent set of controls for getting the best-quality results out of an original. The size of the preview window can be adjusted to fit a monitor and it is a good idea to have this as large as possible — particularly if a Levels adjustment is likely to be made or the Dropper tools used on the fly. Like many scanning software interfaces, it remains open even after a scan has been completed, so that users can continue to work without needing to relaunch. It is

good practice to scan each film frame at the highest possible resolution and save it on CD-R as a digital master. Each time the image is needed, it can be opened from the write-only disk, saved on the hard disk, and interpreted in Photoshop just like a negative is in a conventional darkroom. As film scanning is a laborious process, scanning images only once in this way saves time.

Software tools

Image modes
Three modes are commonly found: RGB, Grayscale and, on the better scanners, the direct-to-press CMYK.

Original
This menu is used to set the type of film being scanned, for example, color negative, color transparency, black-and-white negative or black-and-white transparency.

Input resolution
This menu determines the resolution of the scan and final file size. Notice that the File Size readout changes each time this value is altered.

Output resolution
This menu has no effect on the size of the final image file, but it sets the image resolution ready for its intended use. For ink-jet printing this should be set at 200ppi and for commercial lithographs at 300ppi.

Frame selector

This allocates a number to each frame in the film holder, making it easy to choose which image to preview. Shift-clicking selects more than one at a time.

Preview button

Once a frame has been selected, this runs the all-important preview scan, where contrast and brightness measurements are taken and adjusted.

Scan button

This fires the final scan. On a film scanner, it is possible to undertake a batch scan, where several final scans are made automatically, so users can leave the workstation unattended.

Menus and panels

In addition to Levels, Curves and Unsharp Mask tools, the better scanners have the option of three further image-enhancing automatic processes called digital ICE, GEM and ROC. These functions allow users to minimize the effects of crude film grain, restore lost color and remove physical defects such as dust and hair from older film stock. With each of these processes working on the fly, scan times can increase to several minutes, but this may well be quicker than fixing mistakes by hand in Photoshop.

See also Professional workstation *pages 116–117* / How scanners work *pages 122–123* / Scanning monochrome *pages 128–129* / Scanning color *pages 130–131* /

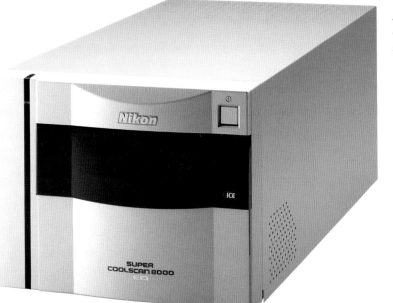

A professional-quality film scanner.

Scanning monochrome

Single color, or monochrome, materials are easy to scan provided users stick to a few basic rules.

Flat originals 1

Scanning properly printed black-and-white photographic prints should pose little or no technical challenge to a new user. There are two types of photographic print commonly in use: the machine print and the hand print. Machine prints are produced automatically by photo labs as a cost-effective way of producing proofs or images for consumers or reproduction in newspapers. Machine prints lack the careful contrast and exposure control of a hand print and may display fully bleached-out highlights and completely filled-in shadows. This lack of detail cannot be rescued in the scanning process. The better-quality hand prints are made by a skilled darkroom printer, who has burned and dodged the print to reveal clear detail in shadows and highlights. This kind of print will produce excellent-quality scans. Occasional problems can occur when images are printed on textured photographic paper, which include a loss of sharpness and perhaps, even, the paper's texture being visible in the digital image, particularly if it has been over-enlarged.

See also Image modes *pages 80–81* / File formats *pages 86–87* / How scanners work *pages 122–123* / Scanners *pages 124–127* /

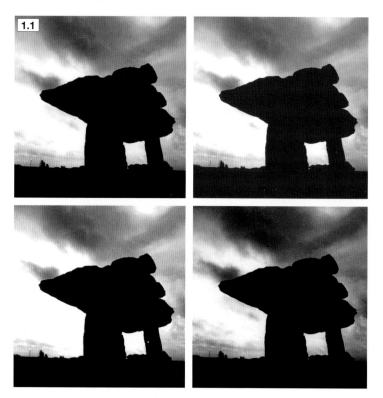

1.1

Different densities can be achieved by using very simple controls, such as Levels. The creative control of contrast can lead to several variations, each with its own merits.

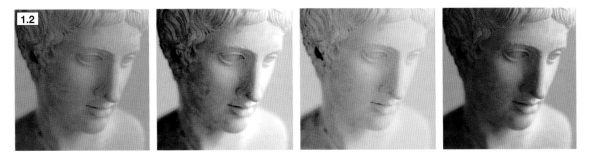

When scanning film, contrast and brightness can be enhanced using the Dropper tools.

Film originals

Black-and-white photographic film also presents a set of innate characteristics that need to be addressed during the scan. This kind of film is available in many different ISO speeds from the fine-grain ISO 25 to the coarse-grain ISO 1600 and beyond. Fine-grain material scans very well, but coarse-grain film may not produce high-resolution results simply because the detail is not present in the original in the first place. Simple over- and underexposure errors are easily solved, but very dense negatives subject to excessive overexposure will not yield good results. Chromogenic black-and-

white film, such as Ilford XP2, although based on a color-negative film technology, will give excellent results when scanned in Grayscale mode.

Preparing material for scanning

How you prepare monochrome material for later scanning can make a crucial difference to the end result. In general terms, all print material should be prepared with a slightly lower contrast than normal, with detail clearly visible in all areas. Bright white highlights and rich black shadows sacrificed at this stage can easily be put back later in Photoshop. Film material, too, should be processed in a low-contrast developer such as Agfa Rodinal, which creates smooth transitions between tones and very fine sharpness. Common problems occur when a specialized film like Kodak T-Max is not processed in the recommended developer, leaving a dense and high-contrast result that will prove problematic to scan. Streaky drying marks left on a negative should be removed with lighter fluid prior to scanning, as should any dust using a blower brush.

Scan settings for monochrome originals

Image mode: Grayscale.
Flatbed input resolution: 300ppi for commercial repro, 200ppi for ink-jet print, 72ppi for Internet or e-mail use.
Film input resolution: Scan at the highest optical resolution available.
Enlargement: Try to scan the largest original possible, but don't expect good results from anything enlarged over 125%.
Filters: Make sure USM and Descreen are both turned off. For grainy film, try the GEM function if available.
Contrast and brightness: Leave as is, but use Levels to correct underexposed (pale) or overexposed (dark) originals, as shown.
File format: Save as an uncompressed TIFF.

Tip

Given the option of scanning in an enhanced 12- or 16-bit mode to create a smoother tonal reproduction, select 16-bit but convert the image back to 8 bits per channel in Photoshop.

Scanning color

Perhaps the biggest challenge in scanning is reproducing color accurately, particularly if it is not correct in the original.

Flat originals   1

Color photographic prints are commonly machine-processed from a local developing and printing outlet. Enprints — a generic term for the 4 x 6-inch standard color print — do not make good originals for high-quality scanning because of their mass-produced nature. The latest printing technology used by photo labs employs a laser-imaging system to beam digital images directly onto conventional photographic paper, rather than the old-fashioned lamp and lens system. This produces excellent results, but problems may occur if these prints are rescanned, because software sharpening that occurred in the laser-imaging lab may become magnified and strangely

visible. In short, this kind of print will be, at best, the same quality after scanning, or worse if over-enlarged. That said, in situations where nothing else exists, the machine-made print is straightforward and trouble-free to scan. The best results are pulled off glossy prints with stipple or luster finish, lacking both sharpness and color saturation.

Tip

If preparing images for Internet or e-mail only, scan in full RGB mode rather than 256 colors and make a compression later on in Adobe Photoshop.

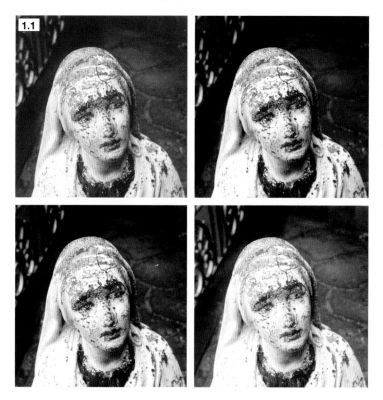

1.1

Pre-set scanning settings can create very different results when applied to the same image.

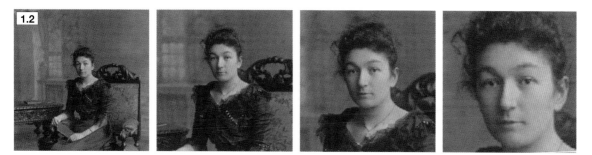

As a small image is enlarged, detail becomes less sharp.

Film originals

Color negative film poses little difficulty for scanning, as it is not prone to excessive overexposure in the camera. With a reasonably average density, accurate colors and contrast are easy to maintain. The better results are gained when good-quality film stock is used, such as professional Fuji and Kodak color-negative products. These have a finer grain structure and are better at recording subtle tones when compared to cheaper film. Color transparency, or slide, is the hardest material to expose correctly in camera, with little room for exposure error. Most commonly, problems occur when shooting under high-contrast sunlight, which may leave dense black shadows and clear white highlights.

Preparing material for scanning

Users with no access to a color darkroom can have little direct impact on the preparation of color material. Instead, a professional photographic processing service for film development and printing should be used to guarantee the best results. Users should look for a local lab that has Kodak Q-Lab status, which guarantees a regular and independent monitoring of their processes. If shooting transparency for later scanning, opt for top-quality material, such as Fuji Velvia or Provia, for fine-grain and richly saturated colors. Make sure all dust is removed prior to scanning using a photographer's blower brush.

Scan settings for color originals

Image mode: RGB color. Only choose CMYK if producing raw scans for use in a tightly controlled CMYK workflow.
Flatbed input resolution: 300ppi for commercial repro, 200ppi for ink-jet print, 72ppi for Internet or e-mail use.
Film input resolution: Scan at the highest optical resolution available.
Filters: Make sure USM and Descreen are both turned off. For faded color prints or film, try the ROC function if it is available.
Contrast and brightness: Leave, but use Levels to correct underexposed (pale) or overexposed (dark) originals, as shown.
File format: Save as an uncompressed TIFF.

See also Image modes *pages 80–81* / File formats *pages 86–87* / How scanners work *pages 122–123* / Scanners *pages 124–127* /

Scanning line art

When scanning drawings, diagrams and other single-tone originals, great care must be taken to maintain fine detail.

Flat originals

1

Single-color line art comes in all shapes, sizes and formats and needs special attention to get good results. Formerly the kind of task undertaken by a repro house or commercial printer, line art scans can be made with any good flatbed scanner. Unlike photographic originals, line art must be scanned at a very high resolution such as 600ppi or 1200ppi or results will display the characteristic staircased pixel effect around curved shapes. With pixels being square in shape, and most artwork containing some curved shapes, aliasing will occur when too low a resolution is set at capture. Good-quality line originals are printed on a kind of photographic material called bromide paper, which offers a sharp, high-quality medium for scanning. However, much line art is hand drawn or acquired from a previously printed book or leaflet and includes such formats as

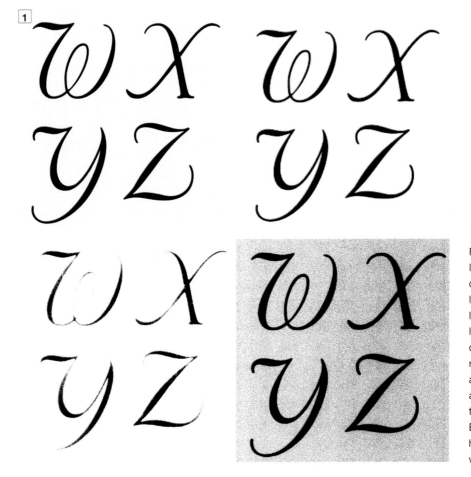

Fine line detail (top left) can disappear during scanning. Too light a scan (bottom left) results in a thinner letter form, while too dark (bottom right) results in letters that are thick and fuzzy and a background that is too dark. Experiment until you have the effect you want (top right).

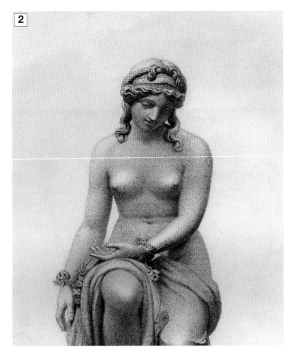

2

Scanned bitmaps can be converted to RGB and colored.

etchings, copperplate or drypoint prints, woodcuts and silhouettes. Any original that has fine line detail is best treated as a line art scan, while pencil drawings are best scanned in Grayscale mode because of their delicate tonal range.

Preparing material for scanning

There is little that can influence the quality of an old original, but working from the largest version will

See also Image modes *pages 80–81* / File formats *pages 86–87* / How scanners work *pages 122–123* / Flatbed scanner interface *pages 124–125* /

give the best results. The print should be squared-up beforehand and positioned parallel to the edge of the scanner bed. This will ensure that straight lines remain straight after scanning and do not have to be transformed in Photoshop later on.

Post-scanning processing   **2**

Once the scanned image is opened in Photoshop, few tools, and hardly any menu items, remain available. Simple cleaning and retouching is best done using the Eraser tool in conjunction with default black-and-white foreground and background color. In order to add color to a bitmap image, it needs first to be converted to Grayscale mode before converting to RGB. Adding color to a high-contrast image isn't straightforward, but any of the painting tools set to Multiply Blending mode can be used. Select a color from the picker and then paint over white areas.

Practical uses

Bitmap scans are a great way to collect decorative edges and textures for later use in montage projects. Saved as a 1-bit document, they take up little memory space and are easily resized to fit. Perimeter shapes gleaned from ripped paper make excellent photograph edges.

Scan settings for line-art originals

Image mode: Bitmap or Lineart.
Input resolution: 600ppi minimum or 1200ppi.
Threshold: Instead of brightness and contrast, the simple Threshold slider allows the user to make the image darker or lighter.
File format: Save as a Bitmap TIFF. The file size will be tiny as the image is created from 1-bit data.

Scanning objects

It is possible to scan three-dimensional objects using a flatbed scanner for results that can be remarkably convincing.

Getting the scanner ready   1

Flatbed scanners can scan the underside of a three-dimensional object in much the same way that a photocopier can make an image of a hand. Yet, unlike the squashed and high-contrast results from a photocopier, object scans can be manipulated carefully in Photoshop to produce very realistic results. For a quick turnaround when it is impractical to shoot a photograph in the studio, a flatbed scan can offer a very cost-effective substitute. Scanner platen glass is easily damaged on contact with hard objects, so cover it first with a sheet of ultra-clear acetate. Surprisingly the sensor can record objects within a plane of about 2 inches (5cm) from the glass. With the lid open or removed altogether, the most interesting facet of an object should be placed face down on the glass. A large sheet of white paper draped over the object will prevent ambient room light from confusing the "exposure."

Choosing objects   2

Natural organic subjects, such as flowers, leaves, wood, together with metal tools, colored plastics and anything that might suit a conventional photographic still life, all make good subjects. Those that might crush under their own weight — for example, flowers — should be clamped in position using clips. Objects with shiny and reflective surfaces don't scan well and include clear glass, ceramics, silver and jewelry.

A wrench (right) and flower (below) scanned as objects, and the scanner software dialog (below left).

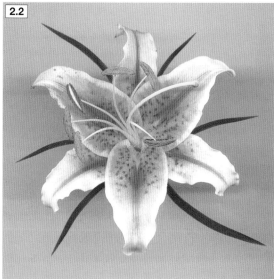

2.1

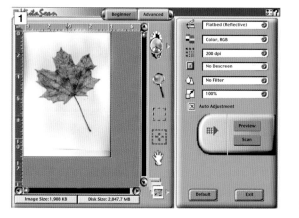

2.2

Scanner settings

Capture mode: RGB color
Input Resolution: 200dpi for ink-jet, 72dpi for Internet output.
Filters: Sharpening OFF.
Save As: TIFF format.

Working method

Fit the Marquee tool closely around the 3-D object and crop out as much of the background as possible. The more background removed at this stage, the better the final scan. Unlike conventional scanning, 3-D objects need considerable processing in Photoshop to rescue faded colors and to remove mistakes. Open the image in Photoshop and immediately rename the background layer. Next make a careful selection around the object using the Pen tool, taking time to trace the edge accurately, and cut the background away. Contrast-correct the remaining image using Levels and restore color using the Color Balance sliders.

Merging with other layers

3

The 3-D object should now sit isolated on a layer of its own, ready for use in later montage projects. Saving it as a Photoshop file will preserve the transparent background. This example (far right) was merged with another scanned object and had a drop shadow applied to create the illusion of studio lighting.

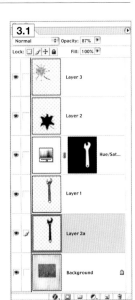

Tip

Keep scanner glass in top condition by wiping off greasy fingerprints with a lens-cleaning cloth or alcohol-free eyeglass cleaners.

Removing errors

Occasionally, a scanner will not be able to find an equivalent color to match part of the 3-D object, so it inserts green or red pixels by mistake. This frequently occurs on shiny surfaces where the scanner light makes a bright highlight. Using the Red-eye Reduction tool or the Sponge tool set to Desaturate, the image will correct this.

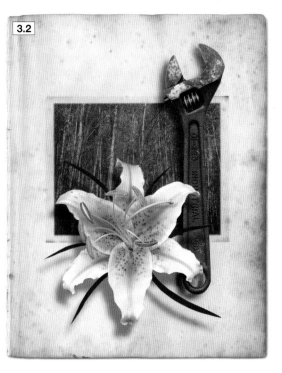

A still-life montage using the enhanced objects.

See also Image modes *pages 80–81* / File formats *pages 86–87* / How scanners work *pages 122–123* / Flatbed scanner interface *pages 124–125* /

Scanning printed matter

When scanning pre-printed materials, it is essential to use the right tools, or the process could run into difficulties.

Flat originals 1

All photographs, graphics and artwork pass through a standard reproduction process before ending up on the printed page. It is not impossible to scan images that have been through repro once already, but results will not approach the quality of scans from film or photographic prints. Many documents of historical importance may only survive in a printed form, so the techniques that follow attempt to make the best of a bad job. Black-and-white photographs, as reproduced in newspapers, are put through a halftone process which splits the continuous tones into a series of tiny dots of variable size. Because the newspaper is printed with one ink color only — black — this is the only way to mimic the appearance of a range of grays. Color images are reproduced using the same method, but using three colors, Cyan, Magenta, Yellow plus black (CMYK).

Scanning problems 2

Close-up, color halftones are arranged in a rosette-like pattern which merges when viewed from a distance. There are generally three different grades of halftone: coarse, as found in a newspaper; medium, as found in a magazine; and fine, as found in an art book. The key problem that arises when dealing with this kind of original is the reappearance of the halftone pattern in the new pixel image. Called the "moiré effect," this results from conflict between two established patterns — in this case the halftone and the monitor screen. During the scanning process, a special Descreen filter blurs these individual dots together and removes all evidence of the previous pattern. The resulting scan is soft focus, but without the moiré.

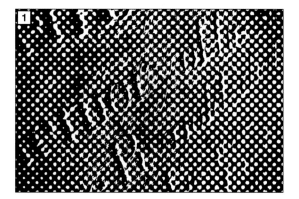

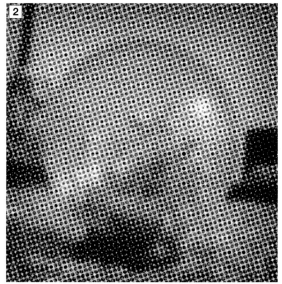

Scan settings for print originals

Mode: RGB for color halftones, Grayscale for mono halftones.
Resolution: 200ppi for ink-jet, 72ppi for Internet and on-screen use. Note: scans of halftones are not suitable for high-quality lithographic reproduction.
Filters: Descreen on and one of the three Descreen filters selected (whichever matches your original).
Save as: TIFF

Preparing material for scanning

There is little that can be done with printed originals other than making sure the book is lying as flat as possible on the scanner. For better magazine scanning, remove the page first. The best results are gleaned from large originals that are reduced substantially before reprinting.

Post-scanning processing ⬜3

If the original is larger than the final requirements, much of the sharpness lost can be rescued using the Unsharp Mask (USM) tool. After adjusting contrast and brightness using Levels, a slight sharpening should be applied before resizing, and another one immediately after.

Rescanning ink-jet prints

Despite the near invisibility of ink-jet dots on a photo-quality print, similar problems can occur when rescanning. Scanning software responds to each tiny ink dot by allocating a brightly colored pixel, which in turn becomes more visible during manipulation and printout. Use the Descreen filter on its finest setting, or a 0.5-pixel Gaussian blur in Photoshop before applying the USM.

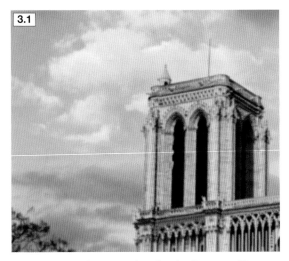

An unsharpened scan made using the Descreen filter.

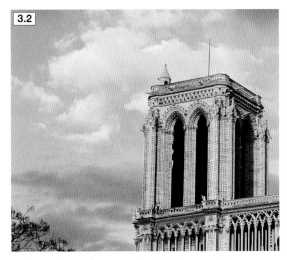

A sharpened scan made using the Descreen filter.

See also Image modes *pages 80–81* / File formats *pages 86–87* / How scanners work *pages 122–123* / Flatbed scanner interface *pages 124–125* / Scanning *pages 128–131*

Lab services

It is possible to get high-resolution scans from photographic film without owning a film scanner.

A more cost-effective way of starting digital photography is to use film-scanning services. Most local photo labs offer an additional scan-to-disk service for an extra price during standard developing and printing. There are two common packages available for over-the-counter film scanning: the Kodak Photo CD and the Kodak Picture CD.

Photo CD [1]

Established now for many years, the Photo CD package is managed by Kodak using a proprietary image file format. After developing and printing, the length of photographic film is scanned and saved in the universal Photo-CD format and returned in a box with a useful cover, containing a reference index print. Each image is saved in five different

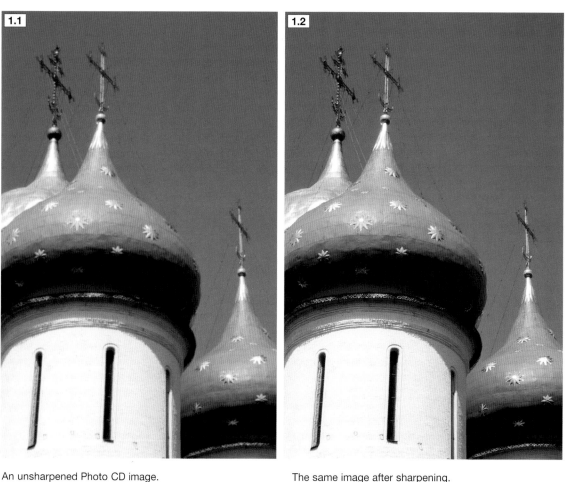

An unsharpened Photo CD image.

The same image after sharpening.

resolutions, with each version drawing upon a common core data pack. The highest resolution scan is 18MB for a color image and is easily big enough to make a photo-quality ink-jet print. Other, smaller, resolutions are designed for on-screen or e-mail use only. Scan quality is usually very good and it is possible to have additional images added to the disk at a later stage, although it is much more cost-effective to have an entire film scanned at one time. Both color-negative and color-transparency material are supported and the Pro Photo CD service is available for an extra premium. Kodak has not licensed its clever Photo-CD technology to any software manufacturer, so it is not possible to save personal files in the Photo-CD format, but the standard TIFF or Photoshop format will work just as well. The disks are cross platform and can be opened from within all of the major imaging applications. All Photo-CD images are deliberately "unsharp" to minimize data, but this is easily rectified using the Unsharp Mask filter in Photoshop.

Picture CD

The cheaper Kodak Picture CD is a similar service, available over the counter or direct from Kodak by mail. The major difference between this and the Photo CD is that images are scanned at a lower resolution and saved in the universal JPEG format. Image quality is not as high and the service is primarily aimed at the family photographer rather than a keen amateur. JPEG files are universally accepted in all imaging applications and can be used for e-mail and for a family website with little additional processing.

Professional scanning services   **2**

Professional photo labs usually offer an independent scanning service for those occasions when one-off scans from medium- or large-format film originals are needed. Professional labs are equipped with super-high-resolution scanners such as the Imacon Flextight which is capable of creating files in excess of 100MB. Results are returned on CD-R or any suitable media of the user's choice. Occasionally using a professional service is a much better idea than investing a large sum of money in a poor-performance medium-format scanner.

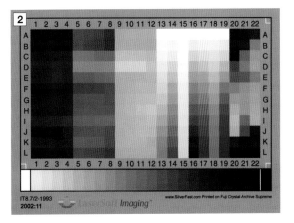

Professional scanning services utilize precise color management tools to ensure the highest possible levels of color accuracy. Standard calibration charts like this example from Silverfast offer a neutral color reference point to base a calibration test on.

See also Packaging image files *pages 90–91* / Budget workstation *pages 112–113* /

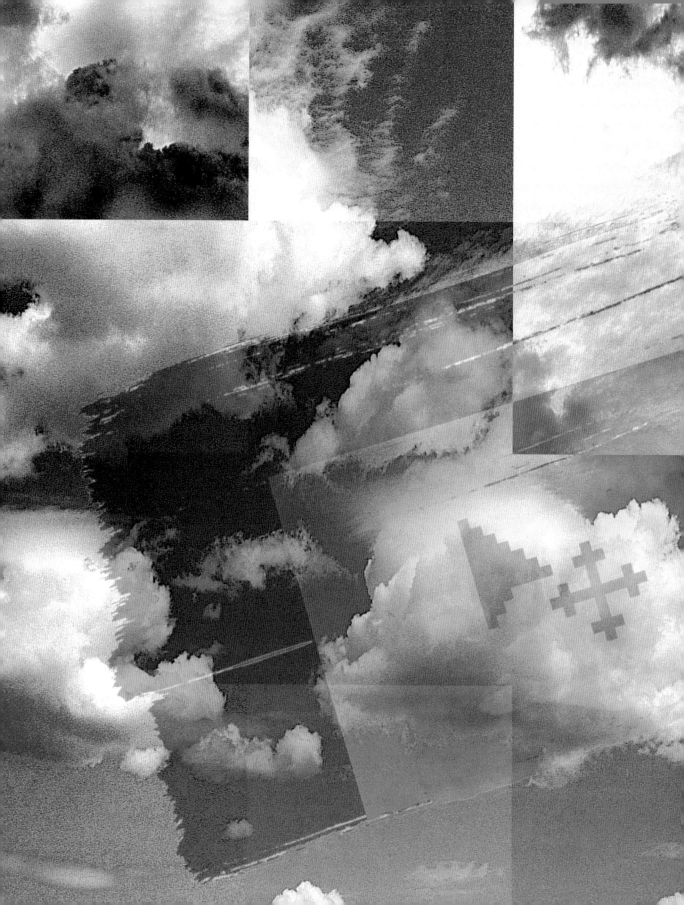

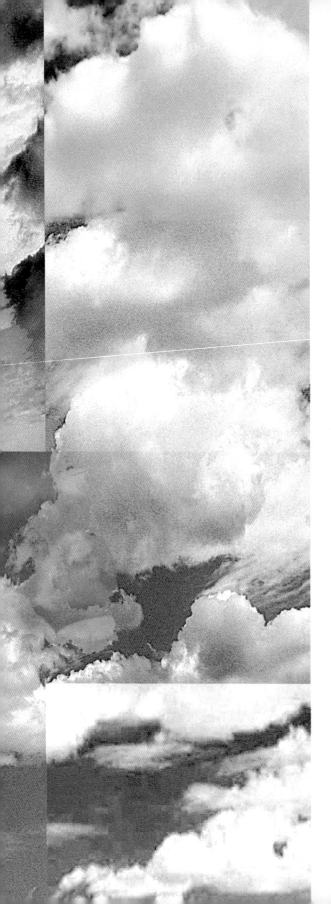

6 Software Applications

Adobe Photoshop

Firmly stationed at the top of the image-editing software ladder is Adobe Photoshop — the best image-editing software money can buy.

Photoshop has been refined through many versions from an early nuts-and-bolts image editor to the latest creative box of tricks for new-media design. Essential for those keen to pursue a design or new-media career, Adobe Photoshop has had an inestimable impact on the world of graphic arts. Photoshop works across both Mac and PC platforms, can read and write all standard image file formats and can work in eight different image modes. For the humble digital photographer, Adobe Photoshop offers a comprehensive kit bag of camera tricks, processing effects and darkroom standards. The downside is knowing where to find them and how to put them to good effect.

Initially, this application was targeted at a very broad range of professionals from the printing, design, television and photography industries and, as a consequence, offered numerous ways of reproducing traditional graphics techniques on a computer. In less than fifteen years, the reprographic industry has totally changed the way it collects, distributes and produces printed matter. With the overnight emergence of the Internet as a dominant method of communication, Photoshop provides an additional set of tools for packaging images for the totally different restrictions of on-line use.

Distinct from its competitors, Adobe Photoshop offers a raft of image-editing tools to suit various

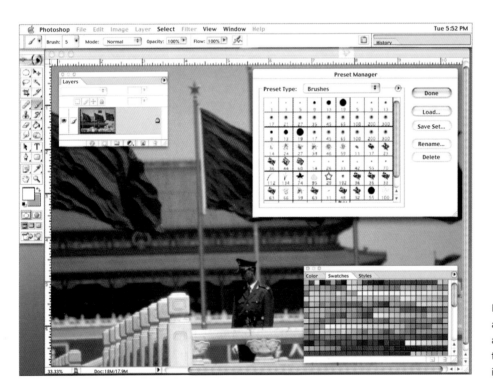

Photoshop offers a comprehensive assortment of tools for precision image editing.

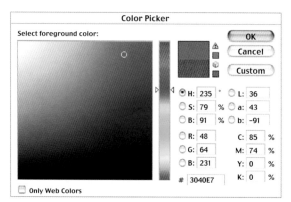

Photoshop's Color Picker is the dialog where color is selected.

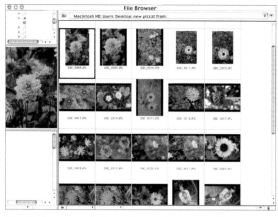

The file browser window offers a visual way of selecting image files for editing.

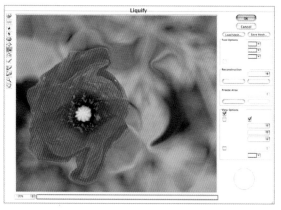

The Liquify Filter dialog offers a comprehensive set of controls in a full-screen dialog.

levels of expertise, starting with basic slider dialogs and progressing to more complex and infinitely variable controls. When learning the basics of one edit, such as color correction, users are introduced to a new and more sophisticated way of doing the same thing. Most encouraging is the error-forgiving History palette, which will reverse up to one hundred previous edits.

The latest versions of Photoshop are packed with color-management tools, so that disastrous profile conversions can be prevented from ruining work. Designed to work with common industry standards, Adobe Photoshop allows users to work on and contribute to other professionals' workflows without complications. Despite the reputation of the application as daunting, the latest versions are designed with user-friendly dialogs and contextual menus that pop up automatically when a different tool is selected. Nevertheless, the best tools are the hardest to get to grips with and they include the Pen tool for making flawless cutouts, the Curves dialog for manipulating up to fifteen independent tonal areas, and the ultra-smooth Duotone Image mode for creating sophisticated tones that rival work by the best darkroom expert.

In addition to all the tools needed for making great images, Photoshop also provides several timesaving automated functions, such as an instant Web Gallery, Picture Package and the very useful Actions palette for writing self-running scripts. Most settings and color recipes can be saved, stored, and then replayed over later images, and there are many plug-ins that can be added to create a highly customized application.

See also Photoshop Essentials *pages 164–191* / Creative Photoshop *pages 194–219* / Photoshop Montage *pages 222–239* /

Adobe Photoshop Elements

Far from being a cut-down version of Photoshop, Elements is a powerful application that has been totally redesigned for the novice user.

Photoshop Elements is a budget version of the original software, but unlike other budget packages it comes with a comprehensive manual. In addition, there are useful Hints and Recipes desktop panels to help users get started. Excellent for absolute beginners, these desktop step-by-steps guide users through the sometimes confusing early days of image editing. At a fraction of the price of the full Photoshop, Elements includes all the best tools for both desktop printing and web-page output.

Ideal for those who intend to graduate to the full Photoshop at a later date, Elements has the familiar Levels, Layers and Filters and the essential History palette for multiple "undos." Designed around the now-familiar desktop environment, with docking palettes and contextual menus that change with the tools, Elements offers an essentially graphical and intuitive interface compared to other old-fashioned applications. For extra assistance, the Hints palette can be left on the desktop to deliver a detailed description of each tool and process in use, just like a desktop tutor. The Recipes palette works by providing an on-the-spot tutorial in a tiny window on the desktop, which directs users through tasks, such as retouching, printing, and using text, in clear steps. Like many of the latest Adobe products, additional recipes can be downloaded free from their website.

Elements displays its tricks and gadgets via a host of user-friendly icons rather than the austere drop-down menus of older applications. This helps users see the potential effects of a command before running it and so avoids wasting time having to undo it immediately after. All filters, layer styles and effects are supplied with their own useful icons

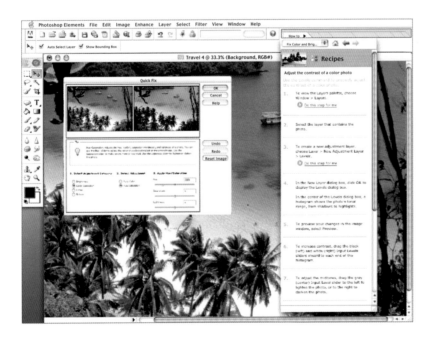

Photoshop Elements provides self-help guidance.

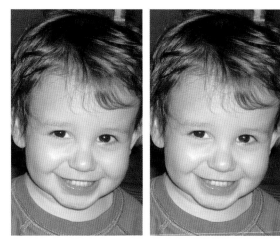

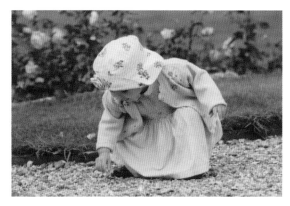

Before red-eye adjustment.　　After red-eye adjustment.

A family photograph before a frame effect.

which can be hidden away in the dock at the top of the screen when not required.

The Quick Fix dialog allows users to find all the color, contrast and image brightness controls at once, instead of having to delve deeply into the manual adjustment controls. Here an image is presented before and after fixing with the option of reversing out at any given time.

On the downside, Photoshop Elements doesn't have the sophisticated Pen tool or Curves controls for advanced tonal manipulation and can only edit RGB, Grayscale, Bitmap and Index mode images. Yet, unless intending to produce images ready for commercial reproduction straight away, users should not find this an issue. There is little control over how images with different color profiles are interpreted within Elements, but users can decide to tag working images with their own system's default color profile. In addition to the general editing tools, there are useful automated commands such as Contact Print, Picture Package and Web Photo Gallery, as well as full support for third party plug-in sets such as Extensis PhotoFrame. For more experimental users the Photomerge command enables the blending together of several different images to produce an effective montage in just a few minutes.

Compatibility

Available for Mac OS from 8.6 onward and Windows 98/2000/NT4.0/ME/XP operating systems.

Upgrade

Users can upgrade from Elements to the full Adobe Photoshop for an additional cost.

See also Budget workstation *pages 112–113* / Midprice workstation *pages 114–115* /

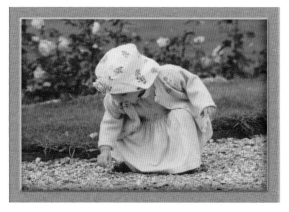

The Recipes menu in Photoshop Elements can be useful to create frame effects automatically.

Jasc PaintShop Pro

Established as a firm favorite of keen photographers worldwide, PaintShop Pro offers a comprehensive set of tools at a very competitive price.

PaintShop Pro is a budget Windows-only application that offers many of the features found only in a professional application such as Adobe Photoshop, including layers, levels and the multiple undo, named Command History. Targeted increasingly at the professional end of the market, the software has grown out of a sustained history of redesign and redevelopment, often leapfrogging its rivals along the way. In fact, the product has sold so successfully, it no doubt influenced Adobe's decision to release the similarly priced Photoshop Elements and package the Image Ready animation suite together with full Photoshop.

Supplied with an excellent manual and shipped with many value-added features, such as an animation feature, PaintShop Pro is designed primarily for the intermediate-level digital photographer who wants to do more than basic edits

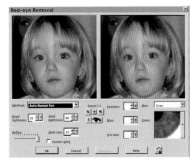

The Red-eye Reduction dialog.

and printing family photos. It comes fully equipped with a sophisticated range of tools for painting, drawing and for retouching basic shooting and scanning mishaps such as red eye and dust. Like Photoshop, it has a familiar barrage of toning and colorizing tools with Hue/Saturation and Color Balance dialogs.

PaintShop Pro is an ideal application to start with and, by using some industry-standard tools, it offers users the chance to transfer skills and knowledge to a higher-level product at a later date. For those keen on swapping images across two different operating systems, or wanting to minimize the cost of buying two full-price software licenses, PaintShop Pro is the ideal low-cost Windows image editor, as it can open and save files in over 50 different formats including Photoshop's own .psd file format.

Not solely designed for desktop print output, PaintShop Pro offers additional tools for packaging images for on-line and network distribution. A built-in GIF animator allows users to create buttons and

PaintShop Command History dialog.

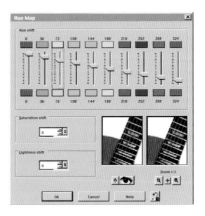

PaintShop Hue Map dialog.

banners that run and loop within their own fixed time frames and a range of tools for compressing images into JPEGs. For already-competent web designers, there is an opportunity to make image maps with built-in hyperlinks to other Internet resources; there is a useful image-slicing function for hacking larger images into smaller chunks for faster download; and there are ever-useful rollover images for making pages look a touch more interactive than they really are.

As a TWAIN-compliant application, PaintShop Pro can be used to offload from a flatbed, film scanner or digital camera directly, and has a good selection of print preview functions so users can tell exactly how printouts will appear on paper. Sold without the full color-management tools of Adobe Photoshop, this product is generally used by individuals rather than a design team within a fully controlled color-management environment.

Cost and compatibility

Available for Windows 95/98/2000/NT/XP only.

Web links

www.jasc.com

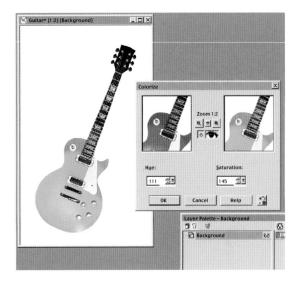

The Colorize dialogs.

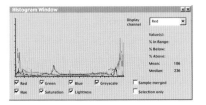

The Histogram dialog.

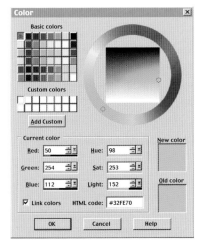

PaintShop Pro Color palette.

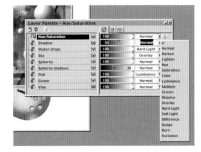

PaintShop Pro Layers dialog.

See also Midprice workstation *pages 114–115 /*

MGI PhotoSuite

Following the sustained success of a worldwide sales campaign aimed at the absolute beginner, the recent MGI PhotoSuite gives users a no-nonsense toolbox for digital photography.

After launching this Windows-only package, users will notice an interface design that owes more to a web browser than to a traditional drop-down menu application. As such, this makes it an ideal starter product for schoolchildren or adult users more familiar with surfing the net than wading through the complexities of a professional image-editing program. PhotoSuite is designed with large, easy-to-see buttons and controls — similar to those in computer kiosk shopping booths or an information center. The interface is much less threatening for a computer novice and, because many newcomers to digital photography also tend to be newcomers to computers, this will help them get started right away.

PhotoSuite is the best of the entry-level image-editing packages and, although the accompanying manual is much less detailed than that of PaintShop Pro or Elements, it offers more than just software tools for image manipulation. The MGI software designers have assumed, rightly, that this level of user may not be confident with storing and filing documents away in the hidden depths of their PC, so useful functions for organizing, storing and keyword-searching images are included. PhotoSuite keeps the most frequently used tools for image repair close by for solving tasks such as red eye and for restoring poorly scanned images.

A bonus feature is the wraparound panorama function, which allows users to stitch together up to 48 different digital images. The result can be printed or saved for later insertion into a web page as 360-degree virtual-reality wraparound. These unique web-image experiences are great for showing landscapes, historic city centers or even the interior space of a building.

Generally, this application does a great deal of processing in the background and does not offer the hands-on control of a more sophisticated image editor. Consequently, very precise commands for cutting out, layering and controlling file compression, color management and linking with other applications are thin on the ground.

Like all other image editors on the market, PhotoSuite offers plenty of do-it-yourself web-gallery commands, so users can share digital images directly on the Internet. There is no need to understand anything about web design or coding, as the program's instant web-page creation and publishing tools do all the complex work. Users will need to set up an Internet account before using the package. Once installed, the program offers a good choice of web-page templates on which to base a home page. For those wanting to make their site more dynamic, there is a basic web graphics GIF editor too.

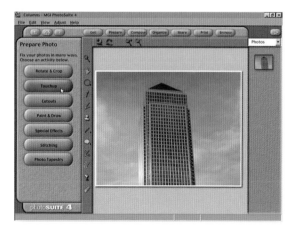

The PhotoSuite dialog.

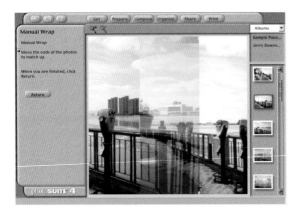

The PhotoSuite Panorama-stitching tool.

The PhotoSuite web-page creator.

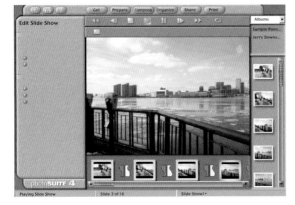

The PhotoSuite slide show.

The PhotoSuite keyword-search function.

Compatibility

Made for Windows PC only. Windows 95,98 ME,
NT/2000.XP. Internet Explorer — essential for all
web-based projects — is included.

Web links

www.mgisoft.com

www.photosuite.com

See also Budget workstation *pages 112–113* / Adobe
Photoshop Elements *pages 144–145* / Jasc PaintShop Pro
pages 146–147 /

Filter plug-ins

All image-editing applications are designed so that users can customize them by adding extra filter sets or functional plug-ins.

Corel KPT 6.0

Formerly known as Kai's Power Tools, this set of versatile filters can be purchased to customize the already extensive selection in Adobe Photoshop. The latest version is distributed by Corel and features wild effects called Goo, Sky Effects, LensFlare and Turbulence, as well as many others. Designed to link with all versions of Photoshop from 4.0 onward, KPT will also work with a range of other Corel-compatible products including Photo-Paint, CorelDraw and Painter.

Xenofex   1

The Xenofex filter set adds a wonderful set of texture filters to an imaging application. The plug-in is accessed via an additional item in the Filters drop-down menu and offers its own self-contained dialog box. Inside the controls are options to vary lighting, texture size and the amount of distortion required. Despite the texture tag, results are remarkably subtle and work well on simple and uncomplicated photographs, such as this shot of a flower head.

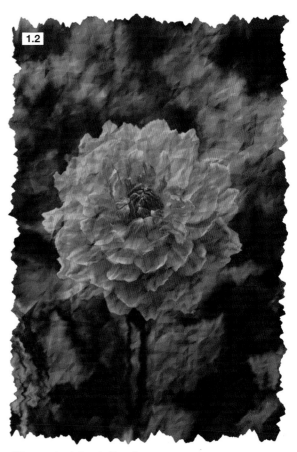

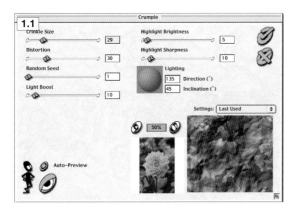

The Xenofex dialog box.

After manipulating in Xenofex.

See also Adobe Photoshop *pages 142–143* /

A trial version of this package can be downloaded from www.xenofex.com

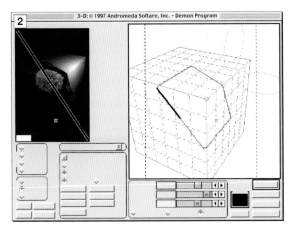

The Andromeda dialog box.

Andromeda   2

Andromeda is another Photoshop plug-in that allows users to drape a photographic image around a 3-D shape such as a cube or sphere. Just like a 3-D design application, the plug-in offers controls for wrapping and mapping, as well as sophisticated ways of lighting an image via a set of virtual studio lights. Users can download a demo version from www.andromeda.com

Lighting effects with Light! plug-in   3

The Light! plug-in from Digital Film Tools is a great addition to any desktop image-editing kit, able to revive a flagging image in minutes. Built to work within Adobe Photoshop as an additional Filter option in the Filter menu, the plug-in uses predetermined pattern files to add subtle daylight effects to an image as highlights or shadows. The trial version comes with several sample pattern images that mimic the light from venetian blinds, Georgian windows and shutters. Identical to the traditional gobos used by studio photographers for casting naturalistic shadows onto studio subjects,

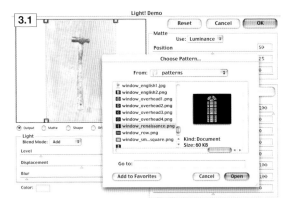

The Light! plug-in dialog box.

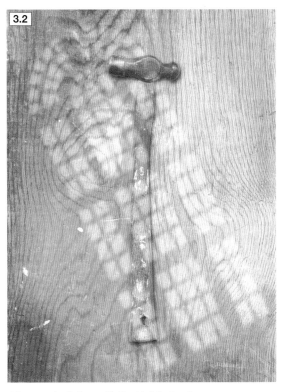

After manipulating with the Light! plug-in.

these patterns are great for adding a convincing daylight feeling to photographs. Users can download a free trial version of Light! from the Digital Film Tools website on www.digitalfilmtools.com

Extensis PhotoFrame edges plug-in

PhotoFrame is one of the best Photoshop and Photoshop Elements plug-ins from Extensis, and is packed with over 2,000 frames, borders and effects on a single CD.

Once loaded, this plug-in works by becoming an additional menu item within Photoshop itself and, when chosen, it becomes a full window-sized creative work area, so users can experiment with a variety of scenarios before committing to any one of them. There are two ways of using the application, either by copying all the sample files to a folder on the hard disk, or leaving them on the installation CD for access only when needed. The selection of effects varies from sensitive and artistic watercolors to wacky and wonderful serrated edges.

See also Adobe Photoshop *pages 142–143* / Adobe Photoshop Elements *pages 144–145* / Media types *pages 244–245* /

Tips on using PhotoFrame [1]

Once a digital image is ready for treatment, launch PhotoFrame and wait for the preview window to appear. The frame files are basic black shapes which transform to fit the exact size and resolution of the image on application. Browsing for a suitable edge can be difficult at first owing to the overwhelming choice and the difficulty of visualizing the end result. Several frames can be loaded at once, so users can toggle between an edited selection to make a choice. Just like a graphic element on a different layer, the frame can be modified infinitely as to size, position, thickness, sharpness and translucency until it meets the desired effect. Frame and border color can be selected from a Swatches palette or sampled from the image itself using the

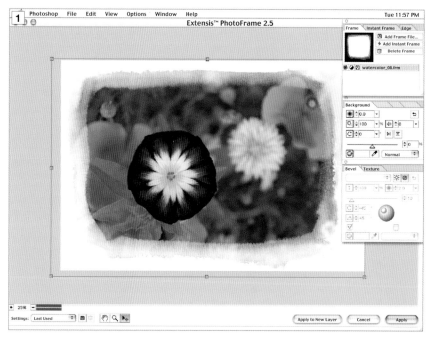

The Photoframe dialog.

Dropper tool. Once complete, the PhotoFrame can be converted into an additional Photoshop layer and further blended or discarded on returning to the main application.

Preparing irregular images for printout and on-screen use 2

Perfect for printout, scratchy or decorative edges will transform a digital image into something quite different. Printing out should prove no problem at all, provided a sensitive paper material has been chosen to accompany, say, watercolor effects. Other jazzy edges are perfect for preparing images for Powerpoint presentations or for personal web-page display. If irregularly shaped images are destined for use on the Internet, border colors should be chosen to fit within the web-safe color range. This same color needs to be nominated as the web-page background color, otherwise the border and background won't blend in together. The only other method of merging an irregularly shaped image is to save it as a GIF file with a transparent region, although this is a much less satisfactory method for photographic images.

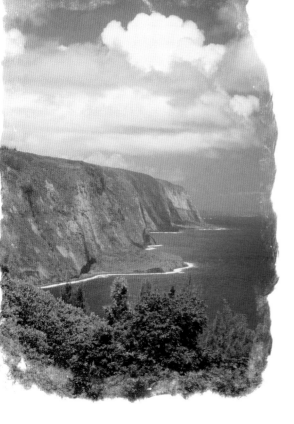

2.1

A landscape image with a rough edge applied.

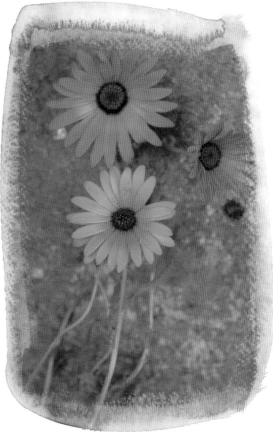

2.2

A still-life image with a translucent watercolor edge.

Finding resources on the Internet

With a software application in place, the next step is to hook up with Internet-based user groups to take advantage of tips, recipes and free downloads.

W eb-based resources are divided into manufacturer-controlled sites and sites set up by enthusiasts. For each of their image-editing products, Adobe has established an on-line resource center, where specially invited guests from the professional world of design offer advice and advanced techniques for free. Pro tips are a great way of learning how to cut through the red tape of image editing and for picking up tips not covered in the handbook.

Both Photoshop and Elements can be customized to fit a user's exact requirements by adding further Recipe files for special effects. All precise settings in Photoshop, such as Levels, Curves and the Channel Mixer can be saved at the dialog box stage, ready to store away, and reapplied to other images. These tiny data files can also be shared with other users over the Internet or sent as e-mail attachments. In addition to saving recipes, users can also design their own filter effects from the Filter>Other>Custom menu. Custom brush sets and swatch palettes are also available for free download from the Adobe website.

The most useful tools users can generate themselves are the self-propelling Action and Droplet scripts. Actions — similar to word processing macros — are a set of pre-recorded commands that can be applied to an image or used to generate artwork from a blank document. A host of Action files come already supplied with Photoshop, but users can record their own using the Action menu. Once saved and stored, these files can be shared with other users, even across different platforms. Actions can be instigated from their own palette, simply by pressing "play," or from within the File>Automate menu for playing over an entire folder of images. Many useful color recipes and print effects can be created through Action files and there are many freely available from the Internet. A Droplet file is

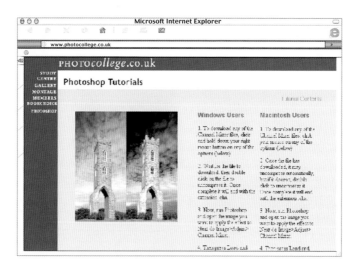

A Photoshop tutorial from the Photocollege website.

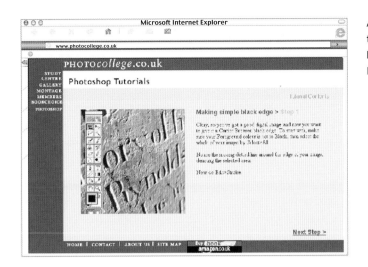

A step-by-step guide to making edges can be found on the Photocollege website.

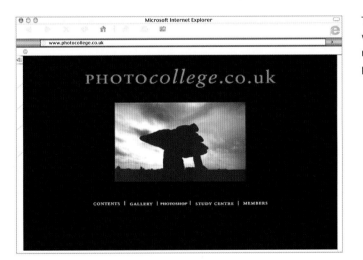

The Photocollege website is a free resource for keen photographers.

a variation of an Action file and, once placed on the desktop of a PC, will apply a pre-set series of commands to any document icon dragged and dropped onto it.

For any interaction with the Internet, it is wise to install a good-quality virus-protection utility on a PC before downloading any files from user groups or enthusiast sites. It is easy for PCs to become infected and even easier not to realize it has happened. Try the well-respected McAfee Virus Scan.

Web links

1

www.adobe.com

www.photocollege.co.uk

See also Adobe Photoshop *pages 142–143* / Adobe Photoshop Elements *pages 144–145* / Internet-based printing services *pages 264–265* /

Web-design software

If digital photography is merely a way of generating images for a website, proper web-design software is essential to make the site more effective.

Since the rapid expansion of the Internet, software companies have been working hard to keep up with constantly changing technology, standards and user expectations. Purpose-made web-design software allows the user complete control over the graphic look of a site — something the useful, but not very imaginative, auto web-gallery functions found within most image editors cannot offer. Moreover, users don't need to understand html code in order to design and publish websites, as the top three products allow work to be carried out with an entirely visual interface, just like a desktop-publishing program (DTP). The three major players are the industry-preferred Macromedia Dreamweaver, the small-office favored Microsoft FrontPage and the less-used Adobe GoLive. Many office applications allow users to save and export html files, but it is much better to create all content entirely in a web-design program created specifically for the task.

Dreamweaver functions like a DTP package and allows the user to place images and text within three types of pre-defined boxes called tables, cells and layers. Just like a complex DTP layout, all the image and html assets for a website must reside in one single site folder in order to maintain the complex links generated within that site. Simple sites are constructed from individual html pages linked together in a linear book-type fashion. At its most elemental, html offers functional tools for the display and positioning of text and graphics, with little interactivity. More dynamic and interactive sites are

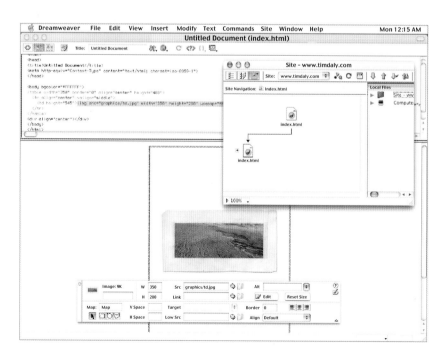

The Dreamweaver interface offers an html code view alongside a much simpler graphical view for making effective websites.

generated using additional code, such as Javascript, or using items prepared in specialized web animation packages like Flash.

In addition to a web-design application, users will need to buy an image-editor program, such as Photoshop or Photoshop Elements, capable of packaging images into the web-friendly JPEG or GIF format files, and a web browser on which to view the html content. Macromedia's own image editor is called Fireworks, but offers far less image-editing control than Adobe Photoshop. Ideally, two or more browser types should be used, to show how pages are interpreted via both Internet Explorer and Netscape. For uploading files to a web server, an additional piece of software called a File Transfer Protocol (FTP) package is required. There are many shareware

See also Adobe Photoshop *pages 142–143* / Adobe Photoshop Elements *pages 144–145* / Making image maps *pages 270–271* /

FTP packages to choose from and Dreamweaver is supplied with its own built in.

Once a website nears completion, users need to arrange a web-hosting service before the work can be viewed worldwide. Hosting packages range from the free space on the back of an Internet provider (IP), such as AOL or Freeserve, or dedicated server space which comes with an annual rental agreement. Finally, a reliable (and preferably speedy) Internet connection is essential for uploading files to the server space without delay.

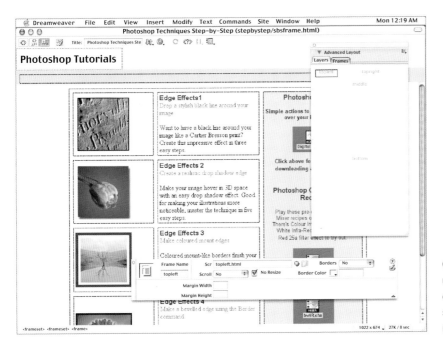

Complex layouts can be built using frames, where some elements on the page — such as menu bars — can remain static.

Maintenance and repair utilities

To keep a computer in tip-top condition and to protect hard-won work, users need to install a maintenance utility program.

Hands-on housekeeping

Despite the terrifying concept of repairing computers, anyone can use a maintenance utility to keep a PC working at optimum speed. Most PCs are fitted only with rudimentary repair and maintenance features, so it is a good idea to invest in a dedicated package such as Norton Utilities from Symantec.

A computer's hard drive is just like a busy public library, where books are constantly being taken off shelves and put back in the wrong places, and it will need to be put through a clean-up process — defragmenting — at least twice a year.

Defragmenting ensures that all data is consolidated in a continuous region on the hard disk, just like library books are reorganized and arranged together for easier access. Defragmenting actually speeds up a PC, as it spends less time searching for data spread across many "shelves." Norton makes the task of defragmenting very simple and helps users through the process in a step-by-step manner with an application called Speed Disk.

It is essential to take the time to spring clean a PC regularly, throwing away any unused files or trial software. Any available hard disk space is used by an imaging application as a scratch disk space, and an application will slow down significantly if the hard disk is overloaded with waste files.

Norton Disk Doctor — part of the utility's package — can also repair removable disks and internal hard drives if failure occurs. After running an initial examination, most problems can be solved automatically by the application itself — unless

See also Computer basics *pages 96–97* / Finding resources on the Internet *pages 154–155* /

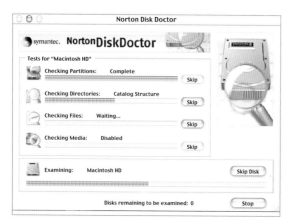

The Norton Disk Doctor application is a software tool that can be used to regularly ward off serious hardware faults. After an initial checking routine, errors and problems are fixed before they start to affect your PC's performance.

The very useful UnErase tool can find files that you have thrown away and, providing no new data has been written over them, can recover the files to a nominated disk.

impending hardware failure looms. If a computer is constantly crashing, the Disk Doctor can be run to rectify some of the issues that would be too complex to solve without expert knowledge.

Perhaps the most useful tool in the box is Norton's UnErase — a simple, but vital, tool for recovering data that has been thrown away by mistake. (Once a file has been deleted, it will still be in the same place on a computer's hard drive or floppy disk, since only the link to it has been removed.) For this task to be successful, it is important that later data has not been written to the same area of the disk before attempting recovery. If the mistake is discovered soon after the event, most files are very easily recovered. UnErase works by recovering files from both removable media and hard drives and works best when the lost data is recovered to another disk in case it overwrites itself in the process.

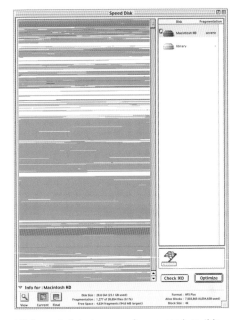

Well-used disks become fragmented, as this stripey orange illustration shows. Large files are stored in many different locations on a disk and can easily become disjointed resulting in slower access time. Defragmenting solves this by reorganizing blocks of data into nearby areas.

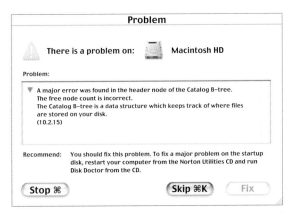

Disk Doctor produces a simple report when an error is encountered and promptly asks your permission to fix it.

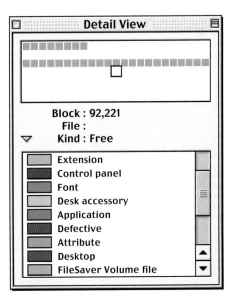

With Speed Disk, a useful graphical representation of your disk is created, so you can see where different data such as applications, fonts and control panels are arranged.

Quicktime VR software

Apple's revolutionary virtual-reality (VR) software has now become the standard tool for creating interactive VR content.

Priced at a low cost and available for both Windows and Mac operating systems, the professional Quicktime VR modeling software offers a far superior set of tools compared to freebie panoramic stitching software. The product works by seamlessly stitching together different digital images to make either a revolving 360-degree panorama for on-screen use or a full-length image for printout. The panorama files can be viewed in a web browser fitted with a suitable plug-in and can be compressed for easy access over the Internet. Once fully loaded, Quicktime VR files can navigate left to right, top to bottom and even zoom in. In addition to promoting luxurious and far-off holiday destinations, current uses of Quicktime VR include showing the interior cabins of new cars, homes for sale and other consumer products.

Preparing to shoot images for a VR panorama [1]

The best VRs result from the careful planning and preparation of a photo shoot. A tripod fitted with a pan- and tilt-head is essential for this kind of project, as is a good grasp of exposure. Arranging the camera in a portrait position (vertical frame) gives a final VR the additional feature of scrolling vertically as well as horizontally. The tripod must be in the center of the environment and level. The zoom lens (if fitted) should be set to the same focal length for the duration of the shoot and a range of images taken in a 360-degree arc with generous overlaps between each. It is essential to try and maintain consistent exposure throughout the series of images, which may mean shooting on a manual setting rather than automatic, to avoid aperture values changing.

Linking together [2]

Quicktime VR takes all the hard work out of assembling and merging the images and automatically renders the final result based on information provided by the user, such as the number of source files and the focal length of the lens used in the shoot. If the images are intended for the Internet, it is worth resizing them down before assembling. The file will then be saved in a web-friendly format or as a Photoshop-friendly flat image, which can then be imported and manipulated.

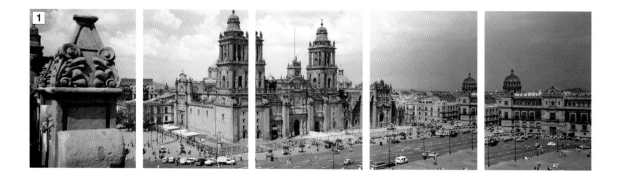

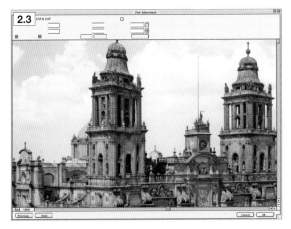

The palette showing the source files for a stitched panorama.

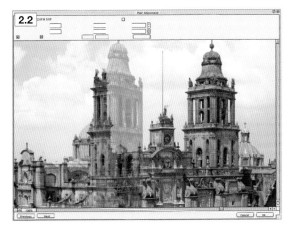

Manual alignment of connecting images gives you the opportunity to make seamless joins.

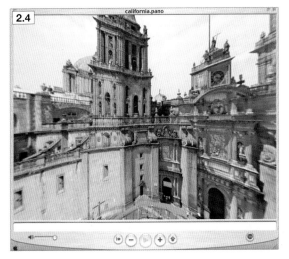

Once dragged into position, the overlap disappears.

The final panorama viewed in the Quicktime movie player.

Hyperlinking

Just like interactive image maps, areas of a Quicktime VR can also be made into hotspots and hyperlinked to other resources on the web. This technology has given rise to on-line VR shops, where users can "touch" an item they want to add to a shopping basket or "walk" from one VR file into another by navigating through a doorway or other such device.

Web links

More examples of the art of VR can be found at the Apple web site on www.apple.com

See also Multimedia features *pages 24–25 /*

Slide-show software

You don't need to be a multimedia programmer to make a slide show of your digital photographs.

iView [1]

There are many shareware applications offering users the chance to sequence digital photos into simple but uninspiring slide shows. A much better alternative is an application like iView MediaPro. This package is very versatile and is a cross between a browser, an image database, a basic image editor and a batch-image processor that can also create very effective slide shows and movies.

How it works

The iView interface allows the user to create slide shows by two means: either by dragging files from the hard disk or from removable media into the preview window; or by downloading them direct from a digital camera. Once imported into the preview window, a small thumbnail is created, giving the user a preview of the forthcoming sequence. The program arranges image files automatically based on their alphabetical or numerical filenames, but images are easily dragged into a new position in the slide show. The software supports all of the major file formats and the package resizes and rotates images to fit the screen, eliminating any need to prepare the files beforehand.

Transition effects [2]

Each image in a slide-show sequence can be timed to appear after a set number of seconds and using a wide range of transition effects. Instead of a plain image replacing another image, a transition effect like Crossfade brings a touch of television editing to the desktop, for more professional and less jarring results. Slow delays make for an ideal slide show in a public space, where each image can be viewed and contemplated before the next one appears. The slide show can also be annotated with a piece of music.

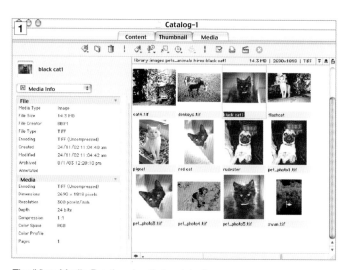

The iView Media Pro thumbnail view interface.

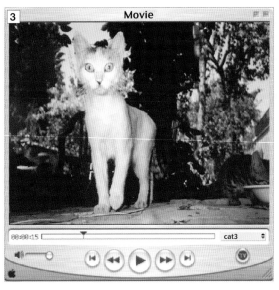

Slide shows can also be exported in the universal Quicktime Movie format.

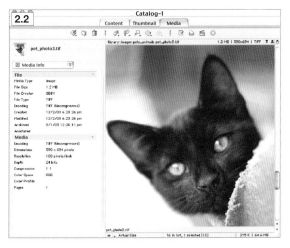

Fig 2.1 caption:
Complex slide-show effects can be created for each frame.

Detailed information for each media clip included in the slideshow can be easily previewed.

Exporting   3

Once a slide show is complete, it can be saved for presentation as a catalog, or exported as a Quicktime movie, compatible with both Mac and PC platforms. Users determine the video dimensions, compression and even prepare the slide show for video streaming. The movie file takes on the slide-show settings, such as frame delay and transitions, and can be made to fit any portion of the desktop. After compression, the movie files are small enough to place on a website or to e-mail to friends.

Details

Available for both Windows PC and Apple platforms, there is a trial version limited to 45 launches on www.iview-multimedia.com

See also Multimedia features *pages 24–25* / File format *pages 86–87* / Compression *pages 88–89* / Storage media *pages 92–93* /

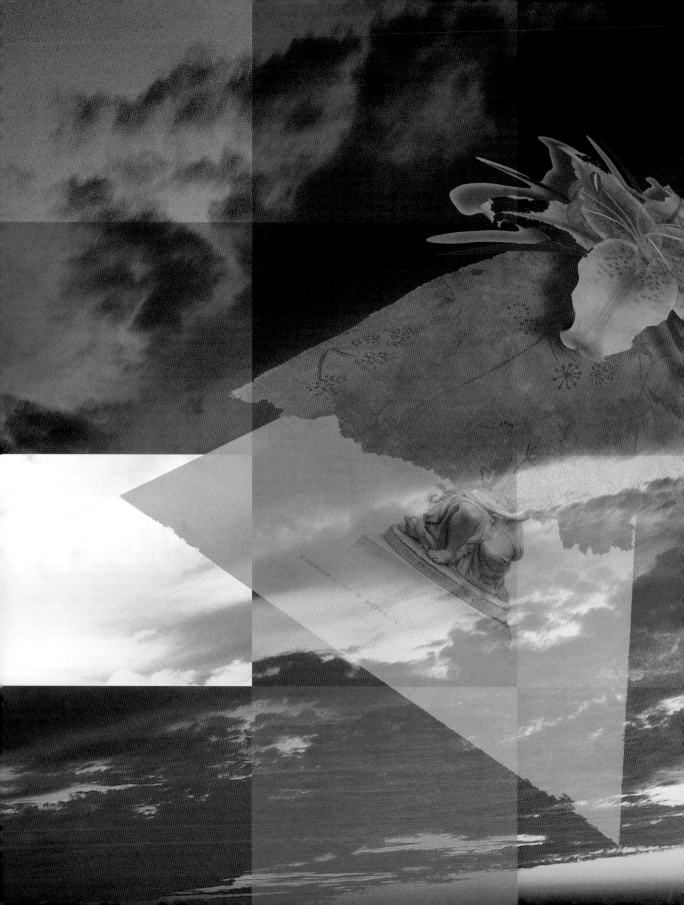

7 Photoshop Essentials

Photoshop toolbox

Packed full of tools and gadgets for creative manipulation, the toolbox is the first port of call when using Photoshop.

The Selection tools

The Marquee tools   1

Four tools can be found hidden under the Marquee pop-out menu and all are used to make geometric selections within the user's images. Both the elliptical and rectangular marquees can be preset with a fixed size or aspect ratio.

The Move tool   2

Shaped like an arrowhead, the Move tool is used to drag selections, non-printing guides, pasted items and layers into place. Select this function quickly by pressing V on the keyboard.

The Lasso tools   3

The Lasso tools are used to define freehand selection shapes by hand. There are three tools in the menu: the freehand lasso; the polygonal lasso — for making straight-line selection shapes; and the magnetic lasso tool which locks onto the edges of an image shape as it is dragged nearby.

The Magic Wand tool   4

The Magic Wand picks up similarly colored pixels like a magnet. Its strength or tolerance can be varied from 0 — the highest attraction — to 255, which has the lowest powers.

The Crop tool   5

Used for recomposing images, the Crop tool darkens the areas a user plans to discard, giving a preview of the likely outcome beforehand.

The Slice and Slice Select tools   6

Used for dissecting large images into smaller pieces for faster web transmission, the Slice tool works just like a scalpel. The Slice Select tool is used for picking the pieces up again at a later time.

The Painting tools

The Healing Brush tool   7

The Healing Brush tool is a more refined way of retouching imperfections on an image than the method offered by the general-purpose Clone Stamp tool. The Healing Brush works by blending copied pixels over a damaged area.

The Patch tool   8

The Patch tool works in the same way as the Healing Brush, but within selected areas. It is very useful when repairs are close to the boundary of a different color.

The Brush and Pencil tools   9

The Brush and Pencil tools are used to apply color to an image or graphic using soft flowing lines or hard straight lines, respectively. Airbrush effects can be set as an option for the Brush.

The Clone Stamp and Pattern Stamp tools   10

Like a rubber stamp, the Clone Stamp paints with a brush loaded with pixel samples from another area of an image. The Pattern Stamp applies a previously saved pattern over larger areas.

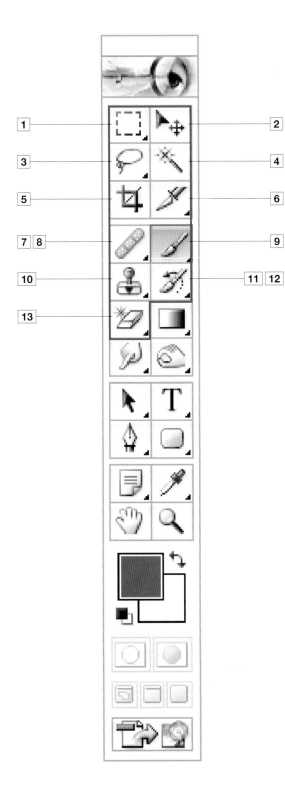

The History Brush [11]

The History Brush restores a recorded state saved in the History palette so the user can retrieve a more suitable section of an image.

The Art History brush [12]

With wild swirling strokes, the Art History brush creates a painterly effect by merging and mixing the colors in an image.

The Eraser tools [13]

With three variations — the Eraser, the Magic Eraser and the Background Eraser — these tools rub away pixels to reveal underlying layers, transparency or the current background color. The Magic Eraser knocks out whole chunks of similarly colored pixels to leave a cutout.

See also Photoshop Essentials *pages 166–191* / Creative Photoshop *pages 194–219* / Photoshop Montage *pages 222–239* /

The Gradient tools

A comprehensive set of five tools for creating precise color transitions, the Gradient tools can also be used in the Quick Mask mode.

The Paint Bucket [1]

For a quick flood of color, the Paint Bucket tool fills pixel areas with the current foreground color.

The Blur, Sharpen and Smudge tools [2]

Like a sharpening or blurring filter on the end of a brush, the Blur and Sharpen tools are useful for enhancing smaller areas of an image. The Smudge tool works by dragging a fingerlike icon through adjoining colors to create a smearing effect.

The Burning and Dodging tools [3]

Borrowed from the photographic darkroom, the Burning and Dodging tools lighten and darken respectively, smaller areas of an image, and are based on brush size.

The Sponge tool [4]

The highly useful Sponge tool can be used either to drain color away or to increase its saturation in local areas.

The Pen tools [5]

Precision instruments for selecting and cutting out complex shapes, the Pen tools are hard to pick up quickly, but will produce top-quality results once mastered. The Pen selection tools are used to modify and make paths fit better.

The Type tools [6]

Photoshop type can be used in two Type tool modes: the scalable and editable vector type and the pixel-based type made using the Type Mask tool.

The Shape tools [7]

The Shape tools are used for adding resolution-independent vector graphics.

The Note and Annotation tools [8]

The Note tool can be used for sticking a "memo" to an image, while the Annotation tool goes one step further and actually records a message — provided there is a microphone on the PC.

The Eyedropper tool [9]

The Eyedropper tool samples, or picks up, color from within an image and sets it as the foreground or background color.

The Measure tool [10]

The Measure tool is used for making precise measurements between given areas in an image, and is just like using a tape measure.

The Hand tool [11]

The Hand tool is used for moving an image around within its own window — especially useful when the image is magnified and larger than the display window.

The Zoom tool [12]

When working on small areas the Zoom tool can enlarge and reduce the image in its window.

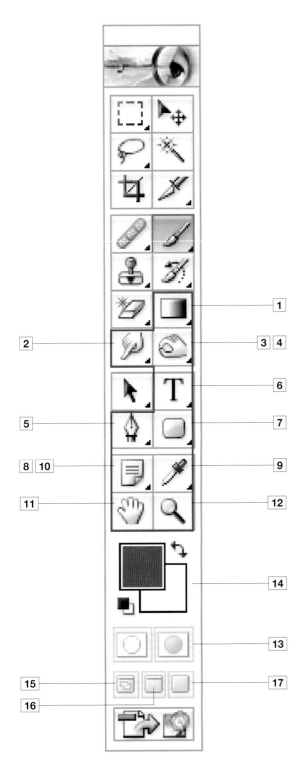

Other tools

The Quick Mask tool [13]

Another entirely different way of making selections is to work in Quick Mask mode with paintbrush or gradients.

The Foreground and Background color pickers [14]

The Foreground and Background color pickers define the current working colors for painting and other editing tasks. To reset colors to default black and white, click the two tiny black and white squares.

Screen Mode options

Standard screen mode [15]

This displays your work-in-progress image with normal menus and tools.

Full screen mode with menu bar [16]

This mode removes any distracting windows or menus from other applications visible on your desktop.

Full screen mode [17]

Like above, but without the drop down menus. If you are well versed in the keyboard shortcuts, you can even remove the toolbox from the desktop, leaving the image at the center of your attention.

See also Photoshop Essentials *pages 166–191* / Creative Photoshop *pages 194–219* / Photoshop Montage *pages 222–239* /

Layers

Layers are a fundamental way of organizing complex image-editing projects for maximum flexibility.

What are layers?

Initially, all digital images acquired from a scanner or digital camera exist in a single layer called the Background Layer. Like most two-dimensional artwork, this is rectangular, intact and can be enlarged or reduced. Yet, for very complex editing and creative montage projects, digital images can be arranged and assembled in different vertical stacking layers, just like a pack of playing cards. Other images can be inserted within the stack as can graphics, stencils and text. When working on a layered image window on a desktop, users can create very sophisticated work by amending and adjusting the relationship between each individual layer in the stack. The downside of using layers is an increase in the data size of an image, as each extra whole layer doubles the file size. With editing complete, layered images can still be printed and saved, but only in the layer-supporting Photoshop file format. The principle behind layers is simple: keep all elements of an image project separate, so changes can be made at any time.

How layers work

Each time a "copy and paste" command is made, a new layer is automatically created in the Layers palette — a process that is repeated when any vector graphics and text are created, too. Individual layers are simply named Layer 1, Layer 2 and so on, but can be renamed to better describe their contents simply by double clicking on the layer icon. Layers can also have their position in the stacking order altered at any time simply by being dragged into a new position above or below a neighboring one. All layers are initially opaque and stop underlying layers from being visible, but this can be altered by cutting holes

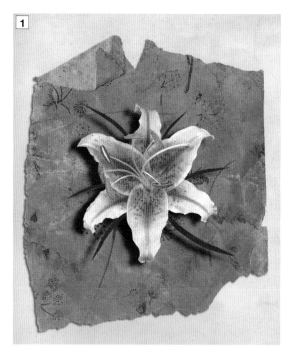

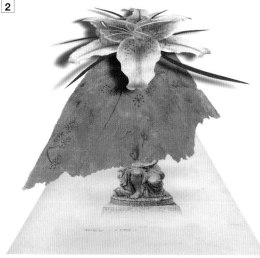

through them or by varying their opacity. The most unusual form layers can adopt is when set with a Blending mode — special preset effects that merge adjoining layers together with a range of colors and contrast. Layers can also be transferred between open images, simply by dragging their icons from one palette to another. However, the color mode, color space and resolution of the destination image will determine how the new addition is accommodated.

The Layers palette ③

The Layers palette can be used as a free-floating desktop palette or can be left docked in the menu bar. The background layer sits at the base of the stack and every new layer created sits on the top. Groups of interrelated layers can be linked together or arranged into a layer folder called a "set" to make for a simpler working process. All the important layer commands are made via the Layer menu, but those most frequently used can be accessed using tiny icons on the palette itself or by using the pop-out menu found on its top right-hand corner. A further subgroup of creative applications called Layer Effects can also add drop shadows and other graphic styles to an image.

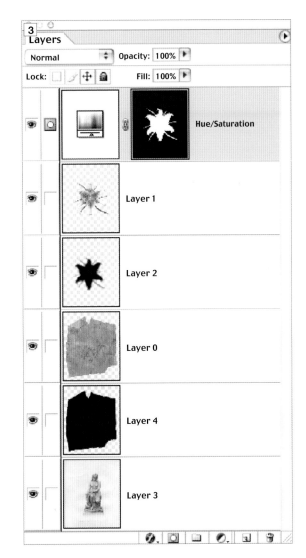

See also Photoshop toolbox *pages 166–169* / Textured backgrounds *pages 206–207* / Layers and stacking *pages 226–227* / Invert adjustment layers *pages 234–235* /

Selections

The first, and most important, task in image editing is defining which areas to change, using a process called selecting.

What are selections?

Unlike a word-processing package, where errant words can simply be highlighted before they are changed, pixel images present more of a challenge. Editing is based entirely on selected image areas — defined by one of many methods — but if no such selection is made, the manipulation won't work. Selections essentially fence off areas of an image, restricting any subsequent editing just to that place while protecting the rest of the image from unwanted change. Selections are not necessary if the intention is to make changes to the whole image at once. Most image-editing packages offer a range of drawing and painting tools for defining selection areas by shape, and the better applications also offer the ability to select similarly colored pixels without the need for drawing.

limited to those areas only, offering a precise and exact method of changing the content and appearance of the image.

Making an accurate selection can be time-consuming. By default, selections are created with razor-sharp edges — perfect if the intention is to move, copy or delete the area in question, but less than ideal if the user wants to apply a subtle effect to the area in question. Softer selection edges can be created using the Select>Feather command, where the higher the pixel radius, the softer the edge will be. Many of the Selection tools can be preset with a feather value before using, but the softening is best applied after. If the marching ants prove visually distracting, they can be turned off, but not removed, by doing a View>Extras command.

How selections work   1

Selection areas are indicated by a moving dotted line, called the "marching ants," and it is possible to select many unconnected areas at once. Following selection, any filter or image adjustment will be

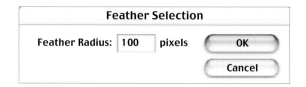

An edit applied to a feathered selection.

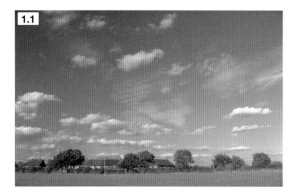

An edit applied to an unfeathered selection.

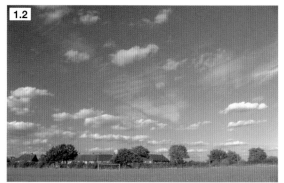

Selection tools

2

All of the selection tools found in the toolbox —
including the Pen but excluding the Magic Wand —
define selections by area. The Magic Wand and the
menu-driven Select Color Range make selections
based on color. For complex and difficult shapes,
the Select Color Range method relies less on an
ability to draw. A further selection tool can be found
when editing in Quick Mask mode. Quick Mask offers
the chance to define selection areas using a
satisfying red paint to mask areas in or out. Toggling
back between Quick Mask mode and normal editing
mode will turn the marching ants on and off. Quick
Mask is a great place to start making selections,
particularly if you find the operation of the drawing
tools difficult. All selections can be modified further
using any of the commands found under the Select
menu, such as expand, contract and grow. Best of
all, complex selections which may have taken time
to complete can be saved and stored for later use as
an Alpha Channel in the Channels palette.

See also Photoshop toolbox *pages 166–169* / Photoshop
Essentials *pages 166–191* / Creative Photoshop *pages
194–219* / Photoshop Montage *pages 222–239* /

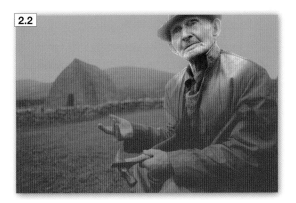

Quick Mask can be used to paint around selection areas.

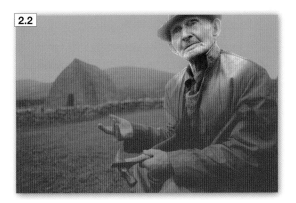

Once complete, the selection of the face can be edited.

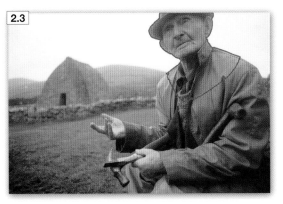

Quitting Quick Mask mode leaves the outline in place.

Choosing color

Finding the right color can be far from straightforward, especially if faced with sixteen million alternatives!

Color palettes 〔1〕

Photoshop offers a multitude of different color palettes, so users can select exactly the right value for the task at hand. All of these palettes can be found by clicking on the foreground color in the toolbox, or directly through most dialog boxes that involve color selection. The Color Picker dialog box presents a range of tools for selection by hand or by typing precise values into the text boxes. Within the Picker are five color models, the familiar RGB and CMYK and the less used HSB and LAB models. Color can be defined using different conceptual models, and the HSB and LAB modes offer an alternative, but no better, way to describe color values. Typing in exact color values is generally done in the RGB and CMYK models for matching the specific requirements of a commercial project. The fifth color model is the very useful Web Safe color palette which presents a much-restricted range for web-only projects. Web colors can also be defined by typing a hexadecimal code into the text box marked with a hash symbol (#). A step on from the Color Picker are the additional Custom palettes such as the universally recognized Pantone scale for defining lithographic ink color.

Defining colors 〔2〕

Color values selected in the Color Picker immediately become the current foreground color — ready for use with any of the brushes in the toolbox. In a regular digital image, over sixteen million colors can be used, but many of these will never print with the intensity shown on screen. For this reason, Photoshop offers a tiny warning triangle that pops up in the Picker whenever a non-printing color is chosen. Users can get the nearest alternative simply by clicking in the

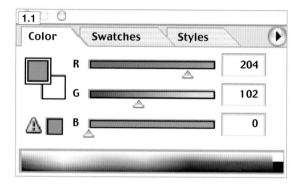

The desktop Color palette.

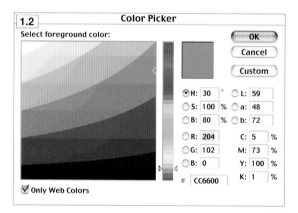

The Web Safe Color palette.

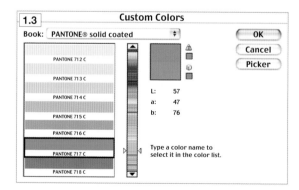

The Pantone Color palette.

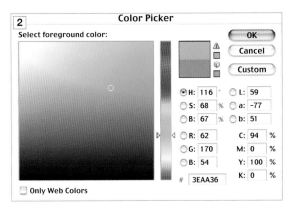

triangle. For Custom colors, such as the Pantone scale, a reference number can simply be typed into the dialog box to avoid scrolling through thousands of unwanted color values. Back in the desktop toolbox, the Dropper tool can also be used to set Foreground color by clicking in the image itself. This is useful for retouching projects where sympathetic colors are best picked from the image itself rather than guessed via the Color Picker. A much smaller version of the Color Picker, the Color palette, can be found under the Window menu and can be set to display all previously mentioned models except the Custom colors.

Swatches

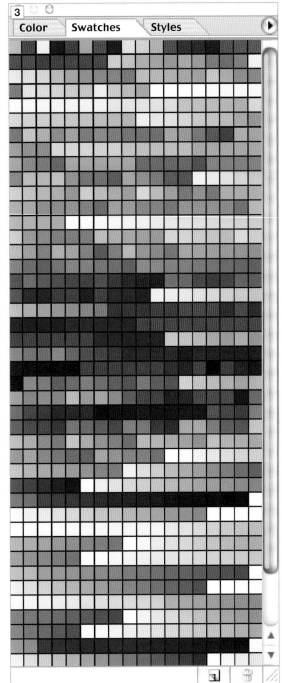

The little-used Swatches palette can be brought to the desktop by a Window>Swatches command and displays a much reduced, but nonetheless useful, color assortment, including many optional palettes loaded through the pop-out menu. Useful for graphic and textile designers for using repeated colors throughout a design, it can be customized and saved for later use.

See also Photoshop toolbox *pages 166–169* / Duotones *pages 196–197* / Channel Mixer *pages 198–199* / Color enhancing *pages 202–203* /

Cropping and image size

The size of an image can be altered for printout, web-page use or simply to improve its composition.

Cropping

1

The Crop tool is used to trim away sections of an image to make a better picture. The tool is used by dragging it across an open image, then modifying the crop using any of the tiny handles at the perimeter edges and corners. The crop can preserve the original image ratio, or proportion, by holding down the Shift key once the crop selection covers the entire image area. Most usefully, the tool darkens down the soon-to-be discarded areas of the image, to show the exact result in advance. Like many other tools, the Crop can be deselected and canceled by returning to the toolbox and clicking on the Crop tool icon. All layers in an image are affected equally by a crop, but if the intention is to edit one specific layer, this is best achieved using the Selection tools with the Edit>Cut command. For very precise projects, where a final image dimension has been specified, the Crop tool can be used with a preset size in either inches or centimeters. It is most important to remember that with every crop, original pixels are discarded and

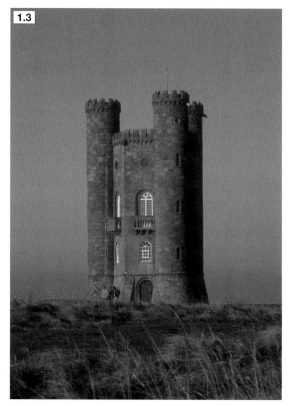

The Crop tool dims down areas to be deleted.

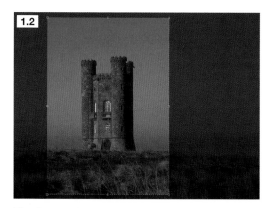

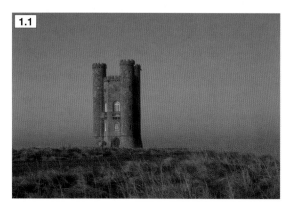

This image could be improved by cropping.

The same image, once the crop has been applied.

the file size reduced. It's also important to save the original image before saving a cropped version, in case you need to go back to the original.

Image size 2

Image size refers entirely to the pixel dimensions of an image and its resolution. Images can be described in inches, centimeters and pixels, as well as a few other lesser-used scales such as Picas and Points. The Image Size dialog is the place to prepare an image at the correct resolution for the target output and it is also where to enlarge and reduce an image. With the Resample button switched off, the resolution of an image can be changed without adding or discarding pixels and so maintaining the original pixel dimensions and file size. When this option is switched on, the reverse is the case and image quality will inevitably drop if a drastic size adjustment is made. It is hard to judge how an image will appear as a printout, but the Print Preview dialog box presents a much easier alternative to changing the document size in the Image Size dialog.

Canvas size 3

Confusingly, Canvas size is always the same size as Image size, unless you decide differently. It is similar to the paper size in a word processing program. Canvas is really a term used for generating additional blank space around an image for adding type, graphics or additional images in a montage project. New canvas space is made from new pixels whose color is defined by the existing background color and this will increase the file size. The exact place the new Canvas appears is determined by the Anchor icon, found in the Canvas Size dialog box. If new Canvas is created with a color and set to appear equally around each side of your image, this can be used to create a quick and effective border effect.

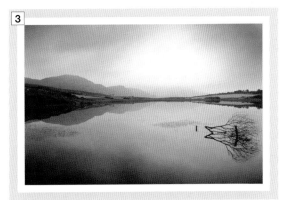

See also Photoshop toolbox *pages 166–169* / Selections *pages 172–173* /

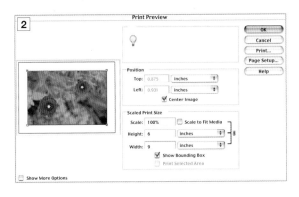

Contrast correction with Levels

Levels are one of the easiest controls to master and are useful for creating subtle tonal changes in an image.

What are Levels?

The Levels dialog is one of the core items in Adobe Photoshop, and has remained unchanged across different versions. This is the best place to adjust the contrast and brightness of a digital photograph, rather than using the cruder Contrast/Brightness sliders. Image contrast and brightness are much more measurable digitally than on traditional film, using a graphical chart called a histogram. In an RGB image, pixel color is mixed from three 0–255 scales displayed in the Levels dialog so an image can be manipulated without guesswork. The real purpose of the Levels dialog is to help process and prepare images for perfect printout and web-page use, using two scales for changing contrast and brightness.

Understanding the histogram

The histogram graph found in the Image>Adjustments>Levels dialog, displays the exact tonal distribution of all an image's pixels along a horizontal 0–255 axis, and their quantity against a vertical scale. As each different image is composed of a wide a variety of colors, so the shape of the histogram is unique to each image. Across the horizontal baseline are three triangular sliders; at the far left, black is used to set the shadow point, in the middle is the gray midtone slider and, set at the far right, is the white highlight triangle. The Levels midtone slider can be used to correct exposure mistakes and scanning errors.

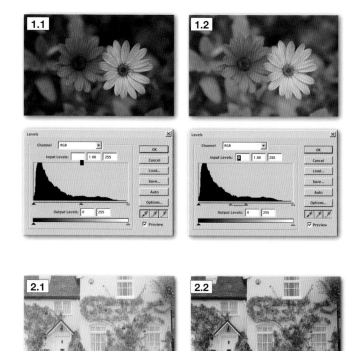

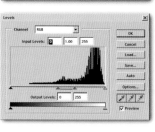

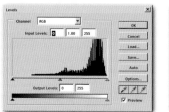

See also Photoshop toolbox *pages 166–169* / Contrast with Curves *pages 180–181* /

Fixing a dark image [1]

The histogram shape of a dark image shows a marked leaning toward the left-hand shadow end of the scale, indicating more blacks and dark grays than lighter tones. To make a brighter image, simply slide the midtone triangle to the left as shown.

Fixing a light image [2]

This histogram shows the opposite effect, with a greater emphasis to the right-hand side, and demonstrating more light tone than shadow. To fix a lighter image, slide the midtone triangle to the right-hand side as shown.

Contrast

Many raw digital images need proper contrast established before printing, otherwise results will be flat and disappointing. When the familiar "black mountain" shape shown in the histogram fails to spread out to both highlight and shadow end points, a low-contrast result will occur. Low contrast can easily be corrected using the Levels sliders.

Fixing a low-contrast image [3]

Lacking in strong blacks and whites, with a histogram shape set more in the center of the scale, this image is flat and dull. Both black and white sliders are moved to new positions, as shown, to create pure shadows and highlights.

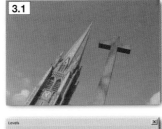

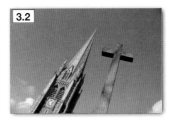

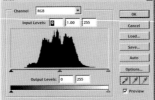

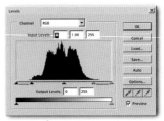

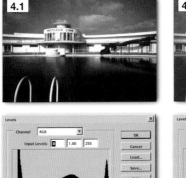

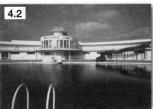

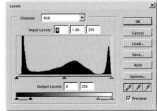

Fixing high contrast [4]

Perhaps the result of a naturally high-contrast subject or an ill-judged scan, this problem can be fixed using the Output sliders found at the base of the Levels dialog box. Both highlight and shadow Output sliders are dragged slightly toward the center of the gradient band, changing black shadows to dark gray and white highlights to light gray.

Contrast with Curves

Where Levels allows only three points of tonal manipulation, the more complex Curves control offers fifteen.

Using the Curves

Curves really come into their own when you want to adjust the contrast of a narrow tonal in a small area of an image. Adjusting image contrast using Curves can seem complex at first with little visible guidance to reassure you. Most new users just pull at the curve like an elastic band and end up canceling their efforts after going too far. Put simply, the straight line graph represents the same 0–255 tonal scale but is arranged in a different way. Highlights are at bottom left, shadow at top right and midtone in the center. Like the Levels gamma slider, you control the contrast by pushing or pulling the center of the curve. Pushing upward decreases brightness and pulling downward increases brightness. If you have images which need only straightforward contrast adjustment overall, that's all you'll need to do.

Sampling a tone from your image

With smaller and individual tonal areas you can use the Curves controls to pick up or sample your desired tone. Once the dialog box is open, move your mouse outside the Curves dialog box into the image window and hover over the problem area. Next, press Control on your keyboard and click to load the exact tonal value as an editable point on the curve. This point can now be pushed or pulled, making the tone lighter or darker as desired. If the rest of the curve moves at the same time, you can click extra points on either side to lock down nearby tones and prevent unwanted adjustments.

Fixing a low contrast image [1]

This image of a cottage lacked vibrancy and saturated colors. To correct this, the curve was

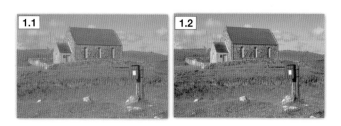

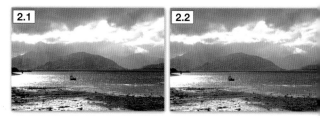

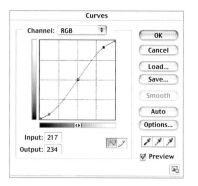

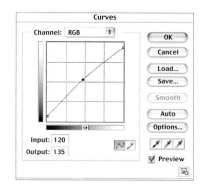

manipulated into a gentle sloping "S" shape as shown. It's essential to click on the central intersection to lock the midtones values first. Next, two extra points were made and dragged into place in the highlights, top right, and the shadows, bottom left. The resulting image shows a brightness without looking oversaturated.

Fixing a high contrast image · 2

With high contrast images, too much white and too much black can prove to be a challenge when printing out. This example of a seascape was dramatic but problematic and was manipulated into a much lower contrast by the following simple process. First, the existing highlight point at the top right of the graph was pulled downward until the whites were made slightly duller. Next the existing black shadow point was pushed upward to make the maximum shadow a lighter shade of gray. Finally the central midtone was pushed upward slightly to brighten the overall effect.

Fixing an underexposed image · 3

When too little light has fallen on the sensor, the result is a darker and duller image than expected. Curves can be used to rectify this simply by clicking a new point in the exact center of the graph and pushing upward. Only a slight push is necessary to enliven the image.

Fixing an overexposed image · 4

When your images are too bright, the Curves controls can be used to correct a simple shooting error. Click a new point in the center of the graph and pull this gently downward. The image will change instantly and will become darker in the midtones.

See also Photoshop toolbox *pages 166–169* / Contrast correction with Levels *pages 178–179* /

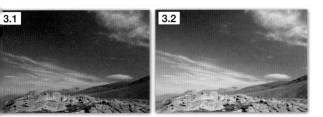

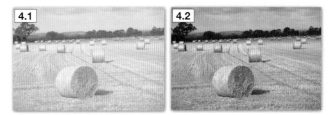

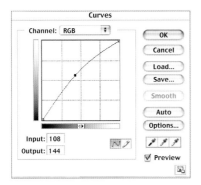

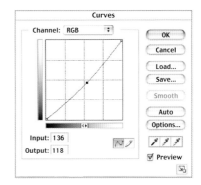

Color correction

Uncorrected images are characterized by dull muddy colors and a total loss of image detail.

The correction principles [1]

Faithful color reproduction is a never-ending task for graphics professionals and a process made much more complex by the introduction of an enormous variety of different cameras, scanners and printers, all working with different standards. Color casts can make an image look dull and muddy, preventing the bright colors expected. Such casts are easily removed, provided users understand the fundamental principles of the color wheel. In all color reproduction are six colors, broken into three opposite pairings: Red and Cyan, Magenta and Green, Blue and Yellow. A color cast will always be caused by an exaggerated amount of one of these six colors and can be removed simply by increasing the value of the opposite color until the cast disappears altogether. There is no mystery to the process, just a straightforward edit.

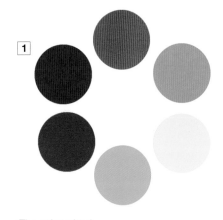

The color wheel.

See also Camera functions: color settings *pages 14–15 /* Photoshop toolbox *pages 166–169 /* Color gamut *pages 184–185 /* Color enhancing *pages 202–203 /*

Where to spot color casts [2]

The easiest place to spot a color cast is in the neutral color area of an image, ideally a gray midtone, since strong white highlights and deep black shadows, or a patch of fully saturated color will never show a cast in its true colors. If no such gray occurs, a skin tone area can also be used.

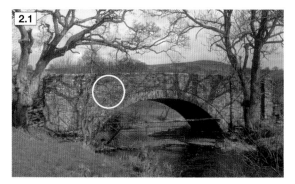

Casts are best observed in neutral tones. This image has a blue cast.

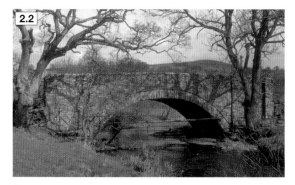

Once the cast is removed, the image looks brighter.

Using the Variations [3]

For those new to color correction, the Variations dialog is the best tool to use. Once selected, an image is displayed in six different variations with the original placed dead center. Casts are simply removed by clicking on the best-looking option and watching the central image change. Users have control over more delicate shifts in color by sliding the scale from Coarse toward Fine, and the best results are achieved working with the Midtone option selected. Pressing the Original option found at the top left of the box allows the user to start again from the beginning.

Using Color Balance controls 4

Users can have greater control using the less visual Color Balance dialog. The success of the command relies entirely on an ability to spot which color is causing the cast and knowing how to correct it. Corrections are made by increasing the value of the opposite color to the cast, the change becoming instantly visible in the image window. For removing casts from artificial light, corrections should be applied with the Highlight option selected. If digital-camera images have persistent color casts, it is worth checking that the white balance setting on the camera hasn't been switched to artificial light by mistake.

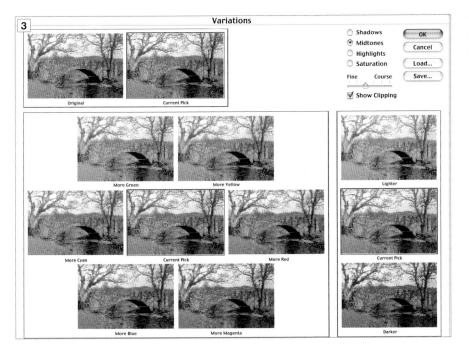

The Variations dialog is a good place to start color correction.

Color gamut

Each input and output device has its own set of limitations for displaying color, called a "gamut."

What is color gamut?

Printed images are viewed as reflected light, while monitors work by transmitting light to display RGB phosphors in often rich and intense colors. Color gamut is another way of describing those colors that fall outside the common color palette denominator between print and monitor. To compensate these colors are reproduced with less saturation than expected or in a slightly different hue. The range, or gamut, of a device can easily be accounted for by using one of Photoshop's many color-management functions, allowing mistakes to be anticipated before they happen.

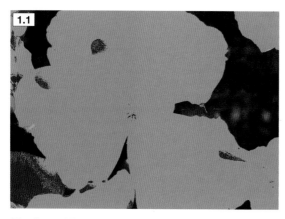

The Gamut Warning tags non-printing colors gray.

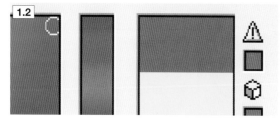

The Gamut Warning triangle appears when the color selected is outside the output device's capability.

How to identify problem colors [1]

There is often the temptation to increase color saturation in order to make images more vivid and intense, or to use richly colored tones to mimic traditional photographic prints, and both actions can lead to trouble. Problem colors are easily spotted by turning on one of two Gamut Warning controls. Once selected, the Gamut Warning option found under the View menu can be left on for the duration of any project and will instantly mark as gray any colors unlikely to print. It is a much better idea to have this selected from the outset, as gamut issues are easier dealt with as individual, ongoing corrections than as a giant, combined task at the end. A much more sophisticated kind of preview function is offered via the Proof Colors option found under the same View menu. This tool modifies the desktop appearance of an image to match the likely outcome in a chosen output media, such as a CMYK lithograph or even specific ink-jet paper types. The user's personal Proof Setup needs to be established before use by picking one of the output options identified under the Custom menu. Once set up, the Proof Colors option can be left switched on to prevent any false expectations.

How to cure gamut problems [2]

Once a gamut problem is identified, it can be cured using the tools within the Replace Color dialog. After the first appearance of gray, select Replace Color from the Image>Adjustments menu and click on any part of the gray area in the image. With the Selection Preview option displayed in the dialog, use the Fuzziness slider to identify the entire gamut area. Try reducing the Saturation as a first step, and if

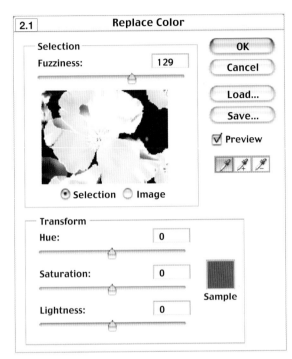

2.1 **Replace Color**

Selection
Fuzziness: 129

OK
Cancel
Load...
Save...
☑ Preview

⦿ Selection ◯ Image

Transform
Hue: 0
Saturation: 0
Lightness: 0

Sample

The Replace Color dialog offers the chance to reverse out of a gamut problem.

that doesn't work, try changing the Hue to a slightly different color. "Overcooked" images — where too much color manipulation has taken place — are difficult, if not impossible, to correct.

Printout problems

If prints still emerge from the printer with unexpected colors, try calibrating the monitor again and double-check Photoshop's Color Settings found under Photoshop>Color Settings.

See also Monitor calibration *pages 110–111* / Choosing color *pages 174–175* / Color correction *pages 182–183* /

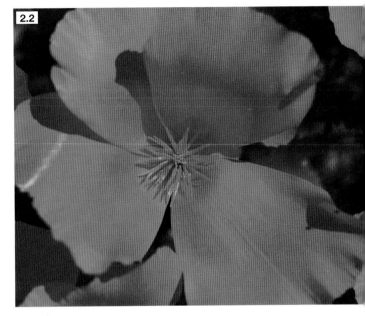

Before gamut correction.

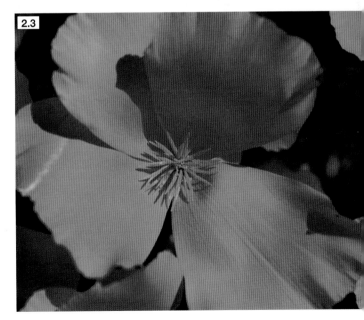

After gamut correction was applied.

Spotting and retouching

If photographs are ruined by the appearance of unwanted items, they can easily be painted out using the Clone Stamp tool.

The Clone Stamp tool 1

Common to both Photoshop and Photoshop Elements, the Clone Stamp tool offers a great way of exploring the magic of digital photography. It works by sampling or copying a section of an image then pasting it over another area — but in real time. Users who have foolishly attempted to paint out an area using an airbrush loaded with color will be familiar with the obvious and poor-quality results of that method. Images are constructed from intricate and complex color gradients that are impossible to reproduce with flat color. Unlike any other painting tool in the Photoshop toolbox, the Clone Stamp tool has no connection with any real-world painting technique and will feel like painting with a brush loaded with "image" rather than color. The real skill of the tool lies not in its application but in the selection of the starting sample area. The tool is perfect for removing physical scratches, dust and hair acquired from flatbed and film scans, and causes much less damage than quick-fix filters such as Despeckle or Dust and Scratches.

Like all other painting and drawing tools in the box, the Clone Stamp can be modified by brush size, shape and opacity and also by its blending mode, although its most useful work is done in the default Normal Blending mode.

Using the tool for retouching 2

With the Clone Stamp tool positioned over to the chosen sample area, press and hold the Alt key and click the mouse once — the tool icon will change as the sample is made. Move the tool cursor away from the sample point and position it over the area chosen for removal. A tiny crosshair will appear to indicate part of the image being sampled. Soft-edged brushes are easier to use at first, but hard-edged ones will cause less blurring of image detail.

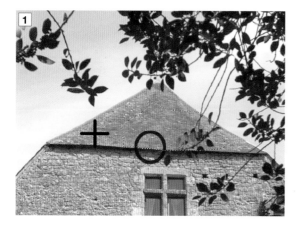

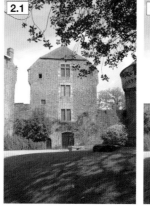

An original image before retouching.

The same image following the removal of some branches.

Using Aligned mode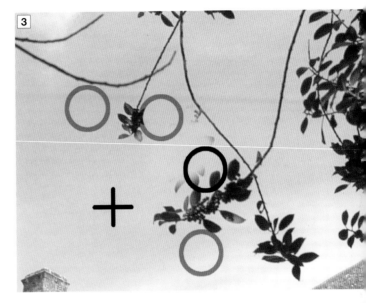

Aligned mode allows the user to continue retouching in a different part of the image, but fixes the distance from sample area to painting area. This means it is essential to watch both what is being copied and where it is being pasted. If the sample point isn't changed regularly, a repeat "herringbone" pattern will appear.

Using Non-aligned mode

Non-aligned mode is set when the Aligned box is left unchecked and allows repeated use of the same sample area in different parts of an image. This is a good technique to use for cloning patterned areas such as foliage or clouds, but will not work well on color gradients.

Working within selection areas

To make retouching more accurate and to stop it from spilling over into unwanted areas of an image, make a selection first to limit its effects. This restricts the painting area precisely, and is ideal for geometric shapes and other hard edges.

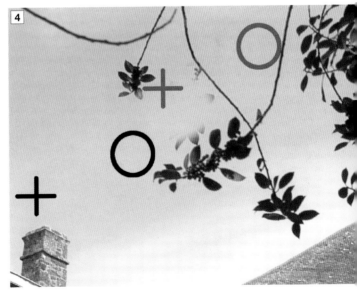

See also Photoshop toolbox *pages 166–169* / Selections *pages 172–173* /

Burning In and emphasis

Adopted from the time-honored skills of the darkroom printer, burning in and dodging help emphasize the main subjects in an image.

What emphasis means

The best traditional photographs undergo an additional stage in the darkroom where individual areas are darkened (burned) and lightened (dodged) to create a much more sophisticated result. Neither natural nor studio light will ever fully draw out each individual part of an image, so this is added afterward. Just like the moody dark and light effect or "chiaroscuro" used by great painters like Rembrandt, burning and dodging can help an image look more three-dimensional. In addition, offending image areas can be darkened down and made less noticeable by burning in, focusing more of the viewer's attention on the main subject. For minor problems caused by shadows or camera exposure, dodging can brighten things up.

The Burning In and Dodging tools 1

Photoshop provides two instruments for emphasizing local areas; the Burning In and Dodging tools. Unfortunately, both tools work with brush characteristics and are limited to regular shapes and standard brush properties. While fine for amending smaller areas of an image, these effects can become visible as a series of circular shapes if used excessively.

Using selections 2

A much more versatile way of doing the same task is to work within hand-drawn selection areas. Selections are made in any shape and, most importantly, to fit exactly the area that needs changing. Using the Lasso tool, selection shapes

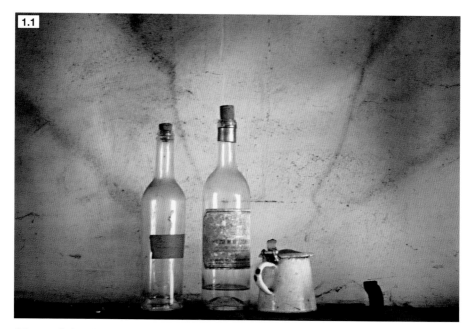

1.1

After gentle burning in, this image looks much more atmospheric.

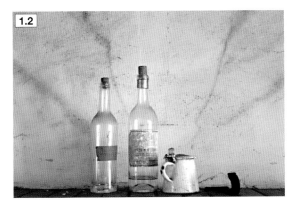

The raw and unedited image.

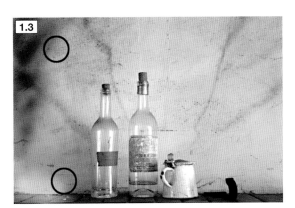

Blotches appear when using Burning In and Dodging tools.

are easily drawn and then softened using the Feather command. Once complete, the area is darkened or lightened using the Brightness slider found in the Brightness/Contrast dialog box. The Brightness command applies the same rate of change to each pixel within the selected area, creating a gradual

rather than posterized result. To mimic the look of a hand-printed photograph, this technique should be applied gradually over several steps rather than in one crude jump. For an even more intuitive working method, deselect Extras from the View menu to hide the marching ants selection line.

Emphasis essentials

For all photographs — color and black and white — darkening the edges helps draw attention to the photograph's central characters. This only needs to be done gently and will appear false if overdone. Empty blank spaces can easily be burned in to prevent attention from wandering, and is best achieved by repeatedly diminishing selections in the same area. Of course, photographers who have spent time in the darkroom dodging and burning with pieces of scrap card will be familiar with this process.

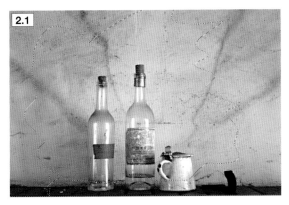

Better results can be achieved using selections.

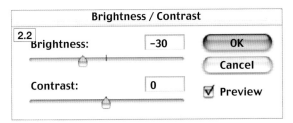

The Brightness slider is used to darken or brighten selection areas.

See also Photoshop toolbox *pages 166–169* / Selections *pages 172–173* /

Sharpening

The magical sharpening tools can be used to tweak an image into fine focus, but cannot be used to correct camera shake or badly focused work.

How sharpening works

Sharpening is nothing more than increasing the level of contrast between edge pixels. In a soft-focused image, colors are muted at the edges of shapes, while in a pin-sharp example, colors are more delineated and have inherently more contrast. Digital-camera images are often soft owing to the anti-alias filter fixed in front of the sensor to prevent jaggy pixel staircasing. All images benefit from software sharpening, applied as the final stage just before printing. Applied too early in an edit, and artifacts caused by sharpening will become magnified, destroying the image quality. All images should be sharpened after resizing, up or down, as interpolation causes an inevitable loss of original image detail. Photoshop has four sharpening filters — Sharpen, Sharpen More, Sharpen Edges and the Unsharp Mask (USM) — all of which can be applied to the image

overall or to a smaller selection area. Only the Unsharp Mask filter can be modified to address the exact problem posed by individual images.

The Unsharp Mask tool   1

Found under the Filter>Sharpen>Unsharp Mask command, the USM has three controls: Amount, Radius, and Threshold. Amount describes the extent of change to pixel color contrast. The Radius slider determines the number of pixels surrounding an edge pixel, with low values defining a narrow band and high values creating a thicker edge. The final control, Threshold, determines how different a pixel is from its neighbors before sharpening is applied. At a zero threshold, all pixels in an image are sharpened, resulting in a noisy and unsatisfactory image. Set at a higher value, less visible defects will occur overall.

See also Camera functions: color settings *pages 14–15* / Photoshop toolbox *pages 166–169* /

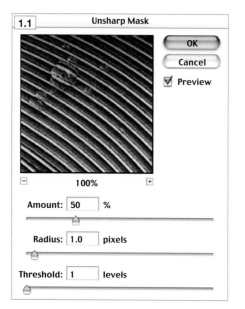

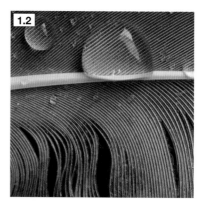

An unsharpened image.

Nine variations using the Unsharp Mask filter.

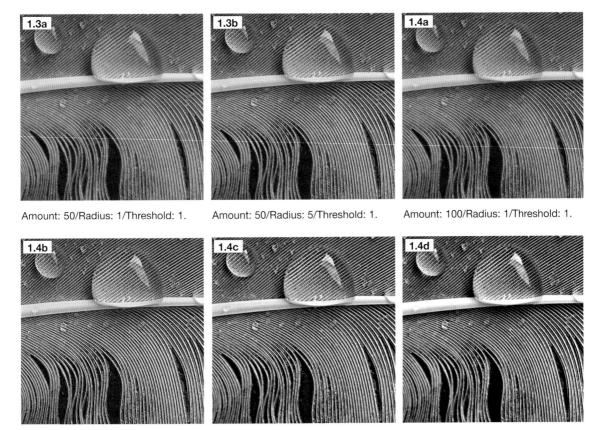

Amount: 50/Radius: 1/Threshold: 1. Amount: 50/Radius: 5/Threshold: 1. Amount: 100/Radius: 1/Threshold: 1.

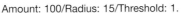

Amount: 100/Radius: 5/Threshold: 1. Amount: 100/Radius: 15/Threshold: 1. Amount: 100/Radius: 50/Threshold: 1.

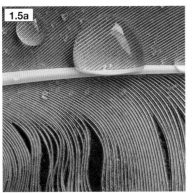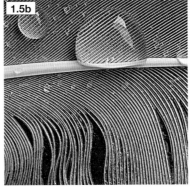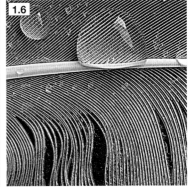

Amount: 200/Radius: 1/Threshold: 1. Amount: 200/Radius: 5/Threshold: 1. Amount: 400/Radius: 5/Threshold: 1.

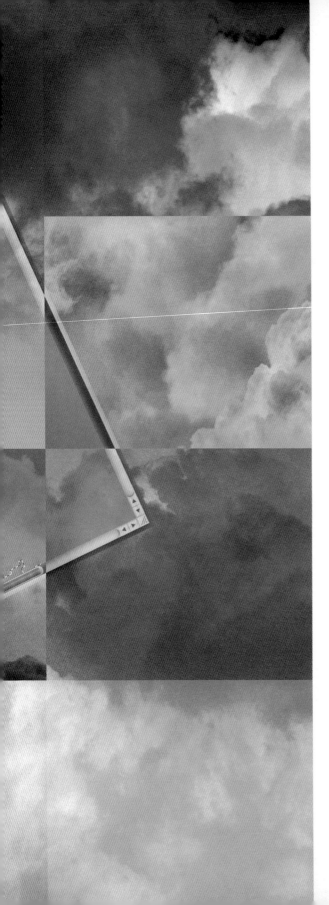

8 Creative Photoshop

Simple toning

Digital toning involves the conversion of an RGB color image into a single color and can be used to dramatic effect.

Changing to sepia

There are various ways that an overall single color tone can be applied to a digital photograph, but the Colorize command — found in the Hue/Saturation dialog box — is by far the easiest. For photographs captured by a digital camera, there is no need to change the image mode from RGB to grayscale, unless the photograph is a monochrome scan in the Grayscale mode, in which case it is essential to convert to RGB mode first. All contrast and lightness corrections should be made in the Levels dialog before applying a new color and all shadow and midtone detail must be clearly visible.

The Hue/Saturation dialog box

Found under the Image>Adjustments menu, the Hue/Saturation dialog presents an array of useful tools and gadgets. Users should work on the Master channel — in the Edit drop-down menu at the top of the palette — which applies a tone to the overall image rather than to just one individual color channel. Choosing both Preview and Colorize options — found on the bottom right of the dialog — presents

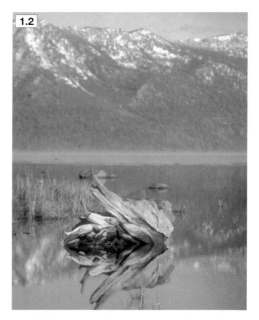

An RGB image was taken as the starting point.

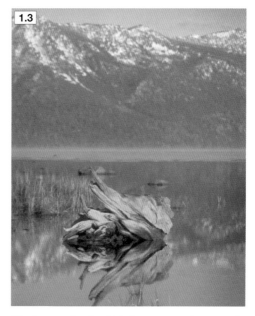

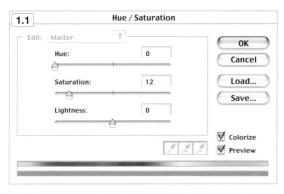

The Colorize check box is the key to this command.

The image after the Colorize command was made.

an immediate transformation of the color image into a toned monochrome. If the image looks too saturated at this early stage, use the Saturation slider to decrease the intensity of color down to a value of 15–25, with the lower saturation settings producing the most subtle and delicate results. Any more than this will result in the appearance of color artifacts in the image, which will be impossible to remove at a later time. Once satisfied with the saturation, select color by moving the Hue slider until a brown or sepia color appears to enhance the image. If all the necessary contrast adjustments were made beforehand, there is no need to use the crude Lightness slider at the base of the dialog.

Applying tone into three sectors   2

Another, more complex, method for applying color tones to an image is to use the Color Balance sliders. Unlike the Hue/Saturation slider, this method allows users to apply different amounts of color in the highlight, midtone and shadow areas separately. First, the existing image color needs to be drained away by using the Image>Adjustments>Desaturate command. This leaves a monochrome image in an RGB color space, so the next step is to pick the Color Balance dialog. New color is applied by sliding the color sliders, checking the midtone option first, then adding subsequent color to the highlights and shadows in the same way.

See also Image modes *pages 80–81* / Photoshop toolbox *pages 166–169* / Choosing color *pages 174–175* / Duotones *pages 196–197* /

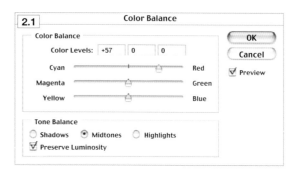

Different colors can be introduced into three tonal sectors by clicking on the Shadows, Midtones and Highlights buttons.

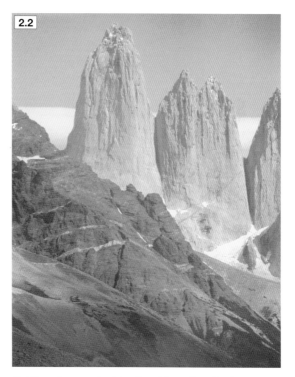

Subtle colors can be introduced to make a landscape image more interesting.

Duotones

Working in the duotone mode allows greater control over image color and tone.

Without doubt, duotones are the best way to tone a digital image and are in part based on a traditional process used in the lithographic printing industry to reproduce toned monochrome photographs for books and posters. Photoshop is packaged with several preset duotone recipe files which can be applied directly to any image and then printed out on any desktop digital printer. The duotone process is based on the use of two colors — usually black and one other color — and even more advanced effects can be applied in the three-color Tritone and four-color Quadtone image modes. The best aspect of applying tone in this way is that users can work with a set of colors, manipulating each one in up to ten different tonal sectors between highlight and shadow.

Using duotones

The image should be converted to grayscale first, and then Duotone selected from the same mode menu. Selecting Duotone from the Type drop-down menu will set black as the base color by default. The color

The Duotone Options dialog box.

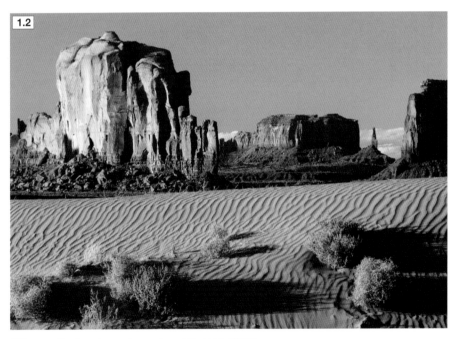

Tritones offer the chance to create subtle tone effects.

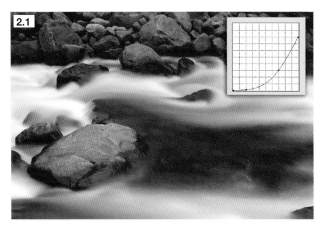

This image shows the effect of orange ink reduced in the highlight areas.

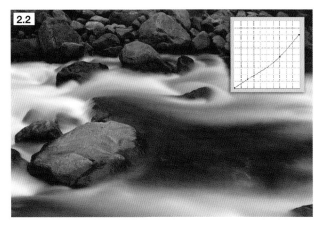

A second variation shows a more prominent orange resulting from a different curve.

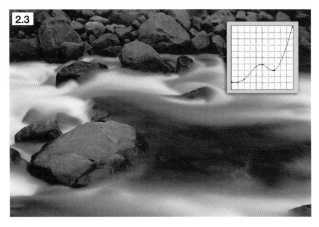

An unusual effect created by making peaks and troughs in the curve.

selection is then made for tone by clicking in the color box, found to the right of the tiny curve icon, and using the Picker — or any of Photoshop's custom color palettes, such as Pantone. A bright color will demonstrate the change immediately.

Using the duotone curves   1

The appearance of this new color is modified by clicking on the tiny curve icon to the right of the Ink 2 text. The duotone curve shows a graph divided into ten sectors, with each square representing a 10% increase in tone. Highlight is 0%, giving white, and shadow is 100%, producing black. The diagonal line means that each original grayscale value is substituted with the same percentage of the new selected color, although this is easily changed by one of the following methods: The first is to click any point on the diagonal line and push or pull the curve up or down. Pushing the curve up will make the new color more prominent, while pulling it down makes it less evident; the second method, for more experienced users, is to change the curve, and therefore the color intensity, by typing numbers directly into the individual text boxes.

Variations on a single color   2

These three images show three variations on a single color using the duotone curves.

See also Photoshop toolbox *pages 166–169* / Choosing color *pages 174–175* / Simple toning *pages 194–195* /

Channel Mixer

The Channel Mixer can be used to mimic specialized photographic films such as black-and-white infrared.

Intensifying colors

Infrared film is an old favorite among landscape photographers, as it changes the dull greens of foliage into bright whites, creating an eerie effect. The result can be perfectly mimicked by the Channel Mixer with a little color intensification beforehand. An image with a good range of green foliage and a blue sky will demonstrate this to maximum effect. For the best results, it is essential to increase the color saturation of all the green items in the original image. There is no need to make a complex selection of green items by area, since they can be selected, instead, on the basis of their unique color by making an Image>Adjustments>Hue/Saturation command. Selecting the Green option from the Edit drop-down menu at the top of the dialog box restricts the edit to one color. Move the Saturation slider to the right-hand side of the scale to increase the saturation, taking it further than for a normal photograph, up to a maximum of +50.

Using the Channel Mixer [1]

The Channel Mixer dialog is then selected to convert the color image into an infrared effect. The Channel Mixer allows users to re-establish the exact amount of each color in its individual color channel, so that green can appear darker or lighter than it would do after a straightforward RGB to grayscale conversion. This is done by clicking on the Monochrome check box where, for example, the quantity of Green can be increased to the maximum +200% while Red and Blue are both reduced to –50. There is no hard-and-fast rule about using the Channel Mixer settings, but a final figure of 100 should be reached once the new totals are added up.

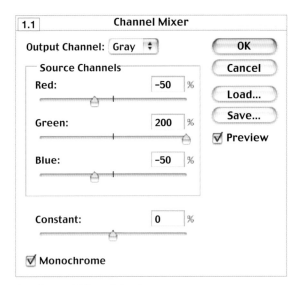

The Channel Mixer dialog box.

Using the Channel Mixer to remix color [2]

As with false-color photographic film, the original color channels of a digital image can be remixed to create unique results. The principle involves changing the quantities of each source color with a new color in order to create effects not seen before using conventional photographic or reprographic techniques. With the example on the right, different effects were applied to change original colors without creating gamut problems or pixel artifacts. Slight color shifts are always much more preferable to exaggerated ones and will print better, too. Special recipes can be saved and applied to future images by clicking on the Save button before quitting.

See also Photoshop toolbox *pages 166–169* / Color gamut *pages 184–185* / Monochrome conversion *pages 200–201* /

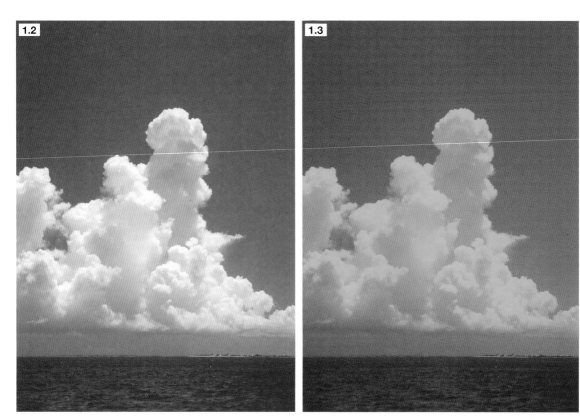

A normal RGB color image.

The same image following a color channel adjustment.

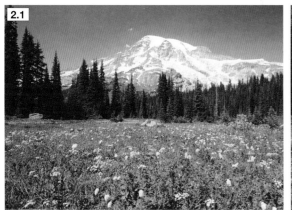

A slightly flat color original.

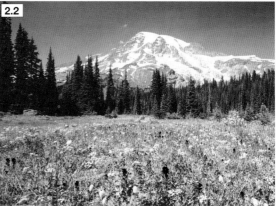

The same image changed into a dynamic monochrome.

Monochrome conversion

Changing color images to monochrome grayscale will leave most digital photographers dissatisfied with the results — but there are alternatives.

Many digital camera images would look much better in atmospheric black and white but, because grayscale is not available as a shooting mode, RGB images have to be converted on returning from a shoot. With the countless possibilities digital color manipulation affords, it is easy to reinterpret a color image as a punchy monochrome using a method other than a simple mode change. Complex color-to-mono conversions can enhance the individual color channels of an image, making the colors darker or lighter than they were in the original subject.

Straight mode conversion 1

Converted from RGB color mode to Grayscale mode, this image has resulted in a muddy and uninspiring variation. Previously bright colors have been interpreted badly, leaving a washed out and disappointing image with little tonal separation. Just like a bad machine-made photographic print on poor-quality paper, all original emphasis has been drained away. An identical effect results if the RGB image is put through the Image>Adjustments> Desaturate command.

See also Image modes *pages 80–81* / Photoshop toolbox *pages 166–169* / Channel Mixer *pages 198–199* /

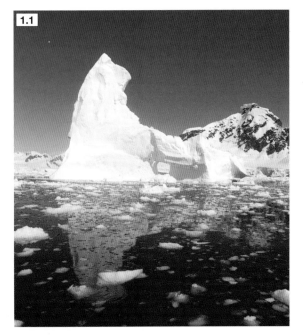

An RGB color image as the starting point.

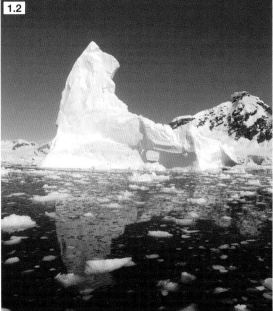

The same image following conversion to grayscale.

Converting to LAB mode

A far better way to avoid drab results is to convert the RGB color image to a different color mode — the LAB mode — a theoretical color space unrelated to any input or output device, which works by separating two color channels from a brightness channel. Following the mode conversion, leave the Channels palette open and discard both A and B color channels by dragging them into the palette wastebasket. Only the Lightness channel remains, together with a brighter result. The image must be converted back to grayscale or to RGB in order to use the full range of Photoshop's tools.

Converting with the Channel Mixer

3

The most inspirational way to make stylish tonal conversions is to use Photoshop's Channel Mixer. Found under Image>Adjustments>Channel Mixer, this dialog box offers users the chance to vary the intensity of original image colors. The variety of achievable results runs from a high-contrast and high-impact monochrome to a softer, subtler color conversion. The key to the dialog box lies within the new values selected. To make a conversion, click the Monochrome check box in the bottom left-hand corner of the dialog and pick a color to emphasize. Decreasing the value in the box darkens the color, while increasing the value lightens it. As each command is made, it is important not to forget that the collective values of the Red, Green and Blue Source Channel text boxes must be 100.

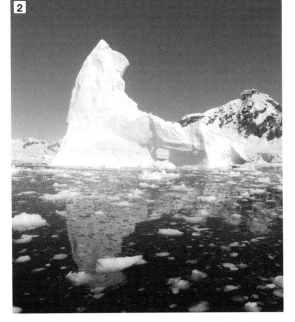

The same image following conversion to LAB mode.

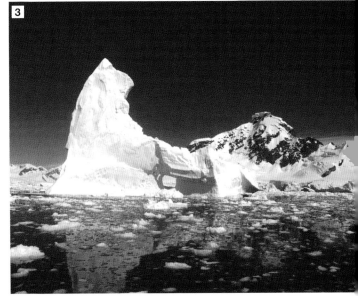

The same image converted using the Channel Mixer.

Color enhancing

Changing the colors in a digital image can produce crude and obvious results if the wrong tools and processes are used.

Warming images up ☐1

Shooting with a full-on flash in cloudy or dull weather will make most images appear bluish and cold. These images are less appealing to look at compared to those taken in sunnier, warmer weather conditions. In conventional, film-based photography, the problem is often counteracted by screwing on a delicate, orange warm-up filter over the camera lens. In digital photography, the solution is simpler still, using the color-correction tools found in the Image>Adjustments menu. If an image appears cold, select the Color Balance option and gradually increase both the Yellow and the Red until the image begins to look noticeably warmer. As a guideline, the value change should read no more than 20 on the scale.

Selective color change

The Selective Color dialog box allows users to control RGB, CMYK and black and white in an image without the need for drawing a complex and time-consuming selection. The Selective Color command is used to pick out all pixels that fall under the color chosen for edit before any edit is made. This is a useful process for making blue skies bluer, but wild color shifts will not always look convincing.

Using Hue/Saturation ☐2

The Hue/Saturation dialog is used to make finer color selections than the Selective Color command. Once the edit color has been identified from the Edit drop-down menu found at the top of the dialog, the precise range of colors can be modified by moving the tiny sliders found within the color gradients at the bottom of the box.

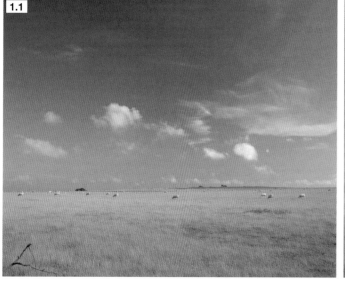

1.1

1.2

An unprocessed, raw file from a digital camera.

The same image following a Color Balance adjustment.

An uncorrected image.

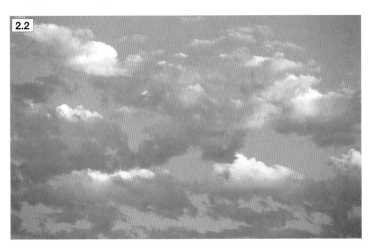

A variation with blues changed to violets.

The same image following a reduction in saturation.

Using adjustment layers

For users who are uncertain about committing to a color change — preferring to return to the adjustment at a later time — the adjustment-layer function is a very useful way of working. Adjustment layers do not contain pixels like all other layers, but contain settings instead. There are many adjustment-layer options for preserving settings without relying on the History palette, which can easily purge a state well into a project. From the Layers menu, choose New Adjustment Layer, make an edit and press OK. The setting is preserved as a layer within the Layers palette, and can be recalled at any time by double-clicking on its layer icon. Holes can even be cut through adjustment layers with the Eraser tool, allowing other layers to show through.

See also Photoshop toolbox *pages 166–169* / Layers *pages 170–171* / Color correction *pages 182–183* /

Hand tinting

For those who want to recreate the look of a hand-tinted photographic print, the effect can be achieved with a few simple commands common to all leading applications.

Preparation

The starting point needs to be a desaturated RGB image, so if the original is in RGB color all original colors should first be drained by doing Image>Adjustments>Desaturate. If the starting point is a grayscale image, the procedure is Image>Mode>RGB Color. The image should not be too dark at this stage or the hand-coloring will look dull and lifeless. Any brightness corrections should be made using the Levels dialog before painting. It is also advisable to make a background Layer copy to work on just in case a mistake is made.

Selecting color   1

Select the Paintbrush tool and give it a soft-edged brush shape. Change the tool's default blending mode from Normal to Color, then reduce the slider to 10%. The Color Blending mode enables a delicate color tint to be dropped onto the image while still preserving underlying image detail — unlike the normal color mode which smears away the image. The Opacity option helps keep colors delicate and less obvious. For this kind of project, it is a good idea to choose working colors from the more convenient Color Swatches palette, which can be left on the desktop for faster access.

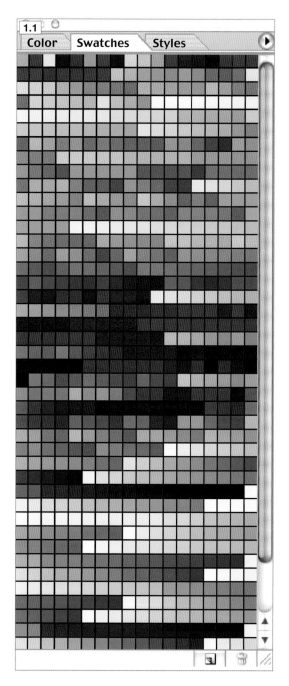

Compared to the Color Picker, the Swatches palette offers a quicker method of selecting color.

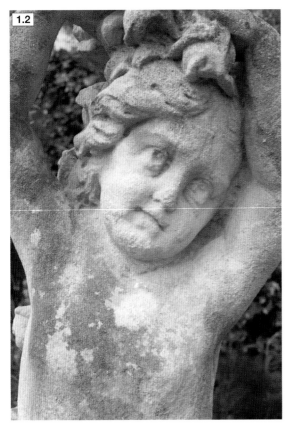

1.2

A desaturated original.

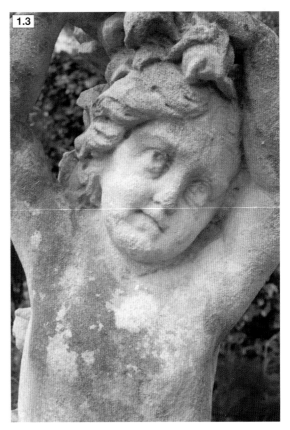

1.3

The same image painted in the Color Blending mode.

Painting

Apply color to the midtone areas of an image only, since shadows will remain largely unaffected. Any mistakes can be removed simply by painting over them with a different color, which removes the previous color as if by magic. When working in Color Blending mode, colors do not mix with each other, they simply cancel each other out.

Using the History brush

The History brush is a remarkable tool that can be used to paint back a previous state, held in the History palette, or any saved "snapshot" that has been taken along the way. A snapshot is a fully saved image state that can be accessed should users want

the option to see a few final variations, or to save several states for later assembly in an animation sequence. The History brush can also be used to bring back an area of original color once an image has been toned or turned into monochrome, in order to create an effective mixture between the two. The tool works just like an eraser, rubbing away previous commands rather than pixel layers.

See also Image modes *pages 80–81* / Photoshop toolbox *pages 166–169* / Layers *pages 170–171* /

Textured backgrounds

For images with the look and feel of a watercolor print, you can cheat a little by using Photoshop's layer-blending modes.

Scanning the source paper   1

Choose an interesting piece of textured or printed paper and scan it using a flatbed scanner. If you want to preserve original colors, then capture in RGB mode, but if it is essentially a single color, like a sheet of writing paper, use Grayscale mode. It is best to make a high-resolution scan large enough to output at 11 x 17 inches, which can be chopped down to size at a later date. Set the scanner input resolution to 300dpi and leave all contrast controls alone.

Modifying imperfect papers   2

It is not essential to scan paper materials that are entirely perfect. After scanning, imperfections — or even large areas of original detail — are easily removed by using the Rubber Stamp tool. Paper shape is unlikely to match the digital image, and this is also simple to modify by cropping with the Crop tool. Paper color can be changed, too, using the Colorize command in the Hue/Saturation dialog box. The example below shows a sheet of textured paper ripped from a book bought at a yard sale. Once scanned, it was enhanced using Levels to make it brighter, while bringing out the rough texture.

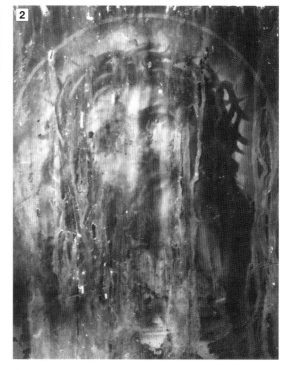

Antique writing paper was used for the background.

This distressed image was used as the overlay.

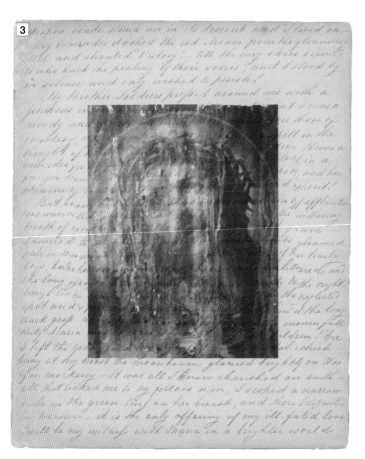

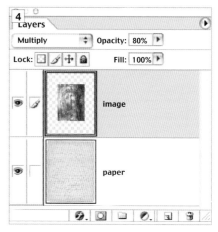

See also Image modes *pages 80–81* / Flatbed scanner interface *pages 124–125* / Layers *pages 170–171* / Cropping and image size *pages 176–177* /

The result of combining and blending the two images.

Applying the image 3

Open the chosen photographic image and make all required contrast and color adjustments. An image with obvious bright highlight areas is best, since these will be replaced by the color and texture of the scanned paper. Keep the textured paper image open on the desktop and simply copy and paste the photographic image on top of it to create an extra layer. The two images will not necessarily be the same size, so use the Transform tool to scale down the photographic image until it sits comfortably in the middle of the textured paper and has a generous border.

Blending the image 4

The next stage is to blend the image in with the textured paper. First change its Layer blending mode — found in the drop-down menu at the top left of the Layers palette — from Normal to Multiply. This has the immediate effect of dropping all highlights that are lighter than the underlying textured paper layer. Now both paper and image layers are merged perfectly together. If the match does not yet look right, reducing the Saturation of the underlying paper layer and the Opacity of the image layer to about 80% are both functions that will merge the layers together further.

Focus effects

In just a few simple steps, Photoshop can emphasize subjects by mimicking the effects of a camera-lens focus.

The Blur tool

The simplest tool to use for applying selective sharpness and focus is the Blur tool. Used with standard brush properties, this is best employed for making minor background corrections when unexpected details appear to take the emphasis away from the main subject. The Blur tool simply merges surrounding pixels into softer and lower-contrast patches, and can look obvious when applied to larger and more prominent areas. The tool is very useful on portrait photographs, where specific sharp details

need to look less distracting. Easier than retouching with the Rubber Stamp tool, blurring retains original pixel colors and hides any mistakes made by the photographer.

Selective zone sharpness

More convincing results can be achieved using the Gaussian Blur tool within carefully selected areas. Just like the depth-of-field effects that result from using a wide-aperture setting on a camera lens, this effect reproduces the ever-shifting zones of

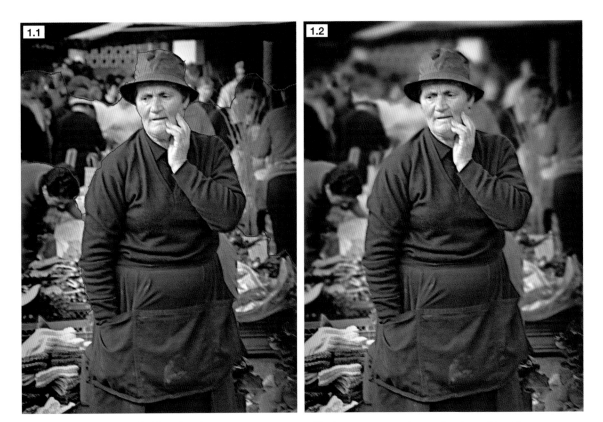

This image has been divided into four focus zones.

The image once each zone has been blurred.

sharpness. The key to this technique is to identify the different zones before doing any sharpening, then apply successively larger Gaussian blurs as you get further into the background.

Making the zones 1

Examine the photograph first and determine at least three different zones receding away from the main subject. Use any of the selecting tools to make a careful selection of each zone and save the selections using the Select>Save Selection command. Each saved selection can be reloaded by repeating the command.

Blurring the zones 2

A much better way of applying the Gaussian Blur filter to each zone is to first Edit>Cut then Edit>Paste each zone into its own individual layer rather than applying the Blur filter to three selection areas in the same layer. The results will not display the telltale sign of the filter creating a slightly different effect at the edge of the selection, but will look seamless and much more convincing. The layers will need reorganizing so that the background layer sits on the top, with the last of the zones sitting in the place normally reserved for the background layer. Each layer needs a recognizable name first, and each layer should have an increasing amount of Gaussian blur applied until the shallow depth of field is created. If any edges look false, use the Eraser tool to rub away edge detail, thus revealing underlying layers.

See also Aperture and depth of field *pages 42–43* / Photoshop toolbox *pages 166–169* / Selections *pages 172–173* /

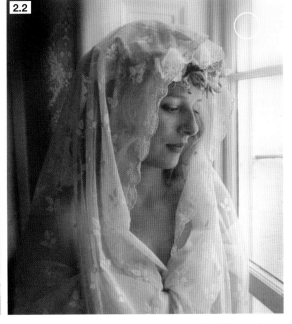

This image has a distracting background.

Sharp detail can be softened easily with the Blur tool.

Texture filters

Digital filters allow you the freedom to vary the visibility of special effects, but unlike conventional cameras, the process is much more reversible.

All digital imaging software applications have a set of filters that can be applied to the overall image, individual layers or even smaller selections. Filters work by applying a precise mathematical formula to each and every pixel in the bitmap, changing their color or position. As such, the results can appear predictable and obvious, just like an old-fashioned screw-on starburst filter for a traditional film camera. But used with caution and care, filters can provide added interest to your digital

photographs. For advanced users, special additional filter sets, such as Xenofex and Corel KPT, can be purchased as plug-ins for Photoshop and other major applications.

Watercolor filter [1]

The Watercolor filter is one of the many artistic filters that apply a brushmark to digital photographs to create hand-crafted effects. The Watercolor filter, unlike others, has a useful dialog box, which can be used to vary brush detail, shadow intensity and texture. The effect in this image was completed using an additional watercolor edge effect from the Extensis PhotoFrame plug-in.

See also Image modes *pages 80–81* / Photoshop toolbox *pages 166–169* / Artistic filters *pages 214–215* /

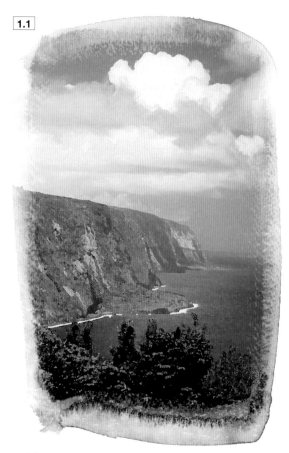

1.1

A landscape image with a Watercolor filter applied.

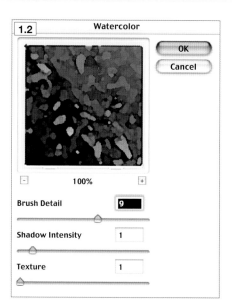

1.2 Watercolor

The Watercolor filter dialog box.

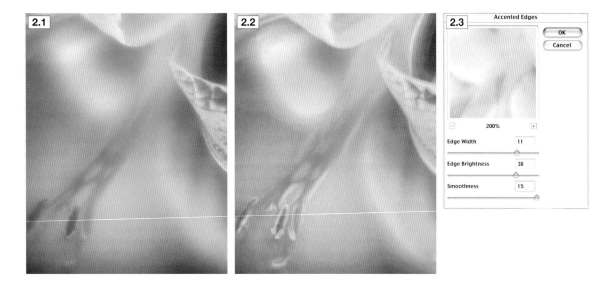

2.1   2.2   2.3 Accented Edges

Brushstroke   2

If you enjoy painting and drawing, then the Brushstroke filters will help make a link between traditional artwork and photography. The results of the Brushstroke filters rely purely on the edges and level of contrast already present in your original digital photograph, giving different results on different images. Experiment by applying a Gaussian Blur filter beforehand to soften sharply focused originals. This example was a close-up soft focus of a flower, which was enhanced with an Accented Edges filter.

Texturizer   3

The Texturizer filters offer a comprehensive set of controls for applying canvas, stone and burlap effects to your original. The filters work best on images that do not have intricate detail or sharpness, as this example shows. Additional texture files can be retrieved from a Samples folder via the dialog box, so you can draw from a greater range of materials. If you do want to create a canvas painting effect, make sure you choose a suitable subject, like a still-life or floral arrangement, for a more convincing result.

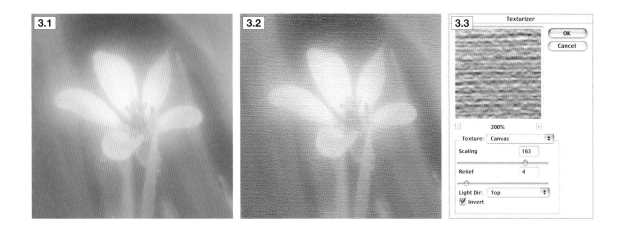

3.1   3.2   3.3 Texturizer

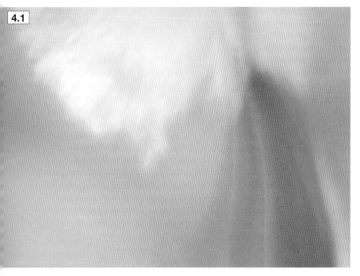

4.1

A delicately colored original image.

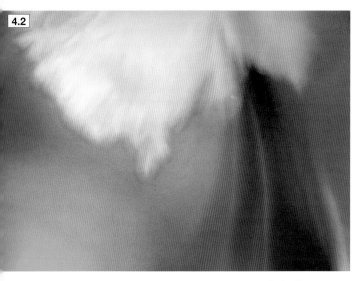

4.2

The same image after enhancing with a Fade filter command.

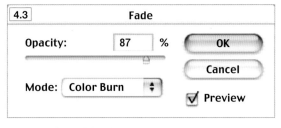

The Fade filter dialog box.

Fading filters

A useful tool for lessening the obvious effects of an overall filter is the Fade filter command. This can be selected from the Filter menu immediately after your filter has been applied. The Fade dialog presents you with the familiar opacity slider and blending modes, as found in the Layers palette. This example started as a diffused flower close-up, then was filtered using Paint Daubs to create a painterly texture. Finally, the Fade filter was employed with both a reduced Opacity and a Burn Blending mode. The Fade dialog is the best control if you want the filtering to look skilful and sensitive.

Filter problems

All filters are available when working in the RGB color mode, but the set will reduce when editing CMYK, Grayscale, LAB or Index mode images. If editing a 16-bit-per-channel image, all of the filters will be out of use. If the filters still seem unavailable, double-check that you are not working on a type or vector layer by mistake.

Filtering in small areas

It is possible to filter smaller selection areas but a much better way to assign the effects of a filter is to apply it to a duplicate layer. Once applied, cut away the excess layer areas with the Eraser tool and let it float over the background layer, while using the Layer variables such as Opacity and Blending modes to make it look convincing.

Blending filters 5

In addition to the Fade filter command, filters can also be modified using the same Blending modes found in Layers. Blending modes can produce very unexpected results by merging the effect with its selection area or layer.

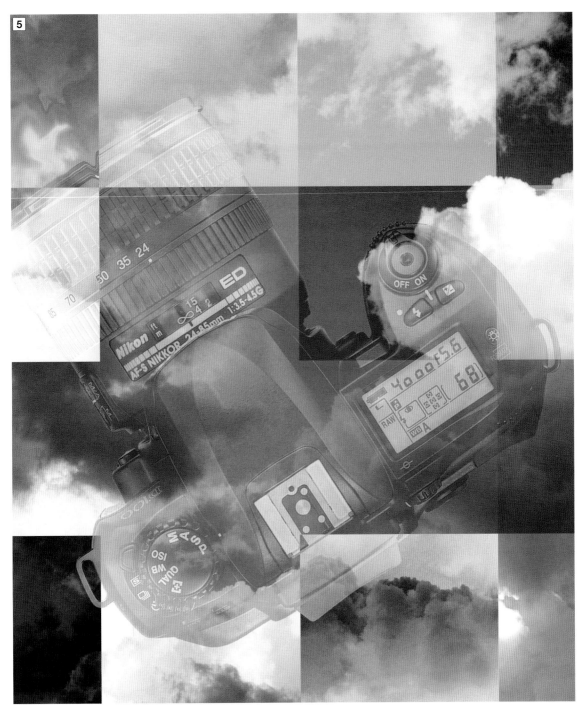

Filtering can also be applied in smaller selection areas rather than across the entire image.

Artistic filters

Software filters work in exactly the same way as conventional camera filters but have the additional advantage of variable intensity.

Artistic filters

The artistic filter set offers fifteen different ways to create a handmade look and painterly effect to images. With paintbrush, pencils and pastel a good starting point for minimal or simplified compositions like a still life or a sparse landscape, these filters will remove most fine details. Most have additional tools within a dialog box such as brush size, stroke length and background texture.

Painting brushes 1

Like the artistic filter set, the brushstrokes offer an additional range of paint application effects such as Spatter, Sumi-e and Sprayed strokes. Brushstroke filters are useful for making rough edge effects when applied to a narrow selection area around the perimeter of an image. The Sumi-e effect creates a heavily textured edge and very painterly effects.

Blur filters 2

Both creative and corrective functions can be achieved using these filters, which work by merging pixel colors together. Gaussian Blur and Motion Blur offer an excellent way of creating depth of field and movement effects, and both can be used on rasterized type layers to good effect. With this example, a static sky was given the appearance of movement by applying the Motion Blur filter to a selection area. In the Motion Blur dialog box, the Angle control offers a chance to determine the sweeping direction of the movement. With this effect it is possible to mimic the look of a slow shutter speed or panning technique.

See also Photoshop toolbox *pages 166–169* / Focus effects *pages 208–209* /

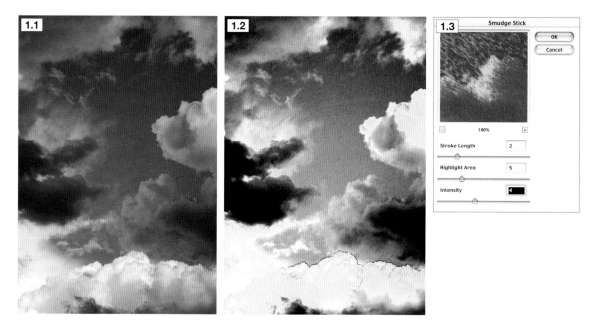

1.1

1.2

1.3 Smudge Stick

OK
Cancel

100%

Stroke Length 2

Highlight Area 5

Intensity 4

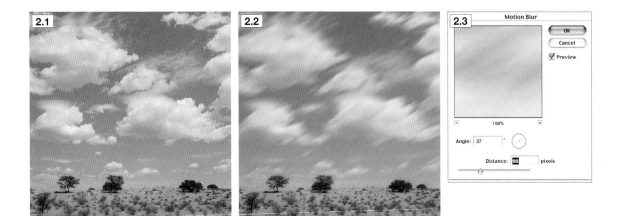

Dust and scratches filter [3]

Old negatives and transparencies can often become dusty and can be very difficult to scan properly. On a high-resolution scan, dust will show up as a white or black mark and will need painstaking retouching with the Rubber Stamp tool. Yet when faced with an enormous task, as this example shows, a quicker method is to use the Dust and Scratches filter. This filter works by blurring the colors of adjacent pixels until rogue black and white marks are blended in with their surroundings. As this process leads to a slight softening of the focus, it should only be applied to areas which are less visibly important, such as a sky. The filter is best used within a selected area, with the Radius value gradually increased until all marks disappear.

Applying filters to duplicate layers

If you are uncertain about the effects of your filtering, make a duplicate layer and apply the filter to this rather than the underlying original. The advantage of working on a duplicate layer is that you can use the Eraser tool to cut holes through the filtered layer to reveal unfiltered parts underneath.

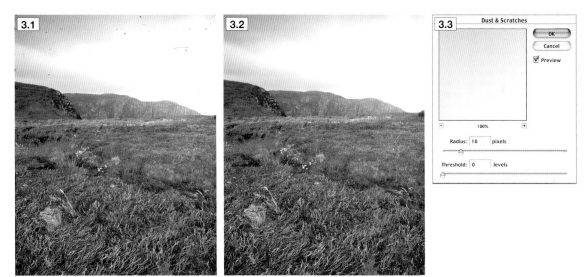

Simple edges

Photoshop can be used in many different ways to create stylish borders and customized edges.

Selection edges   1

Selection perimeters can also be made into an outline of variable thickness and color to become a useful border for containing an image. After choosing Edit>Select>All, set the foreground color to black, then do Edit>Stroke and apply a five-pixel width to create a simple black edge.

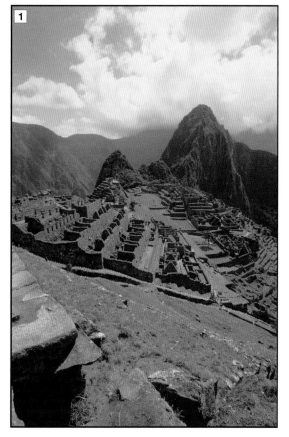

A stroked outline edge effect.

Beveled borders   2

Selection edges can also be modified using an additional Select>Modify>Border command, followed by Edit>Stroke to create a beveled edge effect. Experiment with blending modes, such as Difference or Multiply, to see how the border merges into the background image.

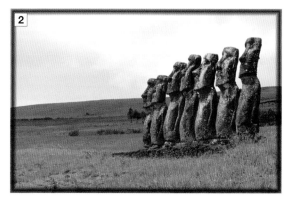

A beveled edge effect.

Colored borders   3

Users can create effective mount-card borders outside the image by increasing the canvas size. After doing an Image>Canvas Size command, add extra but even space around the image using the percentage scale. New canvas space is always created using the current background color and — by making repeated change canvas size adjustments following a background color change — you can create the illusion of card surrounding your image. For sympathetic colors, use the Eyedropper tool plus the Alt key to sample color from the image and set it as the background.

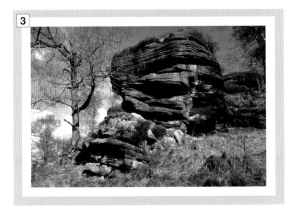

A canvas size edge effect.

Drop-shadow edge

Drop shadows create the illusion of an image floating in a three-dimensional space, and two layers are needed for the effect to work. First, rename the background layer by double-clicking its layer icon and typing in the word "Image." Make a new empty layer and drag this below the Image layer in the Layers palette. Go to Image>Canvas Size and increase both dimensions by ½ inch (1cm), then fill in the empty layer, by doing Edit>Fill, with white. This should surround the image with a white border. Click on the Image layer icon and do Layer>Layer Style>Drop Shadow. In the dialog box, the default effect settings will have already been applied to the image, but the Distance, Spread and Size controls can be moved until the look is right. Once complete, the drop-shadow effect can be changed endlessly by double clicking on the tiny black "f" Layer Effects icon.

See also Photoshop toolbox *pages 166–169* / Layers *pages 170–171* / Cropping and image size *pages 176–177* / Emulsion edges *pages 218–219* /

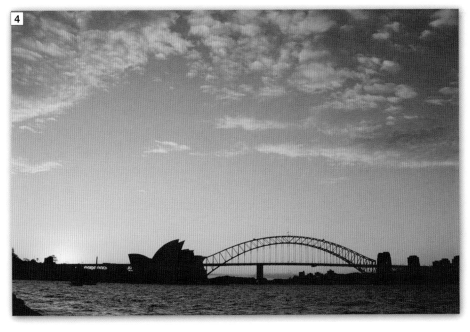

A drop-shadow edge.

Emulsion edges

Get away from straight-edged prints by giving digital photos a liquid-emulsion edge.

U nlike factory-manufactured photographic papers, liquid emulsion is applied by brush in the darkroom, giving conventional photographs a characteristic scratchy look and a hand-painted feel. For digital photographers, the style can be a valuable method of creating an effect that looks somewhere between a painting and photograph and is particularly great for landscape projects.

Making an edge 1

Start by loading the Dry Media brush set in the Brushes window and choose a brush that creates a

dry and bristly effect. Select black as the foreground color and set the brush opacity to 100 percent. Create a new image document then drag the brush around the empty image until you have created a satisfactory shape. It can be as irregular as you want, depending on how you want to use it.

Selecting the edge

With the photographic image open on the desktop, click on the black-edge image window and choose Select>Color Range. The Select Color Range will present a dialog box with a Dropper tool, which must be clicked into a black area of the image. Use the Fuzziness slider to increase the selection area until it includes the entire scratchy black shape. A Select>Similar command followed by a Select>Expand>1-pixel command will ensure that all non-connected blacks and grays are included in the selection area.

Merging 2

Return to the photographic image and do Select>All, then Edit>Copy to store a copy of the image on the clipboard. Next, click on the black image then do Edit>Paste Into. The Paste Into command only places the photographic image inside the selected area, rather than on top of it. Once the image has appeared, use the Move tool and drag it until it is in the right place. The outline selection on the black image works like a stencil (or window), with the image appearing inside the brushy-edged shape only.

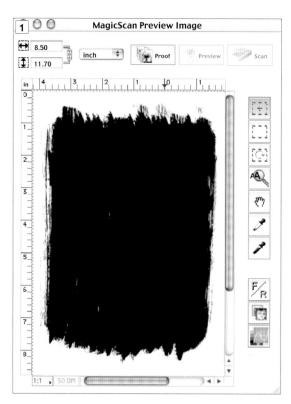

The scanner software dialog box.

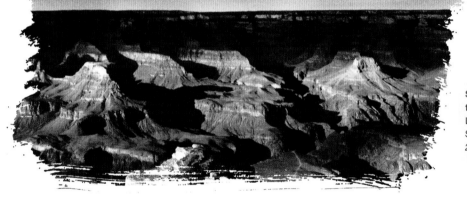

2.1

After both layers have been combined, a brushy emulsion edge is created.

See also Photoshop toolbox *pages 166–169 /* Layers *pages 170–171 /* Simple edges *pages 216–217 /*

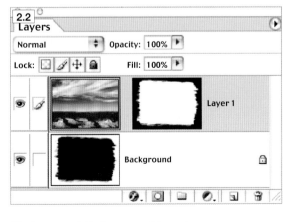

The Layers palette for an emulsion edge.

Fitting

If the image is not the right size, it can be made to fit easily using the Edit>Transform>Scale command. To avoid distorting the image drag corner handles with due care. A better route is to hold down the Shift key while dragging a corner handle, as this will scale the image while keeping its proportions intact. Even handier is to press Alt+Shift simultaneously and watch the image resize from the center. Pushing inward decreases and pulling outward enlarges the image. This is a good opportunity to recompose the image.

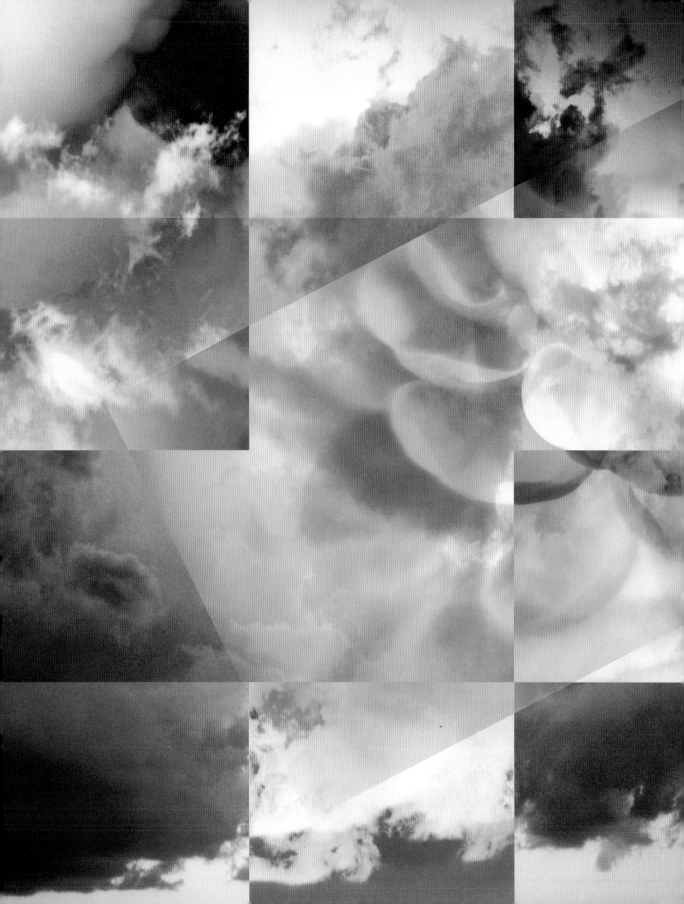

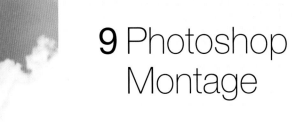

9 Photoshop Montage

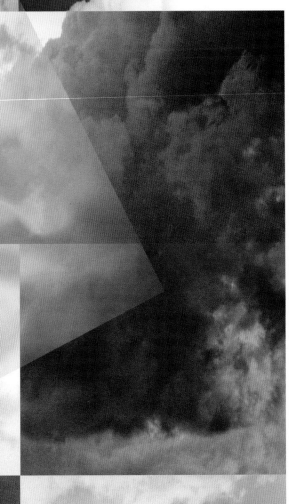

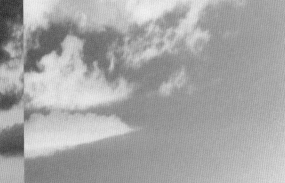

Cutting out

Photoshop offers a wide range of tools for cutting out image elements—the first step in any montage project.

Edit Cut

Once an image area has been selected, the quickest way to remove unwanted detail is by using the Edit>Cut command. This leaves a hole in all layers except the background layer, which is cut back to just the current background color. After the Cut command is made, an Edit>Paste will bring the discarded area back into a brand new layer by default. Sections of one image can be cut and pasted into another image using the same command.

Select and drag

Another way to transfer part of one image to another is to use the Move tool once a selection has been made. Line up two images side by side on the desktop and drag a selection from one to the other. Even though the selected area looks as if it is being deleted from the source image, it is merely being copied and will return to its original place once the command has been completed.

The Eraser tool

Only useful for making soft-edged cutouts, the Eraser tool is too clumsy for precise shapes and perimeters. Set with soft-edged brush properties, the Eraser can be used to reveal underlying layers gradually with a feathered edge, but once holes have been cut through, image detail cannot be put back.

Using Masks

A much more flexible way to use the Eraser tool is to apply it to a Mask layer instead. The purpose of a Mask is to create a stencil effect, allowing layers to appear in full or in part. To create a Mask, simply click on the tiny Mask icon found at the base of the Layers palette and watch it become connected to the current active layer. Click on the Mask icon and select White as the current foreground color, then apply the Eraser tool to the areas for removal. Set with a White foreground color, the Eraser cuts holes into the Mask, but if it is changed to Black the holes can be repaired and original image detail returns. The advantage of using a Mask is that the image layer remains intact while the Mask is cut through like a stencil.

Extract [1]

The Extract command is a far more sophisticated tool to use for cutting out individual layer elements and is presented in a full-screen preview window. Cutting out intricate objects — particularly those with fringed or hairy edges — is a notoriously complex operation and a task not made any easier with the Pen tool. Using the Extract command, you simply identify background and object colors with a highlighter Pen tool and trace around the edge of the object you want to cut out. The highlighter identifies the boundary and decides which colors stay and which are removed. Once completed, simply click to preview the results and the background is removed to leave even intricate edge details still in place. The command works best when there is a clear difference between shape color and contrast, and works less well if similar colors are shared.

See also Photoshop toolbox *pages 166–169* / Layers *pages 170–171* / Selections *pages 172–173* / Using the Pen tool *pages 224–225* /

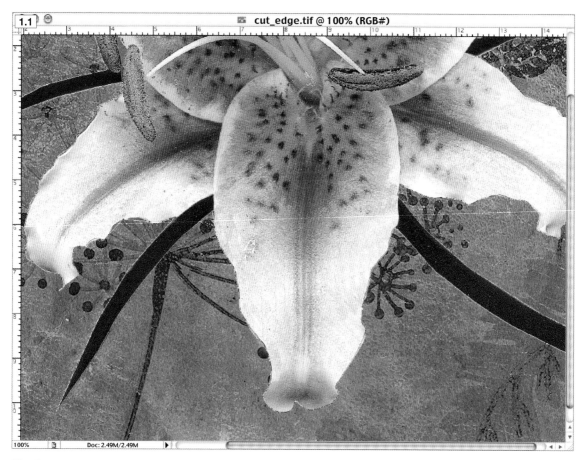

The Pen tool creates a very accurate outline that can be converted into a selection edge.

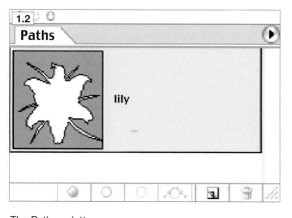

The Paths palette.

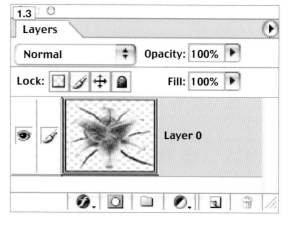

The checkerboard background denotes a cutout.

Using the Pen tool

The Pen tool offers the most precise and professional way of creating cutouts.

One of the hardest tasks is to create an accurate edge selection of a complex object in order to remove unwanted background or to use in a montage project. There are many tools that offer quick-fix solutions to this problem but none are of sufficient quality for professional printed reproduction. The Pen tool is used to create a vector outline called a Path and shares the same kind of line and curve tools as a vector-drawing package like Illustrator or Freehand. In addition to these drawing tools, which plot a dot-to-dot perimeter around a shape, tiny Bezier curves are used for pulling and bending the path into shape. Plotting the line is just half of the task, since pulling Bezier handles into place will make a tighter fit around the image edge. Paths can be saved and stored with the image file, retaining all the time-consuming work for future use. Paths can also be converted into selections and vice versa and, because of the tiny amount of extra data they produce, they are an ideal way to store a complex selection to an image file.

Starting off   1

Work only with the highest-resolution version of an image, as any slightly imperfect edge will be much less visible once the image has been downsampled. Open the image and make sure it is viewed at 200%. Pick the Pen tool from the palette and start clicking points just inside the desired shape. Working slightly inside the edge will prevent any stray and unwanted background details from appearing at the end of the task.

Working the line   2

Straight lines are easy to plot with the Pen tool, but as you encounter a curved edge, click and drag the Pen cursor to create a Bezier handle. The handle can be pushed and pulled to make the line fit exactly around the shape and can be returned to at any time. Complete a fully enclosed Path, joining the last point to the first point made. In the Paths palette, double-click the Path icon and save the work using a recognizable name for later convenience.

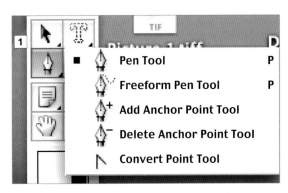

There are five Pen tools hidden in the Pen tool icon.

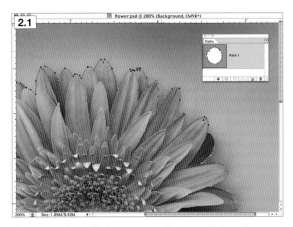

Once saved, the Path can be further modified until an exact fit is achieved.

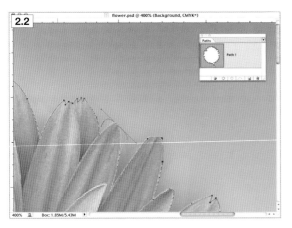

2.2

flower.psd @ 400% (Background, CMYK*)

400%   Doc: 1.85M/5.43M

Close up the Path nodes can be pushed and pulled
into place.

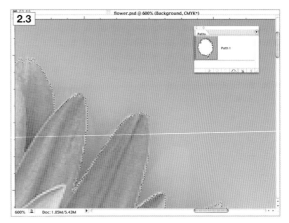

2.3

flower.psd @ 600% (Background, CMYK*)

600%   Doc: 1.85M/5.43M

Better control is achieved when working at 200%.

Cutting away the background   3

Unlock the background layer, or rename it so that
areas can be deleted. Select the saved Path and, from
the pop-out menu, click Make Selection. The dotted
marching ants will now appear, denoting the
selection area. The Path must be deselected by
clicking outside the icon in the Paths palette and,
once switched off, you can make a Select>Invert
command to select the background followed by
Edit>Cut to remove it. Once the background is
deleted, a razor-sharp shape is ready for print
or montage.

See also Photoshop toolbox *pages 166–169* / Layers *pages
170–171* / Selections *pages 172–174* / Cutting out *pages
222–223* /

3

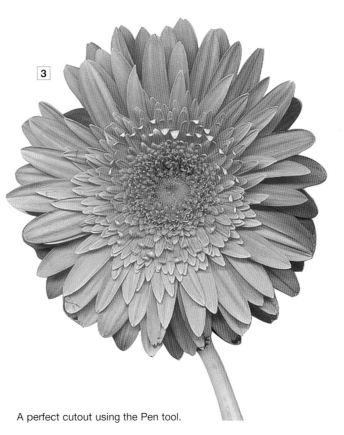

A perfect cutout using the Pen tool.

Layers and stacking

Layers are the best devices to use when starting a montage project as they keep all elements separate and movable.

Background layer

Every digital image is constructed of a single background layer and all processing occurs on this layer until new items are pasted into the image, creating additional layers. The background layer cannot be moved from the bottom of the vertical stacking order if the Layer Lock icon is visible. If not, the background layer can be moved, but must be renamed first.

Changing layer order

All layers occupy their own unique position in the vertical stacking order based on the time of their creation. Users can change the stacking order by click-dragging a Layer icon upward or downward into a new position in the palette, although its contents may be obscured by new surroundings.

Show/Hide icon

The tiny Eye icon fixed to the far left of the layer makes the contents of a layer visible when turned on and invisible when clicked off. Hiding a layer is not the same as deleting it, but is used purely as a way of viewing an otherwise hidden image element.

Link/Unlink icon

If two or more layers need to be grouped together for moving or transforming, they are better linked. With one of the layers the active layer, click on the tiny blank box next to the Show/Hide eye until a tiny chain appears. To remove the connection, just click it off again. For complex projects, layers can be arranged in folder-like sets for better organization.

Deleting layers

A layer is easily deleted by click-dragging it into the Wastebasket icon at the bottom right of the Layers palette. For those uncertain about this kind of action, the layer can be hidden rather than thrown away.

Creating empty layers and duplicating layers

Empty layers can be made by clicking on the New Layer icon found at the bottom of the palette, alongside the wastebasket. To create an identical copy of the current active layer, click and drag its layer icon over the New Layer icon to produce an exact copy.

Adjustment layers

It is possible to create non-pixel adjustment layers to apply settings like Levels, Color Balance and Hue/Saturation to all layers lying underneath. Click on the tiny white/black circle next to the New Layer icon and choose your adjustment layer.

Text layers

The Text tool automatically creates a brand new layer with each individual entry. The editable text layer is shown by a T icon, and it can be changed into a pixel layer by doing a Layer>Rasterize>Type command.

Layer opacity slider

In a complex image, each layer can be set with its own level of transparency, so that it can be blended in. At 100%, a layer is completely opaque and obscures everything underneath, but at 20% it is thin and "watered down," allowing underlying layer details to emerge.

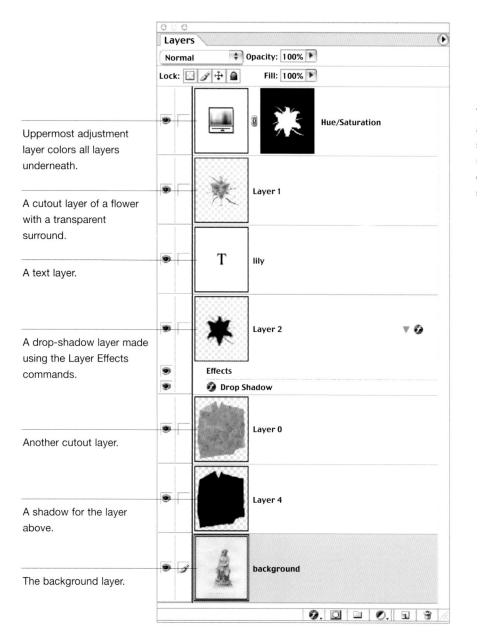

Uppermost adjustment layer colors all layers underneath.

A cutout layer of a flower with a transparent surround.

A text layer.

A drop-shadow layer made using the Layer Effects commands.

Another cutout layer.

A shadow for the layer above.

The background layer.

The Layers palette is arranged in a vertical stack with the uppermost layer sitting on the top, or the surface, of the image.

Layer blending menu

Each of the blending modes defines how a layer reacts to the one immediately underneath and shows how both color and contrast are blended, often with unpredictable results.

See also Photoshop toolbox *pages 166–169* / Layers *pages 170–171* / Opacity and translucence *pages 232–233* /

Shooting for montage

Careful preparation is the key to shooting source images for later montage projects.

Thinking the process through

Most images are not shot specifically for a bit part in a montage project, but cutting out and assembling would often be a lot easier if they were. Photographic images need to be taken with a close eye on scale, viewpoint and lighting direction, especially if many disparate sources are employed in the final montage. Shooting variations is a very good idea, and avoids limiting your options to just one photograph, which may not fit with others that have yet to be shot. These principles apply to most high-budget advertising shoots where cast, backgrounds and special effects are often shot independently and later assembled into a finished piece.

Good background color   1

If later cutting out is likely, objects are best shot against a single-color background that won't deflect colored light onto the edges of the subject. Vivid colors can make cutting out easier, but traces of them are often visible at boundary edges. Simple white or midtone gray backgrounds work best of all in the studio and, if on location, plain and simple backgrounds are preferable to any with a pattern. Cutouts are impossible to do properly if the object is unsharp or blurred. Images should be captured with the fine focus control set and, if shooting in poor light, a flash will help bring out image detail.

See also The lens and focusing *pages 46–47* / Better composition *pages 54–55* / Looking for shape *pages 56–57* / Perspective control *pages 68–69* /

Collecting sources

It is an excellent idea to shoot available textures as an ongoing exercise. These can include anything from clouds and weather conditions to close-ups of natural and manmade textures — images that lend themselves to a wide variety of projects when large areas need to be replaced.

1

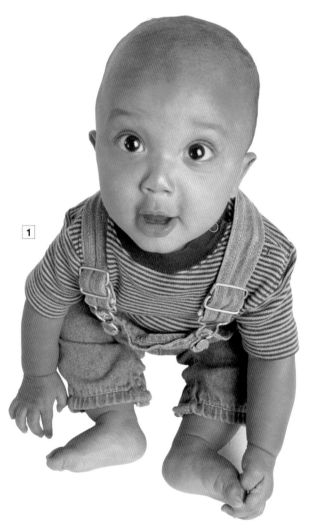

Shoot entire shape

Cutouts are impossible if the entire shape of an object is not there to start with. Missing feet, tops of hats and even partially obscured buildings all can ruin the prospect of later use. Take time to compose an image and always concentrate on the edges of the viewfinder frame. Unwanted telegraph wires, television aerials and satellite dishes all can be removed easily from an image once back at the workstation, but they are best avoided in the first place.

Lenses and distortion

All photographic lenses create distortion of one kind or another, but mixing together different kinds of lens views in one image will look very strange. Keep focal lengths consistent throughout the collection of any source material and if possible use longer lenses, which create less shape distortion compared with wide-angle lenses. Photoshop offers the useful Transform tools for fixing source material into the right size, shape and perspective.

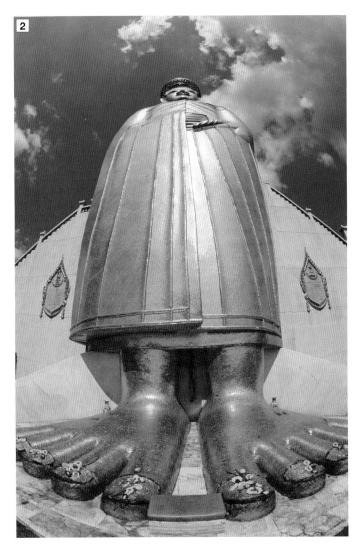

Distorted images can prove difficult to merge with other source images.

Blending effects

Users can mix and merge different digital photographs together by using the universal set of Blending modes found in most good imaging applications.

U nlike conventional photographs, digital images can be overlapped or have their original colors blended to create surreal and interesting results. Much more sophisticated than a simple sandwich of two negatives, Blending modes also provide an easier method of making a montage compared to using the time-consuming cutting tools.

The Layer Blending modes 〔1〕

Layers, by default, are completely opaque, preventing other image detail from showing through. Yet a unique color mix between adjacent layers is reversible and also keeps layers as separate entities. Found within the Normal drop-down menu at the top left of Photoshop's Layers palette, the sixteen Blending modes offer an unpredictable but exciting way to create color effects.

Duplicate layer blending 〔2〕

Users can generate stylish results by blending together two identical layers. This technique is good for intensifying weak or washed-out colors. First drag the background layer icon over the Create New Layer icon found at the bottom of the Layers palette. This will immediately give you an identical second layer. Next, select the duplicate layer, then choose Overlay from the Blending mode drop-down menu. The resulting image will show more intense colors with a slightly higher contrast.

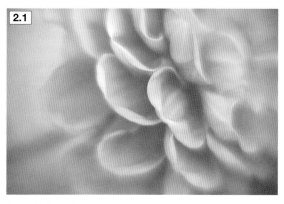

A single layer image.

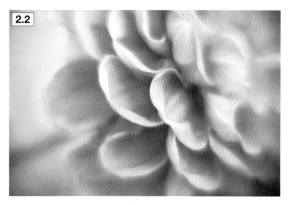

A duplicate layer with the Overlay Blending mode.

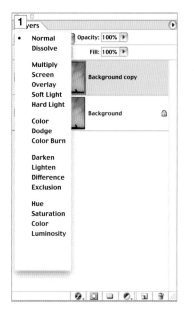

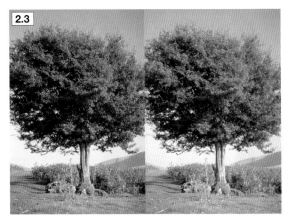

An invert duplicate layer with the Hue Blending mode.

Invert duplicate layers

Invert layers are simply layers that have had all their color and tonal values set to their exact opposite. Negative becomes positive, blue becomes orange and black becomes white. Inverted digital photographs look much like traditional color negatives, with all colors mapped to their opposite values. Yet the effect can be further developed with the addition of a Blending mode. Follow the previous steps for creating a duplicate layer, then select Image> Adjust>Invert to flip the duplicate layer into a negative. Next, apply a Hue Blending mode and watch how the negative and positive combine.

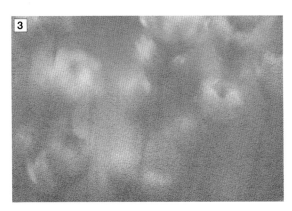

Reduced opacity creates delicate colors.

Opacity 3

The Opacity slider is a simple control for draining away the intensity of an entire layer. Like adding water to watercolor paint, this tool makes a watery and thinned out version of an original, which is both reversible and can be modified at any time without overcooking your image. This project was completed by reducing a layer's full opacity to 50% to show a delicate and barely perceptible version, allowing an underlying texture to show through.

Dropping highlights 4

This project involved the combination of a sheet of music with a flower photograph. After scanning and assembling as two layers in the same image, the highlights in the sheet music appear as distracting white patches. Click on this layer, then choose Multiply from the Blending mode drop-down menu. Notice how the two layers now merge seamlessly together. This technique is useful for similar projects where white paper areas need to be discarded, like drawings, printed type or signatures on white paper.

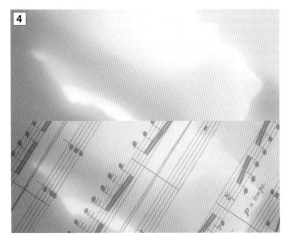

Whites can be removed with the Multiply Blending mode.

See also Layers *pages 170–171* / Color enhancing *pages 202–203* / Layers and stacking *pages 226–227* / Opacity and translucence *pages 232–233* /

Opacity and translucence

Individual or grouped layers can be set with varying levels of opacity to create translucent effects.

Translucent layers are an excellent way of assembling the delicate elements of a photomontage. Once cut out and labeled as an individual layer, each item can be modified to blend fully with its surroundings. Lowering opacity from the default 100% will restrict both contrast and color saturation, making the item in question much less dominant.

Layer Masks [1]

All Masks are essentially grayscale images where white areas let underlying detail show through, black areas prevent it, and gray areas allow varying quantities of translucency. Layer Masks can be created using any of the painting and drawing tools, while the Gradient tool can be used to apply a shaded area. Masks are another level of control that can be applied to montage elements if a simple opacity command doesn't deliver the required effect. Masks can always be modified.

Knockouts [2]

Like Masks, knockouts determine which layer defines a stencil shape to allow underlying detail to emerge through. Knockout properties can be applied to any layer and set of layers, but the defining shape or type must sit at the top of the layer order. Knockouts are like die-cut apertures cut into card and paper.

Clipping groups [3]

Like knockouts, clipping groups offer the opportunity to apply a range of opacity and blending effects to a group of layers before they become masked by an underlying base layer. Members of a clipping group are identified by indent icons, with the base layer shown underlined.

See also Photoshop toolbox *pages 166–169* / Layers *pages 170–171* / Layers and stacking *pages 226–227* /

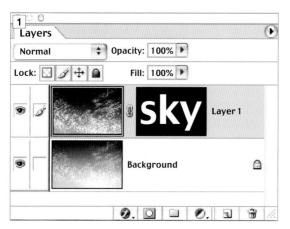

The black Mask was created to protect the underlying layer from the edit.

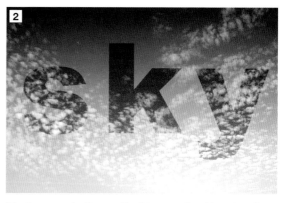

The layer mask allows a flexible way of making stencils.

20% opacity.

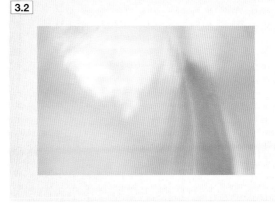

80% opacity.

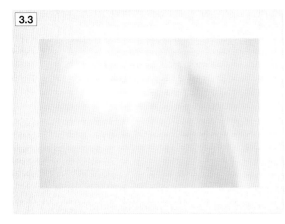

40% opacity.

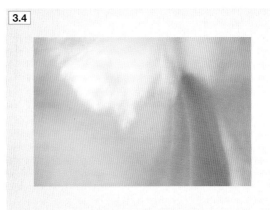

100% opacity.

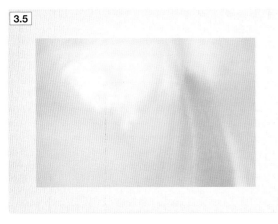

60% opacity.

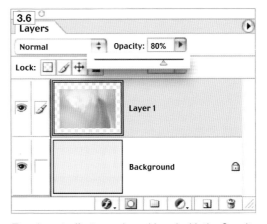

Translucent effects can be achieved with the Opacity slider in the multi-layered image.

Invert adjustment layers

Invert adjustment layers allow users to combine both negative and positive in the same image.

Color reversals

1

Color images can be reversed into opposite color values simply by using an invert adjustment layer. Although not based entirely on a photographic chemical solarization effect, the Invert offers the added chance to merge both negative and positive colors in the same image. Each layer that is placed underneath an invert adjustment layer will be changed, so black becomes white and red is changed to green. To remove a layer from the effect, it must be dragged to a location above the adjustment layer in the Layers palette. Many variations of a single multi-layered image can be made by using this effect.

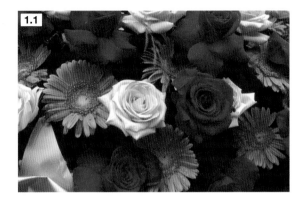

An uncorrected color image.

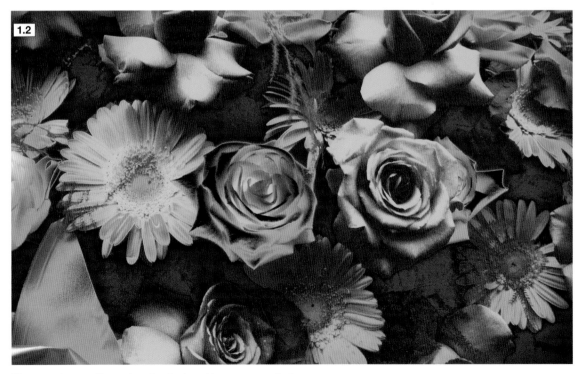

The same image after an invert adjustment layer was applied.

Monochrome reversals   2

Like a traditional solarization- or Sabattier-effect image, a mono reversal can also be made using an invert adjustment layer. This technique creates the appearance of a negative version floating over a positive background layer and is achieved using a cut-through mask. Set white as the foreground color and set the Eraser tool with a soft round brush, then work with low pressure values initially, gently removing the overlying negative adjustment layer. Swap between white and black regularly to amend any holes that appear in the mask as you go.

See also Photoshop toolbox *pages 166–169* / Layers *pages 170–171* / Layers and stacking *pages 226–227* /

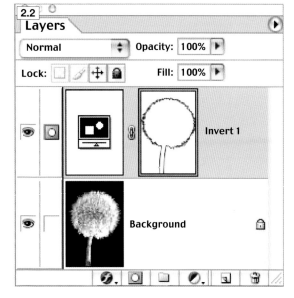

The Layers palette for this project.

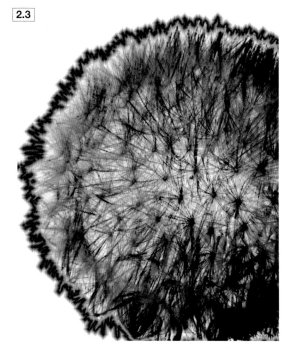

2.1 A straight monochrome original.

2.3 After an invert adjustment layer was applied.

Type essentials

Photoshop offers the same level of type control as a desktop publishing program, and more.

Type fundamentals   1

A standard set of fonts (or typefaces) is installed on a PC and selected for use in most common documents and layout projects, such as reports, posters and leaflets. The type styles have been carefully designed by typographers to undertake very specific tasks, but they can also be used in a much more creative and decorative manner. Two main font styles are common in a PC font pack. The first are the sans serif fonts, for example, plain and undecorated Helvetica or Arial which are commonly used for headlines or public information signage. Next are the serif fonts, such as Times, which are better employed as type styles for the dense blocks of small text found in magazines and books. Serif fonts are designed with tiny triangles or flourishes at the edges of letters, which assist the reader in making a speedy visual link from one word to the next.

See also Photoshop toolbox *pages 166–169* / Type effects *pages 238–239* /

Photoshop type   2

Unlike a graphics or word processing application, type in Photoshop can be highly manipulated and inventive. Like the vector drawing and path tools, type is first rendered as a vector outline rather than a block of pixels and so remains editable. Vector type can be rasterized, however, or turned into pixels, to allow the application of filters and other effects.

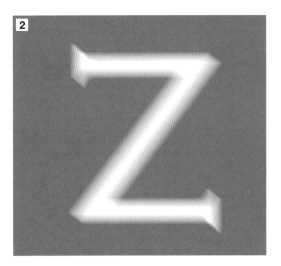

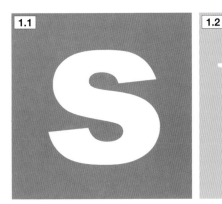

Sans serif font.

Serif font.

Script font.

The Type dialog box 3

To enter vector type, select the Type tool and click in the image window. The Type tool dialog box will appear on the top menu bar enabling the selection of font, color, size and other character modifiers. In later versions of Photoshop, type can be entered directly onto an image without the need for an additional dialog box. To change any entered type, simply drag the cursor over the word or words to be altered and use the drop-down menus at the top. Once satisfied with an entry, click on the Tick icon on the top menu bar to confirm completion of the function.

Type modifiers

Type size is the measurement of each letter's individual height and is measured in points (pt) — a system dating back to when individual metal characters were cast in preset sizes and assembled into sentences by hand. Point size is a measurement from the top of the character to the bottom, with 72 points equaling one inch (2.5cm).

Leading 4

Leading, pronounced like the metal lead, takes its name from the thin strips of metal once used for creating space between horizontal lines of type in a block of text such as a paragraph. This additional space makes small type much easier to read, or can be used to fill a larger page area. Generally, a leading value that is two sizes bigger than the current point size will give balance and readability to text blocks.

Tracking and kerning 5

Individual letters are not surrounded by the same width blank space — for example, the letters w and i. Kerning controls these gaps to create a squashed or spread out space within the confines of a word as needed. Kerning is best left on Auto unless space is tight, as any exaggerated command will make letters look very unusual. The much less sophisticated Tracking tool enables users to stretch words and lines to fill horizontal areas, but always at the expense of conventional balance.

Type effects

Creative type manipulation can add an interesting twist to a graphics project.

Type Mask 1

Individual letter shapes can be filled with an image, rather than a solid color or gradient fill, by using the dotted-edged Type Mask tool. The tool can be applied to any open image using a thicker typeface at a large size such as 72 pt. Once the letters have been created, position them over the area you would like to use as the fill and press the Tick icon. Do Edit>Copy and Edit>Paste the type into a new layer. This type can now be filtered and manipulated but not edited for spelling or font style.

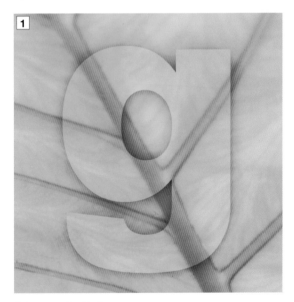

A type mask effect.

Layer Style 2

Type can also be created with an outline around the letter shape in a different color by using Stroke in the Layer Style options. Stroke is just another term for outline and can be introduced in any color and width to both vector-type and mask-type areas. Other innovative styles include Gradient Overlay, Drop Shadow, Bevel and Emboss, Outer and Inner Glow.

Using filters on type 3

If type layers are rasterized or merged with other pixel layers, any filter effect can be applied to the type, creating some very interesting effects. Always aim to keep the rasterized type on a separate layer, or simply apply filters to selected letters from the same layer for more control.

Using Lighting Effects filter

It is also possible to light type, just like using photographic studio lights, to create an embossed or debossed effect across the letterforms. Create a Type Mask selection and save it by doing a Select>Save Selection command. Next, return to the image, deselect the selection and make a Filter>Render>Lighting Effects command. Find the saved selection by clicking in the Texture Channel pop-up menu at the bottom of the dialog box. The letters will appear in the preview window ready to manipulate with the full range of different light types and properties.

See also Photoshop toolbox *pages 166–169* / Filters *pages 210–215* / Type effects *pages 238–239* /

2.1

A drop-shadow effect.

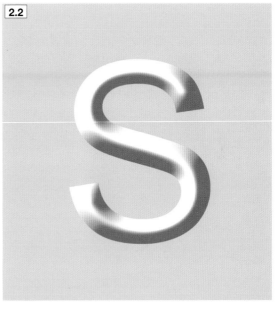

2.2

An emboss effect.

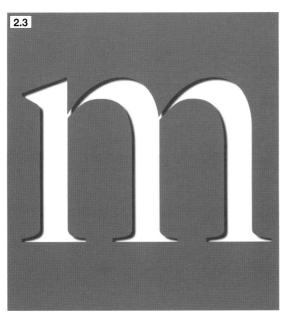

2.3

An inner shadow effect.

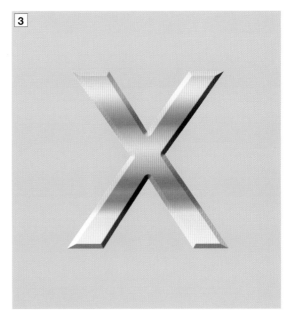

3

A gradient effect.

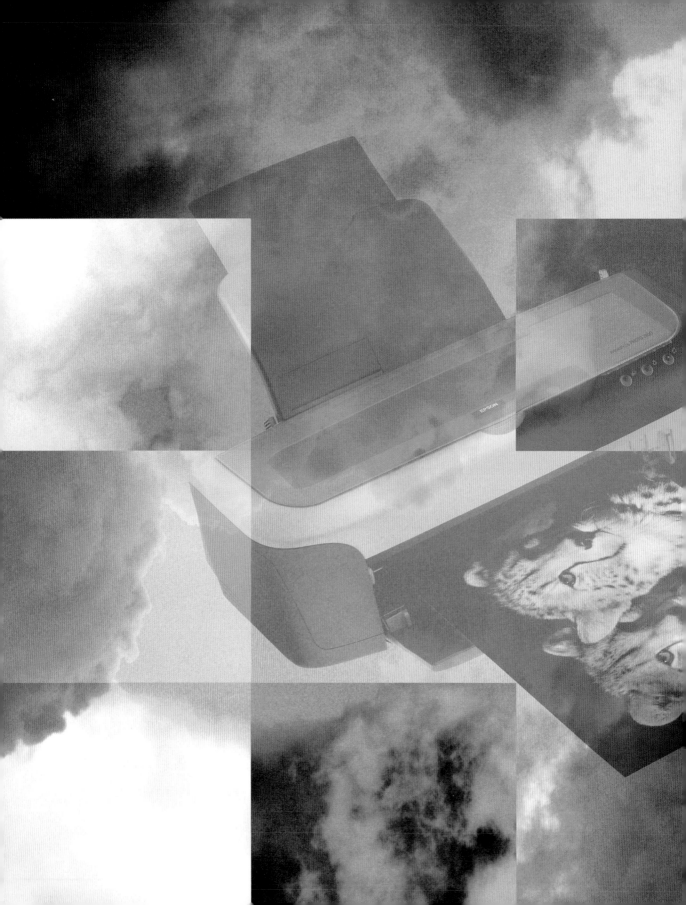

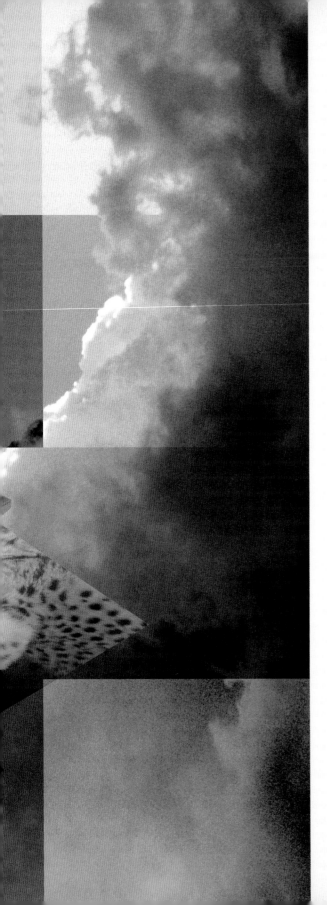

10 Output

Printer types

Ink-jet printers are by far the most popular output devices for digital photographers.

How ink-jets work

Just like the commercial reproduction of photos in magazines, an ink-jet printer uses a variation of the halftone process using the same four CMYK ink colors. The resulting color print is made from millions of tiny drops of color set at different distances from each other and, when viewed from a distance, these minute ink particles merge together to give the impression of continuous photographic color.

Resolution

The word resolution determines the actual number of ink droplets sprayed onto the receiving media, and is expressed in dots per inch such as 2880 or 1440dpi. The bigger this number is, the finer and more photo-real the prints will be. Super-high-resolution printers create ink droplets at different sizes to make a more photorealistic effect but, used with low-resolution settings, this will create speckled results regardless of image resolution. In printer software, preset controls decide resolution, paper type and color balance and have a profound effect on the quality of a printout. Poor results will occur if the wrong media settings are chosen in error.

Media and inks

Most printers can output to custom-sized sheets of paper as well as standard $8\frac{1}{2}$ x 11 and 11 x 17 sizes. The better devices have roll paper feeders for printing panoramic images or a special pop-out tray for printing directly onto CD-R disks. Never be tempted to use cheaper generic ink sets, which will cause both printer software and paper settings to under-perform. For professional ink-jets, special four- or six-tone monochrome cartridges can be bought for the highest quality black-and-white printing.

Computer connector

Printers are connected to a PC via a USB, serial or parallel port and need special driver software installed before being recognized and usable. A recent development is the printer fitted with a digital camera memory card slot, designed to accept the card without the need to transfer images to a computer first.

Home ink-jets [1]

The basic four-color ink-jet printer gives adequate results with graphics and text, but will not be able to match the subtle tones found in a photographic image. With a CMYK four-color cartridge, visible dots will occur in blank highlight areas despite using high-resolution image files.

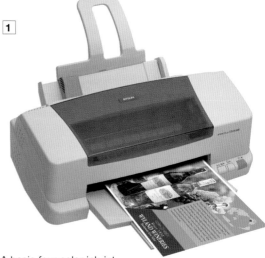

A basic four-color ink-jet.

Photo-realistic ink-jets   2

A much better buy is the printer with two extra colors — light cyan and light magenta — to help mix the subtleties of skin tone. At a slightly higher cost, devices with lightfast inks, such as the Epson Intellidge cartridges, will produce prints with an extended lifespan. Certain brands now offer more economical individual color ink cartridges.

Professional ink-jets   3

Aimed at the professional photographer, these ink-jets are designed to minimize fading. With pigment inks for greater stability but slightly less saturated colors, these devices cost more to buy and operate, but give the highest quality results. Printer software will link with professional imaging applications and provide useful color profiles to ensure a tight control over color-management issues.

3

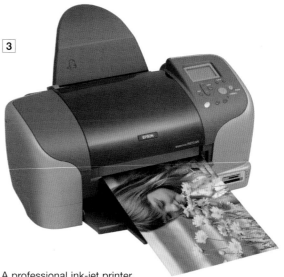

A professional ink-jet printer.

See also Media types *pages 244–245* / Printer software *pages 246–247* / Special ink sets *pages 260–261* /

2

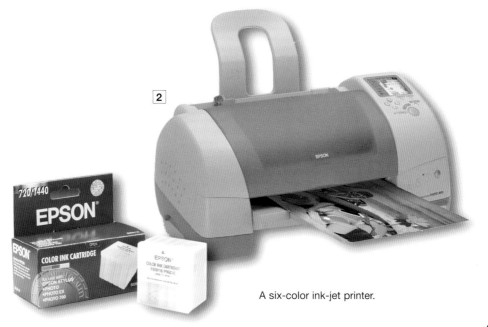

A six-color ink-jet printer.

Media types

Ink-jet printers are versatile because they can be used to print on a wide range of different media.

Printer-branded media

Designed to produce the best possible results when used with same-brand printers and ink sets, branded media by Epson, Canon and Kodak offer the perfect starting point for the novice user. With printer software settings designed to extract maximum quality from own-brand media, far fewer problems will present themselves.

Basic ink-jet paper

At a cheap price, and sold in bulk quantities such as 500 sheets, this kind of paper media is generally sold by the big stationery outlets. Yet, despite the label, it offers only slightly higher quality than copier paper. This is only useful for printing text, graphics and low-quality photos at no more than 360dpi.

Matte photo paper

At a more expensive price, and designed by familiar photographic brands such as Ilford, Epson and Canon, matte-finish photo paper is reassuringly thicker. Manufactured with a high-quality coating of finely powdered china clay, matte photo paper is able to preserve tiny ink dots in their dedicated places. This paper will output at 720dpi and above and is excellent for printing sharp graphics and photographs albeit with slightly muted colors compared to glossy media.

Glossy photo paper

Glossy photo paper is aimed at users with six- or more color ink-jet printers, and has a smooth and shiny surface that reproduces a wider tonal range.

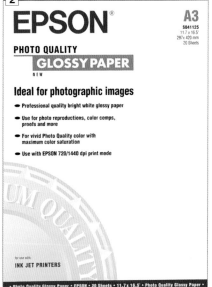

Smooth-coated matte paper.

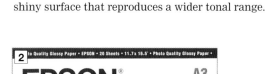

High-gloss photo paper.

Glossy papers are excellent at printing deep blacks and richly saturated colors. Cheaper brands suffer from a puddling effect caused by an incompatibility between ink and coating and can take a little while longer to dry properly.

Premium-weight glossy

Premium-weight paper is much thicker and made to feel exactly like traditional resin-coated photographic paper. With its more rigid feel this kind of paper is best used when frequent handling is expected. It is made by many traditional photographic paper manufacturers including Ilford, Kodak and Agfa.

Glossy photo film 3

This is a material based on a plastic substrate, which cannot be torn or ripped into shape by hand. Photo film generates the most sharply detailed prints compared to any media, but has less of a tactile finish. Good for using in portfolios.

Ink-jet art media 4

Ink-jet art papers offer a more tactile finish. The best brands to try are Somerset and Lyson, and both have been carefully designed to reproduce fine detail and high color saturation with an alluring texture. Very heavy weights up to 300 grams per square meter (gsm) can be used for exhibition printing.

Artists' watercolor paper

At first glance this seems identical to purpose-made ink-jet art media, but artists' paper gives soggy and unsharp results when used with standard printer software settings. Good papers to use are the expensive handmade sheets for artists' printmaking, such as Rives, Fabriano and Bockingford. Much better results are offered by paper traditionally sold by the sheet rather than in sketchbooks.

See also Printer types *pages 242–243* / Calibrating printing paper *pages 250–251* / Test printing *pages 252–253* / Art papers *pages 258–259* /

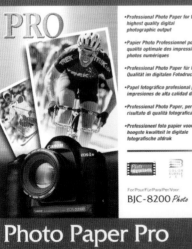

Heavy-weight photo glossy paper.

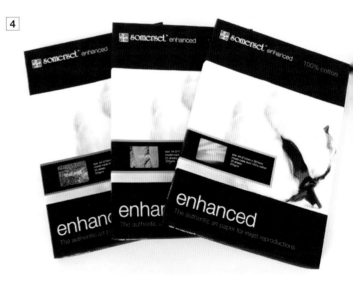

Archival cotton ink-jet paper.

Printer software

Another level of influence is applied by the printer software controls which need careful handling to gain the best results from image files.

Media setting   [1]

It is of primary importance to set the type of paper used to the nearest equivalent media setting found in the printer's drop-down menu. This simple choice will tell the printer head how much ink to drop onto the paper. If the media type is set too high for the paper, the result will be dark and soggy. If too low a quality is picked, washed out and speckled prints will emerge. This also will affect the color balance of the final print.

Printer resolution   [2]

Most printers can be operated in lower quality, or draft, mode for making rough prints or layout proofs, keeping costs down. A printer resolution of 360dpi will drop fewer dots on the receiving paper even if the image is a high-resolution file. The best photo quality is made using 1440 or 2880dpi, but each print will take a lot longer to print and use more ink. Never consider selecting High Speed setting for

photographic quality results. The choice of media may cause some printer resolutions to become unavailable as they are deemed inappropriate for the paper.

Color space and management   [3]

Many printers have a drop-down menu allowing users to set the printer to work in the same color workspace as an application like Adobe RGB (1998). This basic setting will prevent any poor color conversions taking place, but should not be viewed as a method for changing color balance or print quality. Set it to one color space and correct print problems elsewhere.

See also Printer types *pages 242–243* / Media types *pages 244–245* / Using profiles and color management *pages 248–249* / Special ink sets *pages 260–261* /

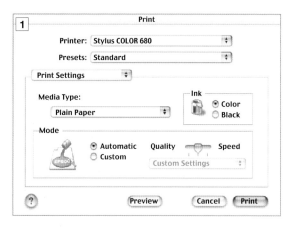

The Media Type menu is a crucial control.

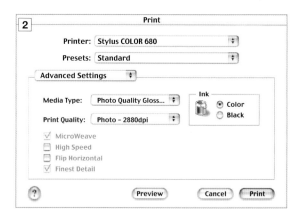

The advanced settings allow users to determine print quality.

Color controls can be used to counteract casts caused by ink and paper combinations.

Error diffusion and dithering

The color halftone process used in magazine reproduction is one of many methods for mimicking continuous tone color with a limited ink set. Error diffusion and dithering are two halftoning methods specifically developed for ink-jet printers and create illusions in different ways. Error diffusion is used to make a random arrangement of ink droplets to mimic subtle colors and is the best method for printing photographic images. Fine dithering places dots in a uniform pattern and is best used for graphics only. To help lower the effects of ink stripes or bands use Microweave or Super Microweave if available.

Auto modes

Many printer software applications offer a raft of Auto print options that make uncontrollable amendments to your image files during printout.

These Auto settings should never be used unless the user has no sophisticated imaging software or is printing directly from a digital camera.

The custom or manual mode

Each and every problem that arises can be solved when operating a printer in the manual mode. Custom mode allows users to drive the printer software tools and establish saved settings and custom paper sizes for future use.

Ink choice

Despite the option to print with the single black ink cartridge, this will effectively reduce a printer's resolution. Grayscale images printed with black ink will be speckled and low quality; far better results can be achieved printing with color ink selected, even for grayscale images.

Using profiles and color management

When digital images are exchanged between different input editing programs and output devices, some shift in color occurs. Keeping control of these changes is called color management.

Color management 1

Digital input devices, such as cameras and scanners, work in subtly different variations of the standard RGB mode, for example sRGB. These subtle variations are termed workspaces, whose precise idiosyncrasies have been developed by manufacturers

Jargon

Profile: A profile determines actual pixel color appearance, be it on a monitor, scanner or printer.

Color Management Module (CMM): Often referred to as the Color Management Engine, this is a tiny program that oversees color conversions. ColorSync and Adobe ACE are both CMM.

Display and output profiles: Designed for monitors and output profiles, these workspaces are sometimes referred to as destination profiles. They are used to set reliable colors to suit an ink/paper/printer combination.

such as ColorMatch for the ColorMatch RGB and the increasingly universal Adobe RGB (1998). Most PCs are set up with different workspaces so that when conversion from one to another takes place, such as from sRGB to Adobe RGB (1998), exact pixel color values are remapped to the new space as the image file is opened. Just like making a color balance adjustment to an image file, bad conversions result in visible color change, loss of color saturation and contrast. To help manage these changes more effectively, a range of software tools can help control the monitor, workspace and printer. Central to this activity is the Color Management Module (CMM) or engine, such as ColorSync or Adobe (ACE), which is designed to standardize a single profile within a workstation and oversee any conversion from or to other profiles.

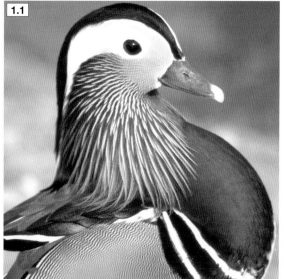

An uncorrected RGB image.

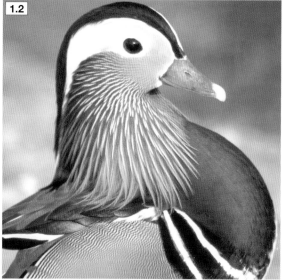

The same image converted into a smaller workspace.

Setting up profiles

Users intending to work within their own workstation — rarely exchanging files with other users on different systems — need make only minor adjustments to their preferences. It is best to work within the most universally recognized color space such as the Adobe RGB (1998). This can be selected in Photoshop by doing Edit>Color Settings>Custom and selecting Adobe RGB (1998) in the Working Spaces drop-down menu. This will now apply the profile to all images and tag them when saved.

Policy decisions

When working with images supplied by others and tagged with a different profile, users have the opportunity to handle them in different ways by setting different color management policies. Three optional policies are to convert the alien profile to your own workspace; to preserve the alien's embedded profile; or to switch off color management altogether. Most users opt for the first of the three options to maintain reliable color output. Yet, if working on a commercial project, it is sensible to agree on a common workspace with a client beforehand.

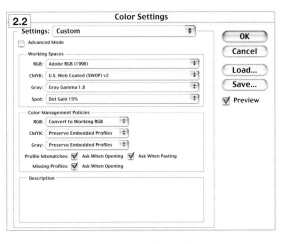

The Color Settings dialog box showing policy decisions.

Workspaces can be set in the Custom Settings dialog.

See also Camera functions: color settings *pages 14–15* /

Calibrating printing paper

Shadow gain and highlight spread are common problems when printing photographs on ink-jets, but spending a little time calibrating paper will get rid of the problem forever.

Paper and printer calibration [1]

Different papers will respond to different printer software settings, but many images still need extra corrections for flawless prints. The idea of testing paper beforehand is a straightforward one and very cost-effective in the long run. Simple testing involves finding the exact points at which the paper cannot separate dark gray from full black and pure white from light gray. Once this has been established and accounted for, prints will no longer burn out in the highlights or fill in the shadow areas.

Testing paper [2]

Select a sheet of printing paper and send a test wedge to print, using the closest media settings options found in the printer software. It is important to make a note of these settings on the reverse side of the paper when it emerges from the printer. Inspect the printout closely in the shadow areas on the black step wedge and try to find the point at which the different steps merge together. On all but the very best ink-jet paper this usually occurs at about the 94% mark, changing any darker tones into pure 100% black. Next, judge the highlights on the black wedge and pick the step before the first sign of any image detail.

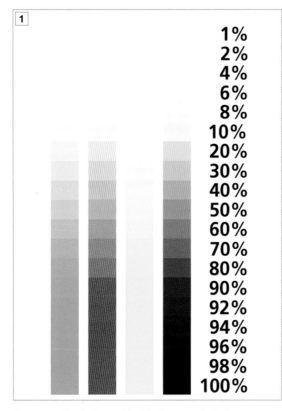

A step-wedge helps to identify the paper's limits.

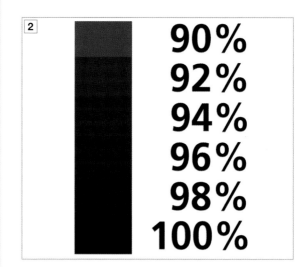

Blacks tend to fill in after 94%.

See also Media types *pages 244–245* / Test printing *pages 252–253* /

Adjusting a monochrome image with Curves [3]

Once the starting points of both highlights and shadows have been established, a digital image can be amended to fit within the new boundaries. Assuming an image is grayscale and the results showed highlights starting at 6% and black

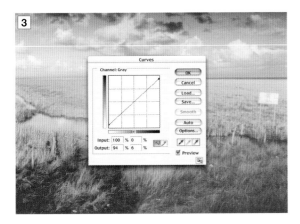

Curves can be used to adapt monochrome images for printing.

appearing at 94%, adjustments can be made by opening the Curves dialog and setting the curve to the new points with Highlight Output shown as 6% and Shadow Output shown as 94%.

Adjusting a color image with Levels [4]

To repeat the same correction for an RGB image, work on the composite RGB channel in the Levels dialog box. As color is not described as a simple 0–100% but on a 0–255 scale, the percentages will need to be converted to fit. Assuming that 1% equals 2.55, adjust the Shadow Output to 15 instead of 0 and the Highlight Output to 240 instead of 255.

Saving Curves and Levels recipes

Once familiar with the technicalities of adjusting output values, you can save them as Curves or Levels recipe files using the printing paper as a reference file name. Once saved, these can be applied to future images by pressing Load in the Curves and Levels dialogs.

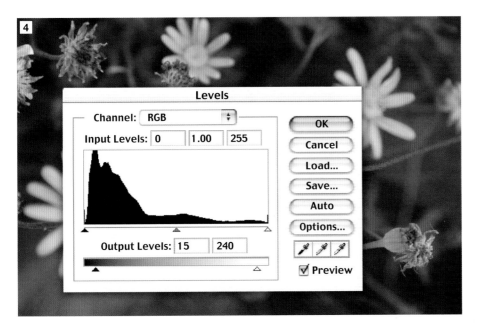

Levels can be used to prepare RGB images for printing.

Test printing

Taking the time to color-calibrate a monitor and working out the best printer software settings for the paper does not always guarantee a perfect print.

Test strips help to solve simple print problems quickly and prevent the waste of costly ink and paper. Central to the craft of darkroom printing is the test strip, where the photographer generates a useful selection of variations to pick from. Digital photographers rarely print out brightness variations and have a bad habit of placing too much trust in the self-correcting nature of printer software. When prints emerge too dark or too light, users tweak the crude printer software settings rather than returning to Photoshop to solve the root cause.

See also Media types *pages 244–245* / Calibrating printing paper *pages 250–251* / Judging test results *pages 254–255* / Common printing problems *pages 256–257* /

Preparing test paper [1]

With this simple technique, there is no need to copy and paste tiny segments of an image into a brand new document for proof printing. Instead, a small selection area from the image being worked on can be printed out onto a small sheet of paper. Any size paper can be used for a test strip, but it is much more economical to set up a custom paper size such as 4 x 6 inches in the printer software beforehand. It is very rare to need to make more than two different test prints to get to the correct recipe but, should this be the case, it is a good idea to label each one with details of the corrections made. Always use the same paper for the test that you intend to use for the final print and never adjust image size or resolution between tests and final print, or you will need to start all over again.

The test print can be made on a more economical sheet of paper.

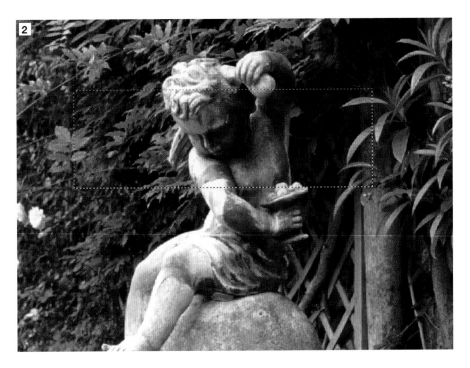

A sharp-edged rectangular selection is made at the start of the test print sequence.

Defining the test area [2]

Open the image and pick the Rectangular Marquee tool from the toolbox, making sure the feather value has been set to zero. Drag this across the image and place the selection in a place that includes highlight, shadow and neutral midtone areas if possible. There is no need to use the Move tool to reposition the selection — simply place the cursor outside the selection and drag it to its new destination. A good idea is to save the selection, so you can return to it once any color or brightness adjustments have been made. Once you have made your placement decision, the image is ready to print.

Sending to print [3]

Make the printer software recognize the selection by choosing the Print Selected Area option in the dialog box. This command will print the selection exactly in the center of the chosen paper size. If results are darker or lighter than expected, return to the image, deselect the selection area and make any amendments. From the Select menu, pick Load Selection and bring back the selection to the same place for the second test, then print.

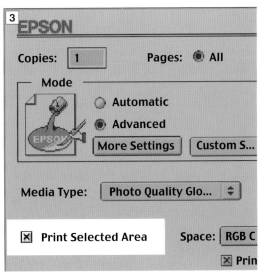

Ensure the Print Selected Area check box is chosen.

Judging test results

It can be impossible to solve a problem if you don't know what to look for in the first place, so what makes a perfect print?

Shooting a wonderful digital photograph is only half the job. Making a print that does it justice is far more time consuming and will never happen by accident. The definition of a good photographic print is the same for both digital and traditional photographs, exhibiting a rich and varied tonal range between smaller areas of full black shadows and clean white highlights. Fine details are present and clearly visible across the whole image without the need to examine at a close distance. The principle subject of a photograph should also be clearly emphasized. Sloppy prints have a compressed and dull tonal range, lack any clear emphasis, and image detail is hidden in dense shadows or lost altogether in burned-out highlights.

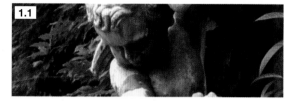

Here, the image is too dark.

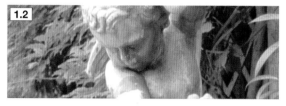

Here, the image is too light.

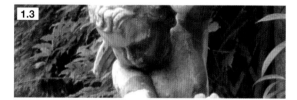

A correct print.

How to judge tests

When test strips come out of the printer, it is important to let them dry before making a decision, since some papers with sticky top coats can take a couple of minutes to absorb ink and dry properly. Always judge results in natural daylight from a nearby window or under color-corrected fluorescent lighting. Avoid viewing in bright sunlight or near any strongly colored walls or furniture.

Frequent brightness problems   **1**

Monochrome or toned images often print darker than expected because of the way RGB image colors are translated into printer ink color. This can also be true with certain duotone colors, where no exact match can be achieved by mixing CMYK inks together. If disappointing prints emerge, consider returning to the duotone dialog and pick another color. On a dark image, shadow areas will fill in and prevent image

detail from appearing, but this can be fixed easily using the Levels controls. Color prints also become much less vivid when dark and can assume a color cast that will disappear once the brightness has been corrected.

Fuzziness

If pin-sharp images print dark and fuzzy, an incorrect media setting has been chosen in the printer software. Too much ink has been dropped onto the paper and ink droplets have merged together to destroy fine detail. Return to the printer software and select a lower grade media and try again.

See also Test printing *pages 252–253* / Common printing problems *pages 256–257* /

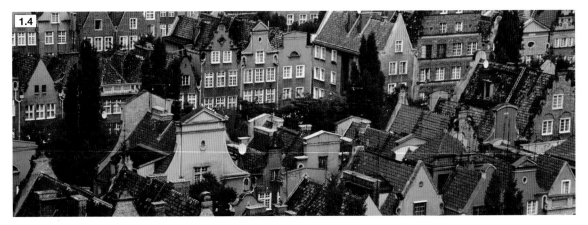

Here, the image is too dark.

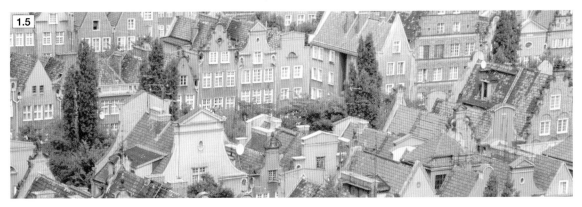

Here, the image is too light.

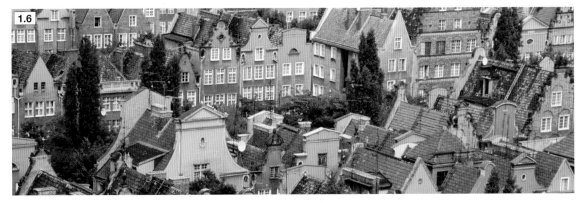

A correct color print.

Common printing problems

There are a host of common print problems listed below for quick reference.

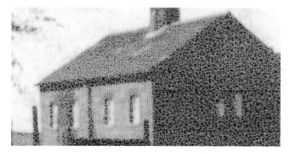

Ink puddling. This is caused by choosing the wrong media setting in the printer software dialog. Pick a lower-grade media setting to correct this. Some cheaper papers are not fully correctable.

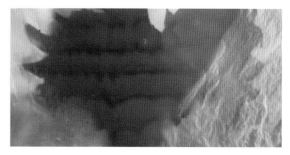

Ink running. This is caused by choosing the wrong media setting when using plastic film or high-gloss paper media, as too much ink will be dropped on the surface. Try a lower-grade media setting to solve this problem.

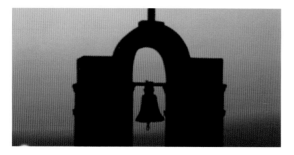

Unsharp. This occurs on uncoated papers, where too much ink has caused a loss of sharpness. Increase image brightness using the Levels slider and if the problem persists, reduce the printer resolution.

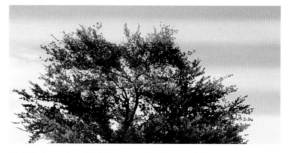

Visible banding. This is caused when printing on uncoated or artists' watercolor paper, especially when combined with too high a resolution, such as 2880 or 1440dpi. Try a lower resolution.

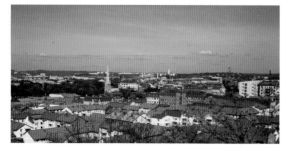

Color run out: yellow. Sudden loss of color occurs when one of the ink reservoirs runs dry during a print. In this example yellow has stopped printing, leaving a color imbalance on the bottom half of the print.

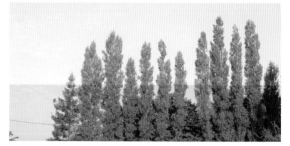

Color run out: cyan. An identical problem, but this time caused by the blue-green cyan ink cartridge running out during a print.

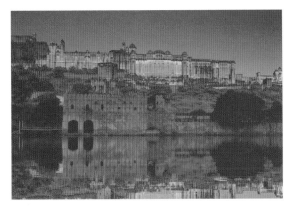

Color run out: black. Loss of black ink makes a significant impact on image contrast.

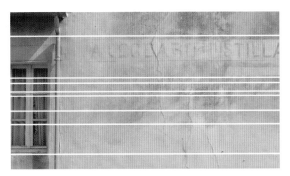

White horizontal lines. White lines are usually caused by an obstruction in the printer head, in most cases blocked individual ink nozzles. Return to the printer software and instigate a printer head cleaning routine.

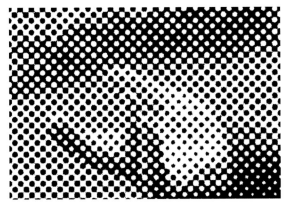

Printing with black ink only. This happens when printing monochrome images using the black ink setting only. Better results are achieved using color inks.

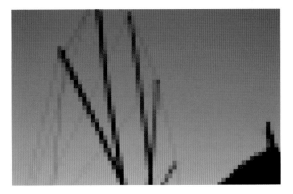

Pixellated printouts. If square pixels are visible on a print this can only be caused by a low image resolution, such as 72ppi. Print the image smaller or reshoot or rescan at a higher resolution.

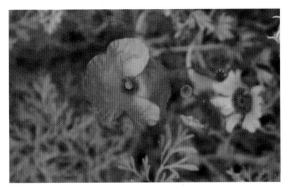

Blocky patterned print. Low-quality JPEG files never enlarge well. Print them at a smaller size or rescan or reshoot if at all practical.

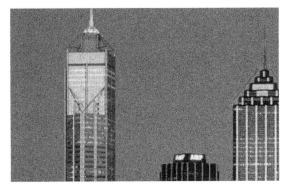

Speckled print. This loss of sharpness is caused by printing out at too low a printer resolution, such as 360dpi. Change to 1440dpi and try again.

Art papers

Cotton papers, intended for use by painters and printmakers, offer another kind of media on which digital photographers can express their creative ideas.

Limitations of the paper

It is essential to realize that cotton, watercolor or acid-free papers will react very differently than glossy ink-jet paper. Art papers are much more absorbent and, as a consequence, much less reflective too. Initial test prints will look oddly dark and have a much less saturated range of colors compared to a monitor image. Due to the open weave of the material, pin-sharp detail will not reproduce well and contrast will be flat and muddy, too. Each art paper has its own kind of base color, ranging from off-white through cream, yellow and even salmon pink. Ink-jet printers never print white ink, so it is important to recognize that the base color of the art paper will become the maximum highlight color and value in a printout.

File preparation

The inherent limitations of the printing media will also determine exactly how each individual file is prepared. It is not essential to have ultra-high-resolution image files to print from, as art papers cannot really cope with anything more than 720dpi. With ink spreading slightly on the paper, there'll be no advantage in preparing images above 150ppi, rather than the normal 200ppi for standard ink-jet media.

Brightness and color

The image will need to be made much brighter than normal to counteract the merging together of midtone areas. This is done in the Levels dialog by moving the midtone slider to the left until the image looks much brighter than usual. To solve the loss of color saturation, use the Hue/Saturation dialog to bump up the colors. Move the Saturation slider to the right and create a much more vivid result than normal.

Loading paper

Most art papers are made beyond an ink-jet printer's maximum media thickness limit of 300 gsm. If you have an Epson printer, move the tension lever (found under the printer lid) from "0" to "+," to accommodate this thicker material. Paper misfeeds are a common issue with art paper but can be prevented by using the Form Feed command to pull paper into position before sending the file to print.

Setting the printer software

Start a thorough series of test prints and start with plain paper as your selected media type then try increasing the printer resolution steadily from 360 and 720dpi until the maximum is reached. Keep a note of all the settings and save the best combination of resolution, media type and color balance as a Save Settings file to replay over future prints on the same paper.

See also Media types *pages 244–245 /*

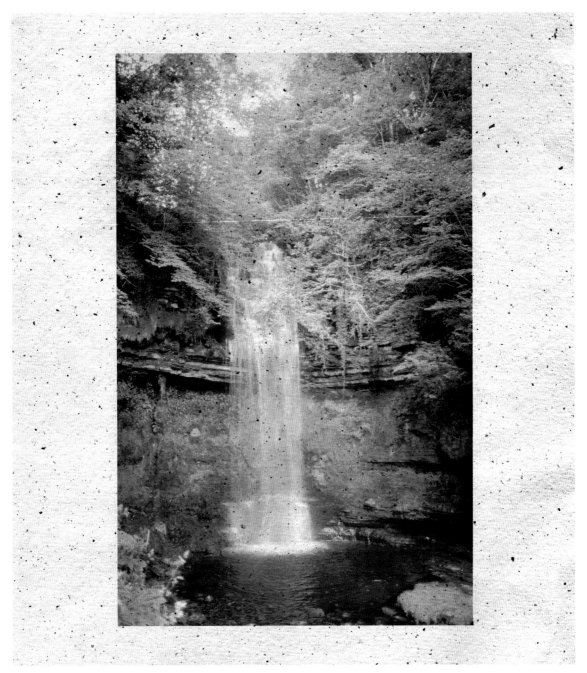

The texture of an art paper can enhance monochrome images.

Special ink sets

Choice of ink is as important to the digital photographer as good-quality oil paint is to an artist.

All ink-jet inks are based on cheap dyes which are inherently unstable in daylight. Printed matter like magazines and newspapers are never designed to last very long and are produced with inks that fade easily. The same problems occur with ink-jet prints made with cheap ink and cheap paper. Better quality and greater longevity is achieved using pigment-based inks, rather than dye-based inks; oil paintings over five hundred years old have survived because of the type of color pigment used to mix artists' oil paints.

Budget inks

Desktop ink-jet printers are calibrated to give the best results using their own brand of ink and paper and will give disappointing results with budget materials. Printer software is painstakingly designed to call up precise amounts of color. They could fail to correct any unexpected color cast caused by a generic product. Refillable cartridges and recycled ink sets are cheap because they are made with cheaper dyes that fade quickly.

Lightfast inks

Much better results can be obtained using products such as Epson's Intellidge ink or Lyson's Fotonic

See also Printer types *pages 242–243* / Media types *pages 244–245* /

Archival Color ink sets, both of which claim to last 25–30 years before fading. Archival inks should be considered for making prints with a guaranteed lifespan such as those for a family photo album.

Individual ink pods   1

Ink-jets that use six- or seven-pod color cartridges are uneconomical because they become unusable once one color has run out. Strong single-color images can easily drain a cartridge after just two or three prints. Better results are offered by printers that have single color cartridges that can be replaced individually when the need arises.

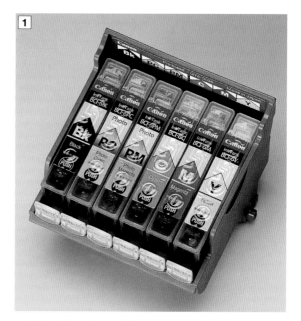

Individual ink color cartridges are more economical to replace.

Warm tone inks

Lyson's Quad Black and Small Gamut Ink sets are innovative inks, filling standard four-pod color cartridges with unusual ink. The Quad Black ink set substitutes the standard CMYK ink colors with four new colors with an identical tonal value, such as black, dark gray, mid-gray and light gray. The benefit of using these products is cast-free prints that have a greatly expanded tonal quality compared to those printed with CMYK. Lyson's Small Gamut inks

are made using a swatch of blue or brown for reproducing traditional photographic printing effects. Currently only a limited number of printers can use Lyson inks, with the list expanding each year.

Independent evaluation

To keep informed about the lightfast qualities of new ink or a paper's archival stability, visit the website of the informative and impartial Wilhelm Imaging Research Inc. at www.wilhelm-research.com

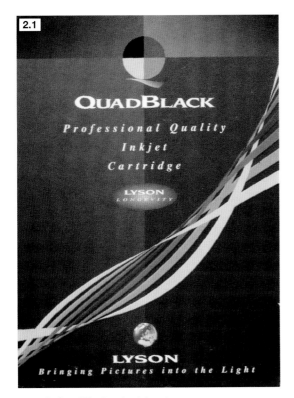

Lyson's QuadBlack color ink set.

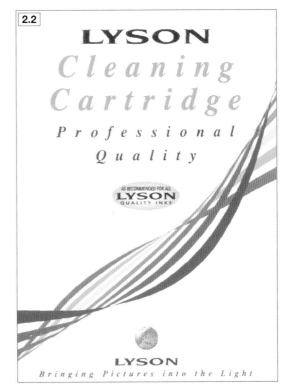

The cleaning cartridge is used to flush residual color ink out of the printer head.

Kiosk printing services

For those who do not have a personal computer, digital photos can still be output using one of the growing number of kiosk printing services.

Kiosk-based print booths can now be found in almost every photographic retailer, and offer a self-service approach to digital photo printing. Based on a custom-made PC, monitor and flatbed scanner linked to a digital miniprinter like the Fuji Frontier, kiosks offer all the tools and services expected from a professional photo lab. Imaged directly onto silver-based photographic paper, this service offers all the hands-on advantages of digital processing with the longevity and stability of traditional photographic paper material.

Accessibility

Kiosks are designed to accept all formats of removable storage media that digital photographers are ever likely to use for transporting image files, such as CD-R, Kodak Photo CD, Zip and 3.5-inch floppy disks, which are formatted for PC rather than Mac use. For ultra-fast turnaround, many kiosks have an additional device for reading both CompactFlash and SmartMedia cards decanted from digital cameras. Many digital photographers use kiosks immediately after a shoot, so they can get to view their results on location or while on holiday. Less common storage formats and memory card formats are less likely to be supported.

Software tools

Kiosks are designed to be used by everyone and do not rely on any previous photographic or computer knowledge. Once the media is inserted into the reader, a host of software tools are available for fixing or enhancing the photographs. Just like a basic image processing application, the kiosk software lets users correct color, brightness and contrast and even red eye. Operated by a touch screen, commands are given in step form, and are ideal for a novice user. The software also offers the chance to make selective enlargements and special crops, providing the new sizes fit within the dimensions of the printing paper in use. For raw and unenhanced images — taken straight from a digital camera memory card — special auto commands can be used to set contrast, color balance and color saturation to prevent washed-out printouts.

Turnaround and quality

Once the image files have been enhanced they are simply sent through an internal network or Internet link to a digital mini-lab station where they are printed out at top quality. Most kiosk services offer very competitive prices compared to professional photo labs and at a lightning fast turnaround, too.

Flatbed scanning

Kiosks can also generate digital image files using a built-in flatbed scanner. Very useful if original negatives have been lost and only a print remains, the flatbed scanner is simply operated via a touch screen interface.

See also Lab services *pages 138–139* / Internet-based printing services *pages 264–265* /

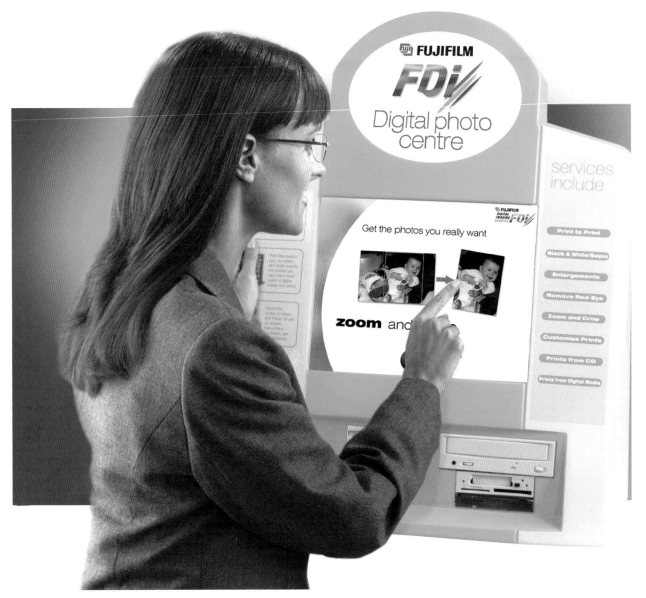

The Fuji FDi Digital photo center offers a simple touch-screen interface.

Internet-based printing services

Just like shopping on-line, it is now possible to order top-quality digital prints from an Internet-based photolab.

Photographers who are confident using a web browser and are comfortable shopping on the Internet, can make use of the growing number of on-line photographic lab services. Digital photographs can be uploaded to an on-line photolab website, such as www.ofoto.com or www.photobox.co.uk, where they are printed out automatically on conventional photographic paper then dispatched by mail.

How the service works

Digital files are received by a high-capacity server linked to an automated mini-lab printer — identical to the machines used in photolabs. After upload, the digital image files are automatically loaded into the mini-lab twenty-four hours a day. Top-quality processors like the Fuji Frontier have a fine laser which is used to "beam" the images onto conventional silver-based color photographic paper. The process doesn't use an enlarging lens, so traditional problems with scratches, dust or poor focus never appear on the prints. At a very low cost, this kind of service offers professional quality output at an affordable price.

Transfer applications

Many Internet photo labs are global rather than local businesses and rely on the use of one of the two common web browsers: Microsoft Internet Explorer and Netscape Communicator, working on both PC and Mac platforms. Uploading image files is just like sending an e-mail attachment and does not require any additional software. A more sophisticated and user-friendly service is offered by the global ColorMailer lab, which uses its own specially devised Photo Service software. This program is free, easy to download and install, and offers a more comprehensive set of tools than either of the two browsers. ColorMailer Photo Service gives cropping and rotational tools, plus useful border options and

See also Lab services *pages 138–139* / Kiosk printing services *pages 262–263* /

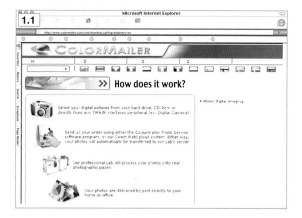

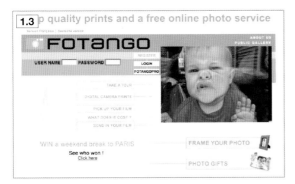

The Fotango log-in.

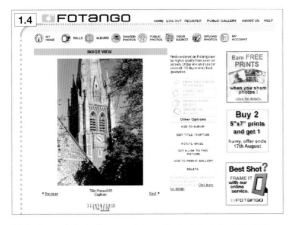

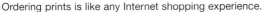

Ordering prints is like any Internet shopping experience.

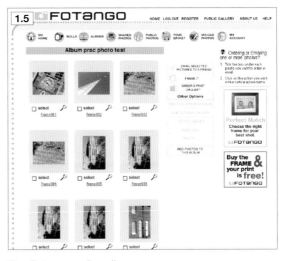

The Fotango on-line album.

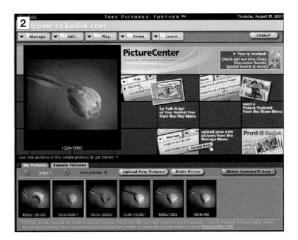

Kodak offers on-line image enhancement.

indicates when the print order exceeds the quality of the digital image file. As with the worldwide network of Kodak on-line labs, users can choose to upload digital photos to a number of ColorMailer labs on most continents, sending photos to overseas friends in a matter of days.

Compressing the files

Uploading large image files via a slow Internet connection can take a long time. The temptation to compress image files for a faster transfer will be at the expense of print quality, but with broadband services becoming more affordable this is less of an issue. Most labs only accept JPEG format images and users should opt for highest quality JPEG settings

such as 80% to 100%. Images must be sent with a resolution of 200ppi or prints will have visibly square pixels.

On-line albums

Internet photo labs also offer a password-protected storage facility allowing users to create their own on-line albums. Once uploaded to an album, access can be granted to friends and family and they can place their own print orders direct.

Preparing JPEG images for the Internet

Compression is the way digital data can be shrunk to make large image files more manageable over a network.

Compression

Broadband Internet, ultra-fast networks and high-capacity storage media may have reduced the need to make digital image compression an everyday necessity, but it is still essential for the Internet. Digital photographs take up huge amounts of data space compared to simple word-processing documents and every single pixel needs a 24-digit number to determine its color. Imagine that a digital camera creates files that have six million or more pixels in every image, and the scale of the issue becomes clear. To counteract this excessive amount of data, images can be condensed into smaller data packages by reducing the need for the 24-digit code for every single pixel.

See also Camera functions: image-quality settings *pages 12–13* / File formats *pages 86–87* / Compression *pages 88–89* / Packaging image files *pages 90–91* /

Joint Photographic Experts Group or JPEG [1]

JPEG is one of many compression routines that are used for photographic images. The process works by assigning an approximate color recipe to a block of pixels rather than each individual one as found in an uncompressed file. The drastic saving on data means a compromise in image quality, but if done properly it can be hardly noticeable. The JPEG routine can be instigated through the Save As command or, for those preferring a preview of the likely result, via the Save for Web command. Within both of these routes, the JPEG file format is offered on a scale of 0–10 or 0–100, with the zero end offering the most data saving but lowest image quality and the top of the scale offering the best image quality but the least data compression.

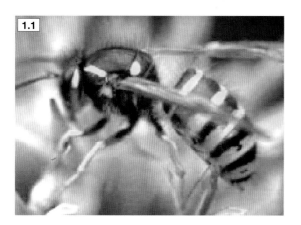

Save As JPEG at 0 quality.

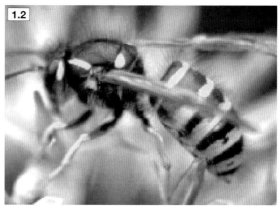

Save As JPEG at 30 quality.

Colors and data size

JPEG compression doesn't reduce the pixel dimensions of an image physically, only the data required to reconstruct it. In fact the very nature of the image itself will determine how much or how little can be saved, rather than the dimensions. A highly patterned or multi-colored photograph with fine details will require much more data than an image of a blue sky, even though they may have been shot with the same digital camera under the same settings. The compression savings will be lower because more colors and sharp edges need more data than images made with few colors and blurred shapes.

Lossy compression

JPEG is also described as a lossy compression routine, since image quality will deteriorate each time the image is opened and re-saved. Blocky image artifacts are unfortunate byproducts of the JPEG compression routine, especially seen in subtle gradients when images have been compressed too far. With the full Save for Web preview function, most images can be reduced to 60% without any significant loss of image quality. JPEG is not suitable for compressing graphic images which have text or logos, as sharp edges and lines will be softened. JPEGs don't deteriorate when used over the Internet, as images are only viewed in a browser and never resaved by the surfer.

Download options

Two further options are available for web-based use: baseline and progressive. To speed up the download of images over the Internet, the baseline option loads a JPEG image line by line on a monitor. The more sophisticated progressive JPEG quickly loads a blurred full-size image, then progressively adds sharp details as the download completes.

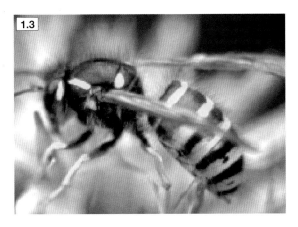

Save As JPEG at 60 quality.

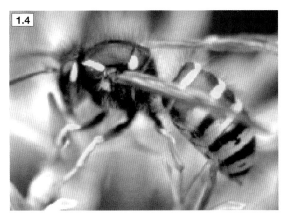

Save As JPEG at 100 quality.

Preparing GIF images for the Internet

The GIF format should be used only for saving web graphics and not for subtle color photographs.

Graphics Interchange Format or GIF

The universal GIF format is commonly used to package graphic images with solid colors and sharp-edged shapes for the Internet. Most web pages have some basic graphics, such as buttons to aid navigation, rather than purely text-only pages which look uninviting. In addition, logos and advertising banners that are constructed with type and bold colors are GIF files. All graphic images created in Photoshop can be saved in the GIF format by using the Save for Web command. The preview window presents the chance to view before and after, plus an opportunity to compare several different settings applied at one time.

Compression

Significant reductions in file size can result from GIF compression and individual web graphics can be made at 5K and under. Photographic images are unsuitable for saving in the GIF format, although many photos are used at a small size within advertising banners. The GIF format works by crunching 16.7 million colors down to 256 colors or fewer in an 8-bit rather than 24-bit file. Despite this catastrophic loss, many images look barely different than their 24-bit versions if compressed sensitively. Images can be reduced slowly to 32, 16 or even 8 colors to help drop data, and individual colors can be extracted from the palette or remapped to another palette for more precise control.

See also Camera functions: image-quality settings *pages 12–13* / File formats *pages 86–87* / Compression *pages 88–89* / Packaging image files *pages 90–91* /

Color reduction algorithm 1

GIFs can be created in a number of different color palettes, depending on the final use of the image file. The Web palette employs the standard 216 web-safe colors and converts pixel color to the nearest web-safe value. Other options such as Perceptual, Selective and Custom offer ways of determining a personalized swatch of colors in a 256-color palette but are much less web-safe. GIFs also squeeze colors into a smaller palette based on several dithering or halftoning methods such as Pattern, Diffusion and Noise, creating very different effects on the same image. Photographic images saved in the GIF format become posterized and coarse and this worsens as the color palette is reduced from 256 to 64 or 32 colors.

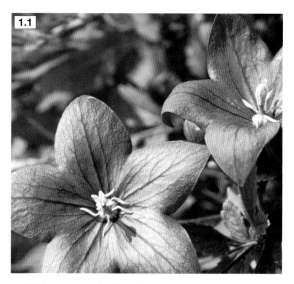

1.1

A GIF image saved with a 64-color palette.

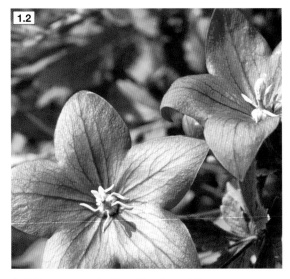

A GIF image saved with a 32-color palette.

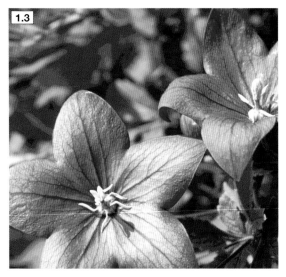

A GIF image saved with a 16-color palette.

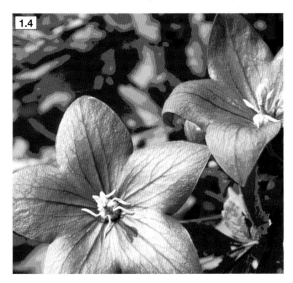

A GIF image saved with a 8-color palette.

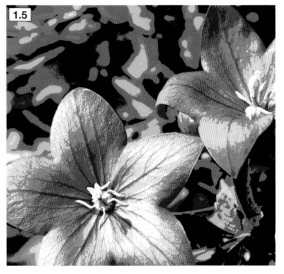

A GIF image saved with a 4-color palette.

Lossless compression

The GIF format is based on a lossless compression routine, so images can be resaved without any further drop in image quality, provided the color palette is not reduced any further. Other variations, such as the useful GIF89a format, permit the use of a transparent background around irregular image shapes to blend in with the web page background color. Interlaced GIFs can also be created with a different attribute to make the image download faster in alternate lines, albeit with a slight increase in file size.

Making image maps

Image maps are interactive image files that can hyperlink to other web resources.

Websites frequently use image maps to create an interactive experience using an image file. Unlike using the whole image as a hyperlink to another web page, image maps are prepared with designated active areas called hotspots, which link separately to other resources. Image maps can be made using any web-friendly image format and are best prepared in Photoshop and linked in Dreamweaver or another professional web-design package.

Making an image map in Photoshop and Image Ready [1]

Open the image, reduce the resolution to 72ppi and decide on a pixel dimension that will fit within the web-page design. Consider picking a web-safe color from the Color Picker as a background color to the image, as this can be matched to the background color of the web page in Dreamweaver. Start the design, keeping all individual hotspots as separate layers, then switch into Image Ready and do Layer>New Layer Based Image Map Area. Add the hyperlink reference to the URL box in the Image Map dialog and repeat the process for each separate layer. Save and preview the html file in your browser.

See also Web-design software *pages 156–157* / Type effects *pages 238–239* /

Defining hotspots in Dreamweaver [2]

Another alternative is to use the image editor to create graphics and image editing, adding the hotspots later in Dreamweaver. Load the image file into the site folder first and launch the application. Open the html file where you intend to use the image and import it immediately. Click on the image and notice the Properties Inspector change its contents to reveal three basic image map-drawing tools. Hotspots can be determined in either an elliptical, rectangular or polygonal shape simply by drawing over the area in question. As each hotspot is completed, type in the URL to define the link.

Internet typography

Image maps are ideal vehicles for experimenting with type embedded into an image file. Text and type style on the Internet is determined by the viewer's browser application, so special fonts can only occur if they are incorporated into an image file. Type designs destined for the Internet must be aliased because of jaggy edges appearing at the edges of curved letter shapes when viewed at 72dpi.

Image slicing

Image slices are used to carve up a larger image or graphic to improve download time. The function is also used to allocate different compression attributes to each individual slice if a design is a mixture of text, flat color and photographic imagery. Slices are made in rectangular shapes and can take a long time to download if prepared at full web-page size.

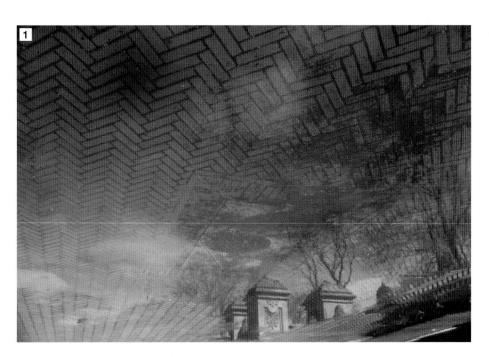

A simple textured background makes an ideal starting point for an image map.

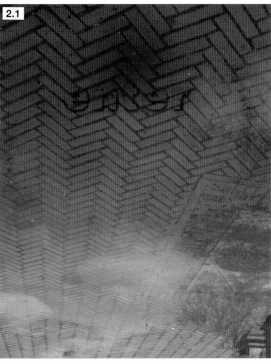

Once a deep shadow effect was placed underneath the word created with the Type Mask tool, it was ready to link.

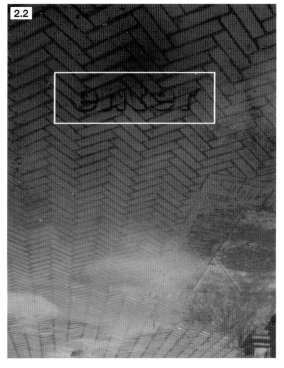

Hotspots are defined by area, such as this rectangle. The word will now function like a normal hyperlink.

Internet animation

Still images form the basis of most web animation.

Animated GIFs 1

Like the simplest form of an animated flick book, GIF animation is made by sequencing a series of digital images together in a shareware package like GIFBuilder or by using the more sophisticated ImageReady. GIF animations are compatible with every browser version and browser type and usually have a tiny file size for instant download and play. Once images have been sequenced in order, each frame can be set to start or stop after a specific number of seconds, and once the final file has been saved, this time factor becomes built-in and irreversible. On more advanced web-animation packages, such as ImageReady, individual frames can be made directly from separate layers in a Photoshop file so users can create complex and dynamic animations. ImageReady also offers the useful tweening function where the user can define a start and end point for a sequence without needing to draw the in-between bits. Once saved and viewed in a web browser, GIF animations will continue playing on a never-ending loop.

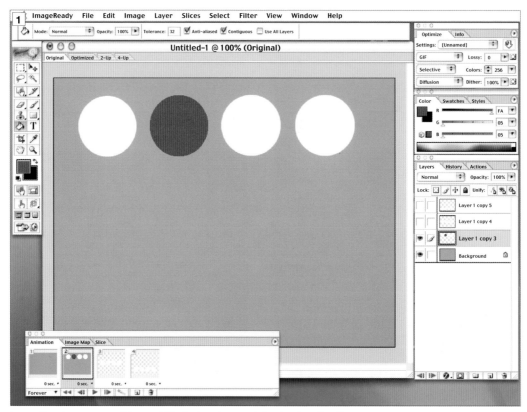

ImageReady can convert layered Photoshop images into simple animations.

Rollovers 2

Most design-aware websites use rollovers to make their pages look more interactive. Rollovers are made in many ways but the most common method uses two near-identical image files that swap places each time the cursor hovers over them. To make a simple button in Photoshop, create the button shape and make two identical text layers, each using a different color. Save two versions of the image to represent the two text color states and to load into the web-design application. The actual rollover is controlled by a tiny piece of Javascript, which swaps the images when prompted by the mouse. The rollover is completed when the mouse moves off again, restoring the original image in its place. When viewed in the browser, both images are downloaded but only one is visible at any one time.

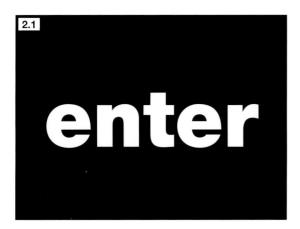

A rollover image in a "down" state.

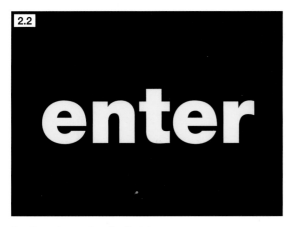

A rollover image in a "up" state.

Javascript driven sequences

While GIF animations are uncontrollable once they appear, sophisticated animations and sequences can be controlled by Javascript. Most Javascript code is freely available over the Internet and can be readily copied and pasted into an html code in an instant. Javascript can be used to create a wide variety of interactive Internet experiences, such as slideshows where each image is allowed to appear for a set time before being replaced, or for presenting a random image from a pre-defined set each time the web page is viewed. Script-driven sequences are infinitely more controllable than GIF sequences and also can be made using JPEG files. Behind this kind of animation are individual image files controlled by time-coded script. Once established, it is easy to change the selection of images by modifying the script to fit the new file names.

See also Preparing JPEG images for the Internet *pages 266–267* / Preparing GIF images for the Internet *pages 268–269* /

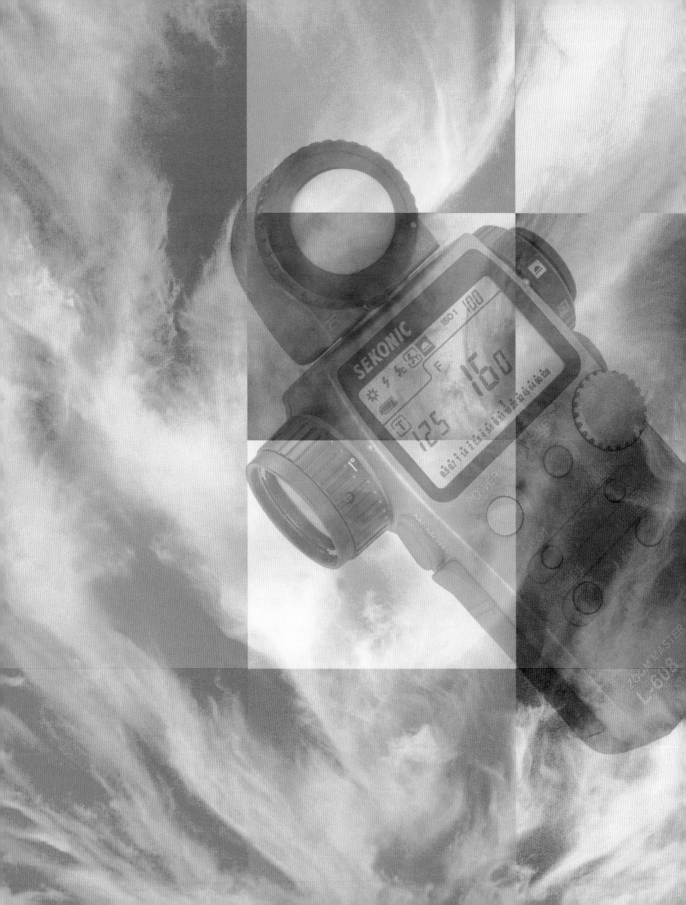

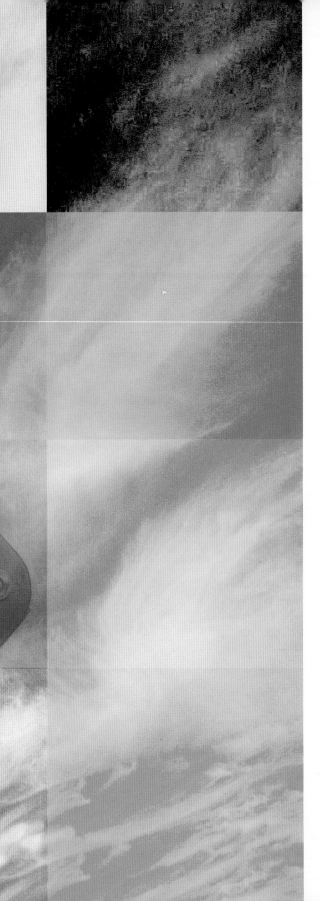

Glossary

Aliasing

Square pixels can't describe curved shapes, and when viewed close up look jagged, like a staircase. Anti-aliasing filters found between the camera lens and image sensor lessen the effects of this process by reducing contrast.

Aperture

An aperture is the circular opening inside a camera lens. It controls the quantity of light passing onto the film or, in a digital camera, onto the image sensor.

Aperture scale

Measured in f-numbers on an international scale as follows: f/2.8, f/4, f/5.6, f/8, f/11 and f/16.

Artifacts

By-products of digital processing such as noise and low quality JPEG compression, both of which degrade image quality.

Background printing

This allows an image document to print while the computer user still retains the ability to work in the current application.

Batch processing

Using a special type of script or Photoshop Action command, batch processing automatically applies a sequence of pre-set commands to a folder of images.

Bit

A bit is the smallest chunk of digital data, which can express two states, like on or off, or if used to describe color, black or white.

Bit depth

Also referred to as color depth, this describes the size of color palette used to create a digital image, e.g., 8-bit, 16-bit and 24-bit.

Bitmap image

A bitmap image is another term for a pixel-based image arranged in a chessboard-like grid.

Bitmap image mode

Bitmap image mode can display only two colors — black and white — and is the best mode to save line art scans. Bitmap images have a tiny file size.

Burst rate

This is an indication of the speed at which a camera can save image data then get ready to capture the next shot.

Byte

Eight bits make a byte in binary numbering. A single byte can describe 256 states, colors or tones on a 0 – 255 scale.

Card reader

Digital cameras are sold with a connecting cable that fits into a computer. A card reader is an additional unit that offers a more convenient way to transfer images to the computer.

CCD

A charged coupled device (CCD) is the light sensitive "eye" of a scanner and "film" in a digital camera.

CD-R

Compact disc recordable (CD-R) is the cheapest and most cost-effective type of media for storing digital images. You need to have a CD writer to write data to these discs, but they can all be played back in a standard CD-ROM drive.

CD-RW

Compact disc rewritable (CD-RW) discs can be used many times, unlike CD-Rs which can only be burned once.

Clipping

Clipping occurs when image tone close to highlight and shadow is converted to pure white and black during scanning. Loss of detail will occur.

CMYK image mode

Cyan, magenta, yellow and black (black is designated as K to prevent confusion with blue) is an image mode used for litho reproduction. All magazines are printed with CMYK inks.

Color space

RGB, CMYK and LAB are different kinds of color spaces, each with their own unique characteristics and limitations.

Compression

Crunching digital data into smaller files is known as compression. Without physically reducing the pixel dimensions of an image, compression routines devise compromise color recipes for a group of pixels, rather than individual ones.

CPU

The central processing unit (CPU) is the engine of a computer, driving the long and complex calculations when images are modified.

CRT monitor

A cathode ray tube (CRT) is a bulbous type of monitor most used for accurate color management.

Curves

Curves is a versatile tool for adjusting contrast, color and brightness by pulling or pushing a line from highlight to shadow.

Depth of field

The zone of sharpness set between the nearest and furthest parts of a scene. You control DOF by two factors: your position to the subject and the aperture value selected on your lens. Higher f-numbers, such as f/22, create a greater depth of field than lower numbers, such as f/2.8.

Descreening

The removal of a halftone pattern from a lithographic image during scanning. This avoids a moiré effect when output.

Diffusion dithering

A dithering technique allocates randomly arranged ink droplets rather than a grid, to create an illusion of continuous color.

Digital zoom

Instead of pulling your subject closer, a small patch of pixels is enlarged, or interpolated to make detail look bigger than it really is.

Dithering

A method of simulating complex colors or tones of gray using few color ingredients. Close together, dots of ink can give the illusion of new color.

Dot pitch

A measure of the fineness of a CRT monitor's shadow mask. The smaller the value, the sharper the display.

DPI (printer)

Printer DPI is an indication of the number of separate ink droplets deposited by a printer. The higher the number, the more photo-real results will look.

DPI (scanner)

Dots per inch (DPI) is a measure of the resolution of a scanner. The higher this number is, the more data you can capture.

DPOF

Digital print order format is a recent set of universal standards allowing you to specify printout options directly from your camera.

Driver

A small software application that instructs a computer how to operate an external peripheral like a printer or scanner. Drivers are frequently updated but are usually available for free download from a manufacturer's website.

Dropper tools

Pipette-like icons that allow the user to define tonal limits like highlight and shadows by directly clicking on image areas.

Duotone

A duotone image is constructed from two different color channels, chosen from the color picker, and can be used to apply a tone to an image.

Dye sublimation

A kind of digital printer that uses a CMYK pigment impregnated donor ribbon to pass color onto special receiving paper.

Dynamic range

Is a measure of the brightness range in photographic materials and digital sensing.

EPS

Encapsulated postscript (EPS) is a standard format for an image or whole page layout, allowing it to be used in a range of applications.

Exposure

Exposure is the exact quantity of light required to make a good picture. This is made by selecting the right combination of shutter speed and aperture value.

F-numbers

Aperture values are described in f-numbers, such as f/2.8 and f/16. Small f-numbers let more light onto your film or sensor and bigger numbers less. F-numbers can also influence your depth of field.

File extension

The three or four letter/number code that appears at the end of a document name, preceded by a period, e.g., landscape.tif. Extensions enable applications to identify file formats and enable cross-platform file transfer.

File format

Digital images can be created and saved in many different file formats such as JPEG, TIFF and PSD. Formats are designed to let you package images for future purposes, like e-mail, printout and for your web page. Not to be confused with disk formatting.

FireWire

A fast data transfer system used on recent computers, especially for digital video and high-resolution image files. Also known as IEEE1394.

FlashPath

A FlashPath adaptor is a 3.5-inch floppy disk which has been modified to accept SmartMedia memory cards and is used to transfer digital camera data to your computer through it's floppy disk drive. Works at a snail's pace.

FlashPix

The FlashPix file format is a Kodak/HP invention used to create digital camera files. It can only be opened in a compatible application.

Gamma

The contrast of the midtone areas in a digital image.

Gamut

Gamut is a description of the extent of a color palette used for the creation, display or output of a digital image.

GIF

Graphics interfilm (GIF), where detail can be coaxed out of overexposed negatives with careful printing. White pixels can never be modified to produce lurking detail.

Gigabyte

A gigabyte is 1,024 megabytes.

Grayscale

Grayscale mode is used to save black and white images. There are 256 steps from black to white in a grayscale image, just enough to prevent banding to the human eye.

Halftone

An image constructed from a dot screen of different sizes to simulate continuous tone or color. Used in magazine and newspaper publishing.

Highlight

The brightest part of an image, represented by 255 on the 0 – 255 scale.

High resolution

High-resolution images are generally made with a million or more pixels and are used to make high quality printouts. These images demand a lot of storage space.

Histogram

A graph that displays the range of tones present in a digital image as a series of vertical columns.

Hot-shoe

A universal socket for attaching an external flashgun to digital cameras.

IBM Microdrive

A high-capacity removable media used in digital cameras, available at up to 1 gigabyte capacity. Like PCMCIA cards, Microdrives are like mini hard-drives.

ICC

The International Color Consortium (ICC) was founded by the major manufacturers in order to develop color standards and cross-platform systems.

Ink-jet

An output device that sprays ink droplets of varying size onto a wide range of media.

Interpolation

All digital images can be enlarged, or interpolated, by introducing new pixels to the bitmap grid. Interpolated images never have the same sharp qualities or color accuracy of original non-interpolated images.

ISO speed

Photographic film and digital sensors are graded by their sensitivity to light. This is sometimes called film speed or ISO speed.

Jaggies

See Aliasing

JPEG

JPEG is an acronym for Joint Photographic Experts Group and is a universal kind of file format used for compressing images. Most digital cameras save images as JPEG files to make more efficient use of limited capacity memory cards.

Kilobyte (K or Kb)

A kilobyte is 1,024 bytes of digital information.

Lab image mode

A theoretical color space (i.e., not employed by any hardware device) used for processing images.

Layer blending

A function of Photoshop layers, allowing a user to merge adjoining layers based on transparency, color and a wide range of non-photographic effects.

Layer opacity

The visible "strength" of a Photoshop layer can be modified on a 0 – 100% scale. As this value drops, the layer merges into the underlying one.

Layered image

A kind of image file, such as a Photoshop file, where separate image elements can be arranged above and below each other, like a stack of cards.

Levels

A common set of tools for controlling image brightness found in Adobe Photoshop and many other imaging applications. Levels can be used for setting highlight and shadow points.

Line art

A type of original artwork, such as type script or pencil drawings, which has only one color.

Low resolution

Low-resolution images have a small file size, produce poor quality printouts and are only suitable for web page display.

Megabyte (Mb)

A megabyte is 1,024 kilobytes of digital information. Most digital images are measured in megabytes.

Megapixel

A measurement of how many pixels a digital camera can make. A bitmap image measuring 1200 x 1800 pixels contains 2.1 million pixels (1200 x 1800 = 2.1 million), made by a 2.1 megapixel camera.

Memory Stick

Sony digital cameras and digital video cameras use their own type of removable media called Memory Stick.

Noise

Like grain in traditional photographic film, noise is an inevitable by-product of shooting with a high ISO setting. If too little light passes onto the CCD sensor, brightly colored pixels are made by mistake in the shadow areas.

Optical resolution

Also called true resolution, this is the measure of the hardware capability, excluding any enhancements made by software trickery or interpolation.

Overexposure

Occurs when too much light is passed onto your sensor due to an exposure error. Overexposure makes images look light with pale and washy colors.

Parallax

Parallax error occurs in cameras fitted with optical viewfinders set to one side or above the lens. When used at close focus, what you see through the viewfinder will be different from the image captured by the lens.

Parallel

A type of connection mainly associated with printers and some scanners. The data transfer rate of a parallel connection is slower than SCSI or USB.

Pantone

The Pantone color library is an internationally established system for describing color with PIN-like codes. It is used in the lithographic printing industry for mixing color by the weights of ink.

Path

A path is a vector-based outline used in Photoshop for creating precise cut-outs. As no pixel data is involved, paths add a tiny amount to the file size and can be converted into selections.

PCI slot

A peripheral component interface (PCI) slot is an expansion bay in a computer used for upgrading or adding extra connecting ports or performance-enhancing cards.

PCMCIA

Personal Computer Memory Card International Association (PCMCIA) is a small credit card-sized device designed to fit into a standard PC laptop.

Peripherals

Peripherals like scanners, printers, CD-writers, etc., are items used to build up a computer workstation.

Pictography

A type of high-resolution digital printer made by Fuji that images directly onto special donor paper without the need for processing chemistry.

Pigment inks

A more lightfast inkset for ink-jet printers, usually with a smaller color gamut than dye-based inksets. Used for producing prints for sale.

Pixel

Taken from the words picture element, a pixel is the building block of a digital image, like a single tile in a mosaic. Pixels are generally square in shape.

Pixellation

When a digital print is made from a low-resolution image, fine details appear blocky, or pixellated, because not enough pixels were used to describe complex shapes.

Profile

The color reproduction characteristics of an input or output device. This is used by color management software such as ColorSync to maintain color accuracy when moving images across computers and input/ouput devices.

Quadtone

A quadtone image is constructed from four different color channels, chosen from the color picker or custom color libraries like Pantone.

RAM

Random access memory (RAM) is the part of a computer that holds your data during work in progress. Computers with little RAM will process images slowly as data is written to the hard drive, which is slower to respond.

Resolution

The term resolution is used to describe several overlapping concepts. In general, high-resolution images are used for printout and have millions of pixels made from a palette of millions of colors. Low-resolution images have fewer pixels and are only suitable for computer monitor display

RGB image mode

Red, green and blue (RGB) mode is used for color images. Each separate color is has its own channel of 256 steps and pixel color is derived from a mixture of these three ingredients.

RIP

A raster image processor (RIP) translates vector graphics and fonts into bitmaps for digital output. RIPs can be both hardware and software.

Scratch disk

A portion of a computer's free hard disk (or an external drive) that acts as overflow RAM during work in progress.

SCSI

Small computer system interface (SCSI) is a type of connector used to attach scanners and other peripherals to your computer.

Selection

A fenced-off area created in an imaging application like Photoshop, which limits the effects of processing or manipulation.

Shadow

The darkest part of an image, represented by 0 on the 0 – 255 scale.

Shadow mask

A type of finely perforated stencil that creates pixels on a CRT monitor.

Sharpening

A processing filter which increases contrast between pixels to give the impression of greater image sharpness.

TFT monitor

Thin film transistor (TFT) monitors are the flat panel type of computer screen.

TIFF

Tagged image file format (TIFF) is the most common cross-platform image type used in the industry. A compressed variation exists, which is less compatible with DTP applications.

Tritone

A tritone image is constructed from three different color channels, chosen from the color picker or custom color libraries like Pantone.

TWAIN

Toolkit without an interesting name (TWAIN) is a universal software standard which lets users acquire images from scanners and digital cameras from within a graphics application.

Underexposure

When too little light is passed onto film in very low light conditions or by error, underexposure creates dark results with muddy colors.

Unsharp Mask (USM)

Unsharp masking is a traditional film compositing technique used to sharpen edges in an image. The Unsharp Mask filter corrects blurring introduced during photographing, scanning, resampling or printing. It is useful for images intended both for print and on-line.

USB

Universal serial bus (USB) is a recent type of connector which allows easier set up of peripheral devices.

VRAM

Video RAM, or VRAM, is responsible for the speed, color depth and resolution of a computer monitor display. A separate card can be purchased to upgrade older machines with limited VRAM.

White balance

Digital cameras and camcorders have a white balance control to prevent unwanted color casts. Unlike photographic color film which is adversely affected by fluorescent and domestic lights, digital cameras can create color-corrected pixels without using special filters.

White out

Excessive light or overexposure in digital images causes an abundance of white pixels called white out. Unlike film, where detail can be coaxed out of overexposed negatives with careful printing, white pixels can never be modified to produce lurking detail.

Suppliers

The following websites offer information on where to find your nearest store or how to buy on-line.

Digital cameras

www.nikon.com
www.canon.com
www.olympus.com
www.minolta.com
www.sony.com
www.fujifilm.com

Storage media and devices

www.nixvue.com
www.iomega.com
www.lexarmedia.com

Plugs, ports and leads

www.adaptec.com
www.belkin.com

Flatbed and film scanners

www.umax.com
www.microtek.com

Ink-jet printers

www.epson.com
www.canon.com
www.lexmark.com

Computers

www.dell.com
www.apple.com
www.silicongraphics.com
www.toshiba.com

Computer memory and storage

www.kingston.com
www.maxtor.com

Computer monitors

www.lacie.com
www.mitsubishi.com

Image editing software

www.adobe.com
www.macromedia.com
www.jasc.com
www.corel.com
www.roxio.com

Plug-in filter software

www.extensis.com
www.andromeda.com
www.xenofex.com
www.corel.com

Ink-jet media

www.inkjetmall.com
www.silverprint.co.uk
www.lyson.com

Index

Page numbers in *italics* refer to captions

3-D wrapping 151

A

Accented Edges filter 211
Adobe (ACE) 248
Adobe Photoshop *see* Photoshop
Adobe RGB (1998) 14, 27, 111, 246,
 248, 249
Andromeda plug-in 151
animation, Internet 147, 272–3
Annotation tool 168
aperture:
 scale/values 42–3, 44, 45, 49, 50
 settings 19, 21, 22, 23, 27, 40, 56
Apple computer 36, 86, 93, 100, 104,
 105, 116, 142
 iMac *96*, 112
 storage in 102–3
Art History brush 167
artifacts 15, 190
asymmetry 55
Auto Contrast filter 125
auto exposure 124
Auto printing mode 247
autofocus 21, 27, 47
 tracking 27

B

background:
 to eliminate detail in 67, 208, 209
 for montage 228
 textured 206–7
backing up 85, 118
Bezier curves 224
bit depth *see* color depth
bitmap 72
 image *76*, 133
Bitmap mode 81, 124, 145
Blending filter 212
Blending modes 230–1
Blur filter 211, 214
Blur tool 168, 208
blurring: background 66, 67
 deliberate 45, 50
 unintentional 44, 49

see also Gaussian blur, Motion blur
borders *see* edges
bracketing 17, 41
brightness 125, 127
 to adjust 179, 254, 258
browser software 36
Brush tool 166
Brushstroke filter 211, 214
burning in 188–9
Burning tool 168, 188

C

camcorder stills 32–3
camera:
 angle 56
 handling 62–3
 settings 17
 shake 44, 49, 62
 tilting 65, 68
cameras:
 digital SLR 26–7, 42, 47, 49, 53, 66,
 117, 119
 large-format 30
 medium format 28
 midprice compact 20–1, 115
 point and shoot digital compact
 18–19, 42
 rotational lens 23
 top-price compact 22–3, 47, 53, 66
Canvas size 177, 216, 217
card reader:
 dual format 37, 75
 external 36, 75, 107, 119
CCD (Charged Coupled Device) sensor
 10, 22, 74, 122, 123
CD-R disk 92, 101, 113, 126, 242, 262
 care of 92
 mini 35
CD-RW disk 92, 101, 116, 118
Channel Mixer 57, 154, 198, 201
clipping groups 232
Clone Stamp tool 166, 186
close-ups 48–9
CMYK inks 242, 254, 261
CMYK mode 80, 81, 91, 126, 174
 filters in 212

color:
 calibration 110–11
 correction 182–3
 depth 73, *76–7*
 to enhance 202–3
 gamut 184–5
 intensification 198
 palettes 58–9, 78, 79, 81, 83; GIF 87,
 268
 primary 64
 profiles 111
 recipe 72, 73
 to remix 198
 reversals 234
 saturation 58
 wheel 182
Color Balance 135, 146, 183, 195,
 202, 226
color balance function 50, 246
Color Blending mode 204–5
color casts 50, 182–3, 254
Color Management Module (CMM) 248
Color Picker 174, 175, 197, 270
color space 14–15, 27, 29, 246
color transparency 131
ColorSync 116, 248
CompactFlash 26, 29, 34, 35, 37, 75, 262
composition 54–5, 56–7
compression 13, 19, 21, 24, 29, 73, 88–9,
 266–7, 268
 on camcorder 32–3
 see also GIF; JPEG; TIFF
computer: all-in-one 112
 components 98–9
 hardware 96, 100, 104
 laptop 118–19
 maintenance 158–9
 memory 98, 112
 monitor 99, 108–9, 112, 114, 116;
 calibration 110–11; care of 109
 operating system 97, 100–1
 peripherals 106–7
 platforms 100–1
 software 97, 100–1
 viruses 100, 155
 see also Apple computer; Windows
PC connectors 11, 36–7, 104–5;

T

telephoto lens 46, 47, 48, 68, 69
text layers 226
Text tool 226
texture filters 150, 210–11
textured background 206–7
Texturizer filter 211
TIFF (Tagged Image File Format) 13,
    21, 22, 86, 87, 88, 91, 139
time-lapse function 20, 24
toning 61, 194–5
tracking 237
Transform tool 69, 207, 229
transition effect 162
tripod 44, 47, 49, 62, 68, 160
TWAIN (Toolkit Without An
    Interesting Name) software 36, 115,
    147
type:
    effects 238–9
    fonts 236
    for Internet 270
    styles 238
Type Mask tool 238
Type tools 168, 237

U

underexposure 41, 129, 181
Unsharp Mask filter 79, 125, 127, 137,
    139, 190–1
upgrade card 105
USB (Universal Serial Bus) connector
    11, 32, 36, 37, 93, 104, 105, 107, 112, 115,
    122, 126, 242
USB personal storage device 93

V

Variations 182–3
video out function 11
viewfinder 11, 19, 40, 46, 47, 58, 62
    to avoid cropping by 65
    framing in 66–7
viewpoint 68–9
virtual reality software 25, 160–1
visual weight 54

W

Watercolor filter 210
web color mode 124
web-design software 156–7, 270

web page image 15, 18, 19, 33, 74,
    178, 270
web-safe color range 153, 174, 268
webcam use 18, 24
white balance function 14, 21, 22, 27,
    50, 183
wide-angle lens 46, 48, 68
Windows PC 36, 86, 93, 104, 105, 114, 142
    storage in 102, 103
Windows-only package 146, 148
wireless transfer 25, 37

X

Xenofex filter 150, 210

Z

Zip disk 92–3, 101, 116, 262
    care of 93
zoom function 10, 18, 20, 23, 26, 46–7,
    64, 67, 160
    on camcorder 33
Zoom tool 168